Food Justice Undone

CALIFORNIA STUDIES IN FOOD AND CULTURE
Darra Goldstein, Editor

Food Justice Undone

Lessons for Building a Better
Movement

Hanna Garth

UNIVERSITY OF CALIFORNIA PRESS

University of California Press
Oakland, California

Library of Congress Cataloging-in-Publication Data

Names: Garth, Hanna author
Title: Food justice undone : lessons for building a better
    movement / Hanna Garth.
Other titles: California studies in food and culture 88.
Description: Oakland, California : University of
    California Press, [2025] | Series: California studies in
    food and culture ; 88 | Includes bibliographical
    references and index.
Identifiers: LCCN 2025038146 (print) | LCCN 2025038147
    (ebook) | ISBN 9780520396685 cloth |
    ISBN 9780520396692 paperback |
    ISBN 9780520396708 ebook
Subjects: LCSH: Food supply—Social aspects—
    California—Los Angeles | Social movements—
    California—Los Angeles | Social justice—California—
    Los Angeles | Racism—California—Los Angeles | Food
    security—California—Los Angeles
Classification: LCC HD9008.L6 G37 2025 (print) |
    LCC HD9008.L6 (ebook) | DDC 338.1/979494—dc23
    /eng/20250911
LC record available at https://lccn.loc.gov/2025038146
LC ebook record available at https://lccn.loc
    .gov/2025038147

GPSR Authorized Representative: Easy Access System
Europe, Mustamäe tee 50, 10621 Tallinn, Estonia, gpsr.
requests@easproject.com

34 33 32 31 30 29 28 27 26 25
10 9 8 7 6 5 4 3 2 1

For my father,
Byron L. Garth
(1948–2019)

Contents

Organizations and People   *ix*

Prologue   *xi*

Introduction   *1*

Interlude 1: Journee   *30*

Chapter 1: History   *33*

Interlude 2: Wendy   *64*

Chapter 2: Justice   *66*

Interlude 3: Ms. Veronica   *97*

Chapter 3: Whiteness   *101*

Interlude 4: Kween   *127*

Chapter 4: Placemaking   *129*

Interlude 5: Ms. Bernetta   *159*

Chapter 5: Liberation   *161*

Conclusion: The End(s) of Food Justice   *194*

Acknowledgments   *211*

Notes   *215*

Bibliography   *241*

Index   *267*

Organizations and People

The names of organizations and people used throughout this book are pseudonyms. Those with first and last names were more central to my analysis, and those with first names only played more minor roles in my research. While these individuals appear in the book, I also spoke with many other people who are not mentioned. The order of organizations and individuals listed below is based on order of appearance in the book.

Food for All
Miguel
Lindsay Adams
Sunny
Build It Better
Randy Johnson
Clara
Growing Health
Julian
Barrio Bite
Federico Jimenez
Javier
Magdely
Rooting Change
Jamarcus Green
Bettering Life
David
Matt Smith
Produce Power
Sarah Cunningham
Chase Bledsoe
Hyejin Kim
Candace

Mission Marathon
Ms. Mary
South Central Residents
Andrés
Journee
Ms. Judy
Ms. Corrinne
Wendy
Ms. Veronica
Kween
Ronica
Ms. Bernetta
Nzinga
Additional People
Josh Anderson
Raimi
Hazel
Jorge
Mary Louise
The Chef
Melissa
Alejandra
Cristianos

Prologue

On a mild fall day in 2008, I spent an afternoon unloading a manure truck as a volunteer at a South Central Los Angeles community garden that was part of the food justice nonprofit Food for All. I was the only volunteer willing to work with the manure that day, so I spent a lot of time talking to Miguel, the staff member unloading the truck. Born and raised in South Central, Miguel started at Food for All as an intern in high school and was working his way up in the organization. He did not say much but had a gentle, calming presence that made me feel at ease in the garden. As we shoveled manure into the wheelbarrow, which we rolled into the garden and dumped into various vegetable beds, I asked him basic questions about Food for All: Why does the organization do the work that it does? What kinds of people volunteered there? Who did they hope to serve? And why? I felt excited to be volunteering, to literally put my hands in the dirt and use my body in a way that was very different from my everyday life as a doctoral student.[1]

That day was one of my first volunteer experiences with a food justice organization, and I was immediately struck by the demographics of the other volunteers. Three college students came from West Los Angeles; it was also their first time volunteering with Food for All. A graduate student from a local state college had been a semiregular volunteer. All had traveled from more affluent parts of Los Angeles, like the beach community of Santa Monica or Brentwood, Westwood, and Century City, nestled between the ocean and Beverly Hills. They had traveled by car along the 10 eastbound or via Santa Monica Boulevard or Wilshire to a southbound street like Western, Normandie, or Vermont, taking them from the center of the city through Koreatown, Mid-City, the University of Southern California area, and into South Central Los Angeles.

I left the garden that day with complicated thoughts and emotions. Physically I felt good—my body was sore, and my skin was caked with dirt and sweat. I enjoyed the work and found it fulfilling. Gardening has been a part of my life for as long as I can remember. Growing up in the Midwest, my family always had a summer garden at home. My grandmother's garden was extensive, allowing her to put together meals with fresh ingredients all summer and canned vegetables in winter. I moved to Los Angeles in 2008. Living in an apartment in West Los Angeles, I had a strong desire to grow my own food. Without access to outdoor space, my small collection of potted herbs and hanging tomato plants on the enclosed balcony did not satisfy my habituated desire to grow food. When my landlord found a volunteer tomato plant I had been nourishing behind the building's landscaped bushes, he threatened eviction, claiming the tomatoes would attract rats, and removed the plant. So I signed up to volunteer at Food for All's garden in South Central Los Angeles, which led to volunteering with other food-related organizations. I stumbled into the food justice movement when I met other like-minded volunteers.

That day in 2008 awoke a nagging curiosity that coincided with my academic training in anthropology, which gave me tools to analyze it. I was struck not only by the volunteer demographics but also by the racial dynamics of the work. The two nonwhite people, me and Miguel, ended up shoveling shit. The other volunteers pulled weeds and chatted while sitting on the edges of garden beds. While Miguel became a fixture in the food justice movement, I never saw the other volunteers again. Later, I would reflect on the fleeting nature of some peoples' relationship with food justice work, which might involve swooping in and posting on social media but never engaging beyond the superficial. These racialized dynamics and varying connections to South Central Los Angeles and the food justice movement are part of what has pulled me to study the movement.

At the outset I did not intend for this food justice work to become a research project. I began this journey as a genuine volunteer interested in working toward food justice. At one point I was offered a job at a food justice organization that I seriously considered taking. I spent a lot of time looking for people and communities I ideologically aligned with. Along the way I encountered many food justice activists who saw things differently from me, and I wanted to understand why. I was captivated and intimidated by the complexity of the food justice movement, the vast number of people who were interested in it, and the many diverging ideologies and logics that compelled them. The spaces where food activists converged in Los Angeles did not reflect a movement in the sense of a single shared idea about what food is, how it should be grown, and who should benefit and why. Nor were these spaces an organized social and nutritional system where the relationship between "food" and "justice" was commonly understood. Instead, the movement grew haphazardly and rapidly, with a diverse group of people involved in food justice for many reasons, and there was rarely the time or place to come together and build a unifying vision across the multiple threads.

I studied the work of seven core food justice–related organizations over twelve years. This involved ethnographic research, including participant observation and interviews, where I spent long stretches of time hanging out and volunteering alongside people, trying to understand how they built meaning around the work they were doing. I tracked the organizations' work via newsletters, events, emails, and social media.[2] Beyond the seven organizations, I studied dozens of smaller and larger organizations with which they partnered for specific projects. These organizations tended to focus on creating sustainable interventions and long-term solutions that would empower residents of South Central to tackle the problem of food access. The organizations centered collective practices like community gardens and corner store conversions as well as cooking demos and K–12 educational interventions focused on individual behavioral shifts such as eating more vegetables and cooking homemade meals.

My research focused on the people doing food justice work and their organizations, which sought to intervene in South Central or East Los Angeles. Most of the people doing food justice work who participated in this research identified as white. Most did not live where they intervened. Part of what drove me to pursue the research was to understand why so many different organizations and activists coming from outside South Central or East LA were keen to intervene in Black and Latinx areas. Given South Central LA's many problems, from high poverty rates and a lack of well-paying jobs to under resourced schools and the lack of affordable housing, why was increasing access to healthy food and teaching people to consume healthier meals seen as crucial? To understand this, I conducted interviews with executive directors, staff members, volunteers, and key players in their collaborations and projects, including temporary consultants, clients, students, and interns. I attended board meetings, small group meetings, planning meetings, workshops, and public events. I offered my own sweat equity in the form of shoveling manure, filling community supported agriculture (CSA) boxes, creating budget spreadsheets, translating documents into Spanish, and assisting organizations when asked.

Many of the people I met early in my research, working together as volunteers or as students in class together, would go on to become the leaders and drivers of the food justice movement in Los Angeles. After graduation from their various programs, they landed food justice–related jobs. As I was working on this project, running into them at events, I asked for interviews or to observe their work. When I decided to turn this into a formal study of the food justice movement, I assumed that it would reveal fruitful possibilities for building justice and freedom, enable hopeful kinds of "horizoning" work, and fall within what anthropologists have called "anthropologies of the good."[3] I was interested in how radical worlds emerge and offer hopeful possibilities for alternative futures. However, the ethnography did not unfold as I expected. Instead, over years of ethnographic engagement and reflection as an anthropologist, the people, projects, and programs I observed aligned more with what Sherry Ortner has called "dark anthropology" or the "questions of power, inequality, domination, and exploitation."[4] The anthropological lens offers an opportunity to attend to the often taken-for-granted ideologies and logics behind social justice interventions. Ethnographic attunement provides a way to better understand why interventions are ineffective, despite the best intentions of those working to "help" others, and to make sense of why inequality persists.

Although I observed harmful effects of food justice work, I know that those working and volunteering in the movement did not intend to create harm and, for the most part, genuinely sought to make the world a better place. Revealing the dark underside of good intentions is an outcome of the research; critiquing the people in the movement is beside the point. Committed to studying the problem from the actors' point of view, I dug deeper and tried to understand what kinds of systems, structures, and processes embedded in nonprofit and development work facilitate some projects and create barriers to others. I saw how well-intentioned people were caught within a system that prevented them from doing the work that was most helpful to communities they served. Many people involved in the movement knew they were stuck but did not know what to do about it, struggling to make sense of the relationship between food and justice. I watched them come to terms with the culpability of their own positions or the tensions, contradictions, and even violence of their work. Many of these well-intentioned people struggled with dawning reflexivity that shadowed their sunny commitment to "the good" through food into the realm of the dark. They often came to question what they were doing and to what end in ways that resonate with the stories I tell throughout this book.

My analysis builds on both my anthropological training and my life experience as a Black woman with family ties to farming and urban gardening as well as twenty years of ethnographic and public health–based research on nutrition, cultural foodways, and food access in marginalized communities. By contrast, I found that there were a lot of people involved in food justice work who seemed completely unaware of both the racial significance of what some scholars and activists term "food apartheid" and the fact that their work might do more harm than good. This book asks how it is that such a set of actors, with little knowledge of food and little to no experience in South Central, could become the driving force of community interventions. I ask why these community interventions rarely consult local residents, and why intervention leaders make assumptions based on stereotypes about the communities they serve. The book unpacks the food justice movement from the multifaceted social and political positions of those working in the movement to illuminate their ways of understanding the deeper purpose and meaning of their work.

The research shows how varying polyvalent meanings of the work were continuously renegotiated and changing over time. This book follows my journey as a researcher and thinker as well as a person in the movement. At the outset I made a false assumption that I would share political ideologies with those in search of justice and that we would agree broadly on what constituted justice through food. The research participants and I share many things, including similar educational backgrounds and socioeconomic status. Like me, many were starting families and looking to buy houses in neighborhoods with good public schools. Publicly—on social media, through bumper stickers and yard signs—we rallied behind similar progressive politicians and local causes. Despite these similarities, however, over time I found that I was more politically aligned with a small subset of food justice organizations that were building from grassroots-organizing techniques and working toward liberation more broadly. Although I was not as ideologically aligned with most of the food justice activists I worked with, I still listened to them, observed their practices, and tried to understand their perspectives.

The research changed as the unraveling of political solidarity shifted the grounds through which I would relate to and understand my interlocutors. Many of the people who participated in my research became my friends and, for some, our social circles remain enmeshed. This work completely overturned the traditional lines between home and the field. I was doing fieldwork at home, but I was also living my life while doing fieldwork. Although I am critical of some of the work of food justice activists, I have found a place where I can hold that critique while simultaneously caring about them as well-intended people. In many ways the boundaries between familiar and strange were overturned and always partial and in flux. This required a particular ethical commitment to the ethnographic project and its ebbs and flows.[5] As I became more aware of this misalignment with my main interlocutors, I still conducted ethnography with the assumption that both ethnographic study and activist interventions can be grounded in radical, liberatory praxis. The research, writing, workshopping, teaching, and organizing that we do as ethnographers can be serious, rigorous, academic work done with an eye toward healing and emancipatory futures, even if that is not what our interlocutors are doing.[6]

My own positionality ultimately builds on anthropologist Deborah A. Thomas's approach to ethical ethnography, which takes seriously Black and Brown "embodied ways of knowing." However, while I understood food consumption practices in Black and Brown communities as rooted in our own knowledge, tradition, and intentional practices of nourishment and commensality, most of the food justice activists I studied did *not* operate from that position. Therefore, to take this ethical approach seriously, I had to extend and invert it. In other words I had to focus on the ideologies and logics that saw Black and Brown communities as ignorant, deficient, and flawed and home in on the microtechniques through which such frameworks are embedded into all kinds of social practices, including movements for social justice. Only by unearthing misguided logics could I show the importance of longstanding Black and Brown approaches to nourishment, ways of knowing, and being in the world. In turn, this should illuminate that the communities being intervened upon by food justice organizations *do* have their own understandings and agency around what foods they should have access to and be consuming and that those positions should be respected.[7]

Given the dynamics of the food justice movement, this research involved a unique approach to ethnographic work. If the premise of anthropology was historically to make sense of the Other, this project turns that premise on its head. Instead, this book questions who the Other is. The book reveals how food justice activists see those they are intervening upon as a generic, stereotyped Other, while South Central residents view those intervening upon them as "outsiders" who could not possibly know their situation. While many traditional approaches to ethnography might focus on the residents of South Central, this book follows the lives and work of the outsiders as well as a smaller subset of residents who are organizing for food justice in different ways.[8] Attending to all these different approaches to food justice is crucial for understanding the failures of food justice and the forms of power that undermine grassroots and community-based organizing.

This book challenges the directionality of knowledge production within ethnographic work. Rather than focusing on the suffering and struggles of the people of South Central, I focus on the lives, identity formations, and work of a group of people who imagine themselves as producing justice and the ways they end up reproducing forms of structural violence. By studying food justice through their vantage point, I came to understand how South Central and its residents continue to be misunderstood, often cast by food justice activists into a "suffering slot" and at times a "savage slot"—both terms used to critique the ways anthropologists have all too easily "slotted" people into different categories.[9] However, in my research I saw how the activists themselves were "slotting" people into such categories. This sustained ethnographic attention to the logics and practices of those who ended up controlling this social movement offers a critical intervention to ethnographic practice more broadly and theorizes why social movements fail and why the potential for radical change is foreclosed.

My experiences in South Central, beyond volunteering in gardens and doing this research, were radically different from how food justice activists characterized life there. Like most residents, I knew the area by the name of "South Central," a historical moniker that the city tried to rebrand, officially renaming it "South Los Angeles" in 2003. The City Council tried to take things further by calling the area "SOLA." However, residents never really transitioned to calling it anything other than "South Central" or "the Hood." For me, how various people named the place often indicated their relationship to it; "South Central" was where residents called home, "South LA" was an imagined place to be intervened upon. Once while describing my research as "a study of food justice in South LA," a friend born and raised in South Central asked for clarification: "Where is South LA?" Genuinely confused, as someone from South Central, she was completely unfamiliar with the "South LA" moniker and imaginary. Throughout the book I use "South LA" to refer to the imagined place that those who are not familiar with South Central Los Angeles are attempting to change, or "bring justice to."

I use the term "South Central" to refer to the area as it is broadly understood and referenced by residents and grassroots-oriented food justice organizations. The first three chapters of the book are more focused on "outsiders," those people and organizations who have attempted to bring justice to South LA and the various ways that they have misunderstood South Central and the problems it faces. Chapters 4, 5, and much of the conclusion focus on those individuals and groups who view food justice as part of a broader, collective envisioning of a liberated South Central, as well as the problems they face as they come up against structures and systems that thwart their efforts. These different approaches, both operating under the banner of food justice, are framed within different but parallel histories and ideologies. This book analyzes the power dynamics between the approaches to show how different groups within the movement jockey for power to shape the movement.

Although the research for this book ended in 2020, I started a different project on food access for South Central households in 2021, which gave me a much deeper understanding of local families' everyday realities. This book is not about those families but the five interludes between chapters are rooted in their lived experiences and offer a glimpse into the lives of residents outside of the food justice movement.[10] The food justice terrain is complex and despite some of the language used within food justice circles, there is no clear-cut divide between good actors and bad actors. There are gradations, flows, influxes, and waning. Some systems and structures facilitate bad outcomes, and there are good people whose actions create harm. My goal is to illuminate the nuances of the food justice movement, including the systems and processes that prevent it from flourishing. I hope to offer lessons for the next generation organizing around liberation and food futures.

Introduction

After exiting the 110 freeway onto West Slauson Avenue, Julian and I drove into South Los Angeles onto a side street in his silver Prius.[1] The street was lined with single-story bungalows, most with chain link or wrought iron fences around their yards of yellowed grass that became green only during increasingly rare winter rains. Cars were parked along both sides of the street, intermixed with emptied trash and recycling bins. Lining each block were a few palm trees and giant ficus trees, commonly planted in the City of Los Angeles. The air was crisp, and the Southern California sun was shining bright. As I looked up toward the palm tree tops against the blue sky, I could recognize this as the opening scene of any number of films or shows based in LA. A few blocks down, Julian slowed to a stop and rolled down the passenger-side window so I could see more clearly. Flowing from the open windows of nearby homes, I heard the sounds of music playing, daytime TV shows, lunch cooking in hissing pressure cookers, and muffled conversations. The air smelled of jasmine and passion fruit vines growing along fences and in backyard gardens.

Julian pointed and said, "Look at that." He was showing me a small field of dead grass littered with faded junk food wrappers, plastic bottles, and cans. He noted the multiunit apartment complexes on all three sides of the field. I must have looked uncertain about what he wanted me to pay attention to. "It's a vacant lot," he said. With a pause for effect, grinning from ear to ear, he elaborated: "Just imagine that this

FIGURE 1. A vacant lot in Los Angeles. Photo by the author.

land in the middle of a food desert is transformed into a lush community garden. The people from all these buildings could be growing their own food, working together to cultivate the garden, and sharing the harvests. We are trying to figure out who owns the land and if we can use it to start a community garden."

Julian and I were carpooling to an on-site meeting of an organization that was trying to increase access to healthy food in South Central Los Angeles. He wanted to intervene in South LA and was in the early stages of creating his first project. Julian hoped to build a new food justice organization focused on K–12 nutrition education and school gardens. I met him through my university networks. A faculty member who knew we were both interested in food justice introduced us at a party. Julian had finished a master's degree and wanted to leverage his technology, design, and business skills to "bring justice" to South LA. He made a few more turns, taking us down Hoover Ave. past Augustus F. Hawkins High School. I noticed that school was in session, and the gates around the relatively new, modern-looking building were closed.[2] Julian pointed at the school, and said:

> That building has fifteen hundred young people inside. Imagine those kids working in the community garden after school, helping out elders, connecting with neighbors, learning skills, and with access to fresh fruits and vegetables right here in their neighborhood. It's beautiful because California's growing season is really aligned with the school year, summer is kind of a dead time anyway. But if we can just figure out how to get the city or owner to give us access to that lot, we could have a dream food justice program—teaching kids about gardening as a way to bring community together and create a way for these communities to have access to fresh fruits and vegetables grown right here in South Central.

I was intrigued by Julian's vision, but when I looked at the school, I could not help but dwell on the closed iron gates, the police car parked outside, and the reports that were cropping up about the school-to-prison pipeline at the time. My early experience shoveling manure at Food for All's garden primed me to pay attention to racialized differences in the experience of food justice work. Given that context, I felt hesitant about using those kids for garden labor, but I could also see the value of getting outside and building community. Julian did not seem to notice the securitized school or think of potential problems with using school kids as labor in his envisioned project. Instead, he focused on his vision of transforming South LA.

Julian rolled down the windows again. I heard the faint sounds of Nipsey Hussle's "Hussle in the House" coming from a car parked nearby. I smiled and thought about our route into South LA that day and the track's opening line about coming "straight outta Slauson." Julian heard the music too and commented that someone was playing Kris Kross's "Jump," the 1992 hit sampled by Hussle. He smiled and asked me if I remembered the song from elementary school. I nodded but did not correct what he had misrecognized. As we drove off, I noted the differences in what I had been attuned to—specific smells, music, and the vibrant pulse of South Central—and what Julian had fixated on—vacancy, his vision, and misplaced nostalgia. I did not dwell on the different ways we interpreted the place; instead I kept my ethnographic focus on Julian's vision of food justice.

Julian and the people from the organization we met that day were part of the growing social movement for food justice in Los Angeles. "Food justice" is popularly understood as a movement to ensure that everyone has access to healthy, affordable, and culturally appropriate food at a reasonable distance from their homes. Although community gardens, neighborhood food distribution programs, and political organizing around food have long histories across the globe, at the historical moment when I started doing this research, organizations like Julian's were specifically focused on increasing access to healthy foods in low-income communities of color. As I moved deeper into this research, I became increasingly interested in the paradigms that inspired people like Julian and how those converged and diverged from the legacies of Black, Indigenous, and other people of color who have organized for better food systems for hundreds of years.

I eventually came to see that the term "food justice" was used in such a variety of ways across diverse sets of actors that in the end the term had very little shared meaning. However, I began this research with an understanding that "food justice" was about correcting the injustices of a deeply inequitable food system. Food access inequality and the right to access affordable, healthy food is a complex problem that needs significant attention. I understood that "food justice" could be applied broadly across the many dimensions of the food system—from inequitable distribution to safe working conditions across sectors of food work to land access and the ability to determine what kind of food is produced locally. For food justice to build into a social movement, I thought it would simply mean that a critical mass of residents was organizing behind efforts to create a more just and equitable food system.[3] However, more than a decade into the research, I learned that movement building is much more complicated. I would grow to see how the different frameworks, ideologies, and power structures shaping the movement would significantly influence the radical possibilities for multiracial coalition building toward change.

To me, a radical approach would involve understanding the root causes of a problem, not just the symptoms of the problem. "Radical change" refers to fundamental deep-seated shifts in the existing structures that cause problems like food access inequities. Radical approaches require a critical analysis of existing power structures and seek to overturn imbalances of power. Multiracial coalition building is solidarity-based organizing work across multiple racial and ethnic groups.[4] These collective efforts tend to position those most impacted by the problems as the most important voices in organizing for change. Multiracial coalitions must be dynamic and responsive to contexts and changing needs. But much of the work I observed that was called "food justice" was not doing this kind of work, which I found puzzling.

It is important and revealing that those involved have consistently referred to this as a food *justice* movement rather than just a food movement.[5] Scholars of food movements categorized different approaches across a spectrum of "motivational frames" ranging from radical, secessionist, progressive, eco-central, entrepreneurial, developmentalist, and so forth.[6] Although there are many possible approaches to improving the food system, the "justice" framework is a prevailing force in various parts of California. The concept of "justice" may hold greater political power in places like South Central, which have longer histories of radical organizing against racial discrimination and systems of oppression. Although some activists might see a "justice" approach as radical, other people were motivated to get involved in food justice to serve those they saw as "in need," which drew a particular kind of person to "help" the people of South LA.

Thus "justice" was a way, for some, of shaping their work around food as something more meaningful than charity to people deemed in need of help. "Justice" became a way of giving that work an aura of significant social and political meaning. Although food justice is often framed as better than charity, which is frequently stigmatized and disparaged as "handouts," I found that in practice the label "justice" can simply be slapped onto charity work or other forms of food activism. "Justice" loses meaning in this process, and people can become confused about what goals, if any, they share with other activists. This kind of co-optation of grassroots movement language can take people's own desires to organize and slowly shift them away from radical possibilities toward more mainstream approaches. Some of the work operating under the "food justice" moniker could actually be worse than charity because it undermines social justice's potential.

Like Julian, many people involved in my research did not live in South Central or have ties to the community. Most of the food justice work that I observed was *not* resistance by those who struggle with the injustices of the food system but instead the actions of well-meaning outsiders who assumed they were helping by envisioning the transformation of South LA and its residents. Many interventions I observed were based on assumptions about the everyday lives of people in South LA rather than research or first-hand experience. The problems were already assumed to be known. My own experiences in South Central sat in contrast to the vision of South LA that some food justice activists were attempting to change. Through friends and family connections my experiences in South Central and adjacent areas (like Leimert Park, Baldwin Hills, Ladera

Heights, and the Crenshaw district) consisted of backyard barbeques, birthday parties, baby showers, Thanksgiving gatherings, Superbowl parties—all gatherings that brought friends and family together and featured food, which was always in abundance and delicious. My personal experience with food in South Central was centered around commensality—that is, sharing food as a community. I knew of other long-standing programs in the area that were rooted in the rich history of strength and resilience in these communities. I realized that I would have to reckon with the meaning of "justice" across multiple subject positions and different experiences with and imaginaries of the food system.

The free breakfast program of the Black Panther Party (BPP), which began in 1969 and continued into the early 1970s, stood out to me and others from South Central as the exemplar of what food justice could look like. The program arose from a clear need articulated by the community, developed by folks who understood the patterns and struggles of daily life who sought to serve the needs of their community. The program, also known as the Free Breakfast for School Children Program, started in West Oakland, California, as part of the vision of BPP founders Huey P. Newton and Bobby Seale to feed the community mind, body, and soul. The initiative was based on research showing how essential breakfast is for optimal school learning. The logic of filling children's bellies and alleviating hunger also served the BPP's goal of teaching the tenets of the struggles for Black liberation while the children ate their breakfasts. The program was one of the BPP's many "survival programs," which included delivering free bags of groceries, free clinics, and housing cooperatives.[7] The effort was systematically attacked and eventually dismantled through the actions of the FBI's COINTELPRO (Counter Intelligence Program) under J. Edgar Hoover.[8] Nevertheless, the BPP breakfast program is the precursor to the federal School Breakfast Program (SBP), which provides free or reduced-price breakfasts to children, authorized in 1975.

In addition to the BPP, I knew friends and family members in South Central who had been influenced by holistic health practitioner Queen Afua's call for a plant-based diet as part of a broader set of practices to harness the power of food to heal Black women's bodies and nuture spiritual health. I also knew that many folks in South Central had been influenced by the African American Hebrew Israelites of Jerusalem and the Nation of Islam's emphasis on healthy eating, which discouraged pork and fried food consumption and encouraged beans, turkey, brown rice, and a more plant-based diet.[9] In 2010, A. Breeze Harper's book *Sistah Vegan* made the rounds in both the food justice community and folks I knew in South Central. Later, in 2014, Bryant Terry's books *Afro-Vegan* and *Vegan Soul Food* added to the broader circulation of information about Black veganism.

Although I encountered some organizations that approached food justice as a community-led project, which I detail toward the end of the book, most food justice activists I worked with saw South LA and their work through a different lens. Many people had experienced the area as a place they drove through on the freeway and learned about only through the nightly news and popular media. The freeways that cut and structured the racial and social geographies of the city also facilitated the interest of people enacting food justice movements in those neighborhoods. Like Julian, they viewed it as a place of lacking, consisting of people "in need." Vacant lots, like the one I drove by with him, served as a metaphor for food justice activists. To them, South LA was a vacant place that awaited their help, a blank canvas upon which they could test their ideas, experiment with programs, and "serve" this imagined community in need of help from outsiders.

My ethnographic sensibilities were piqued by stark differences between my own experiences and the way the food justice activists I worked with framed South LA. Like those I was studying, I did not spend much time at the cookouts in South Central for this research. Instead, I flitted in and out of South LA between planning calls, brainstorms, and meetings, just as the activists I worked with did. Much of this research occurred while riding in cars with activists as we rushed from meeting to meeting, site to site, fighting LA traffic. Simultaneously, in my personal life, through friends and family, I experienced South Central as a place for gatherings, camaraderie, and commensality.

"WE USE THE TERM 'FOOD APARTHEID'"

Nine years after first meeting Julian, in March 2017, I attended a gathering of more than two hundred people working in food justice across Los Angeles. They had come together to unpack and examine the state of healthy food access in LA's so-called food desert communities and to consider ways the food movement could play a role in addressing socioeconomic and racial disparities in health and food access. The event took place at a venue off of Central Avenue, just blocks away from Nickerson Gardens, known as the largest public housing project west of the Mississippi. Many food justice activists I had been formally studying or informally observing were there, including Julian, who by 2017 had been doing garden education in area schools for several years. In the crowd I saw Sarah Cunningham and Chase Bledsoe, both working for Produce Power at the time, and Josh Anderson and Matt Smith, who had been involved in several interventions with different organizations, seated together in the back of the room.

I arrived at the gathering just as the opening remarks started, waving from across the room and mouthing "hello" to many people I knew. After the initial welcome, Andrés was introduced as a community member and invited to speak about his role in a local nonprofit doing work that he called "adjacent to food justice" and his history working within the community. To me, Andrés had positioned himself and the organization he worked for as doing food justice work, but not in the same way as many of the people in the room that he critiqued. He articulated his food justice work as part of a bigger and longer tradition of struggle for liberation, which was tied to histories and ideologies different from the food justice movement that had cropped up in the 2000s. Andrés knew he was a part of that new group too, but he wanted to ensure people understood that he was doing something different. He paused and added what seemed to be an off-script point to his remarks:

> Today, we're talking about the food desert and the areas of progress we made. . . . At least from our vantage point—from the vantage of our residents, is that the food desert [label] always seemed kind of confusing and even contested, certainly contested over the last decade. Kind of felt like some white liberal came up with that term while they were making some vegan, organic food and making sure that there were none of our foods present because, for us, it didn't feel like a desert because a desert is a naturally occurring state and certain animals can actually live and do well in the desert.

As Andrés mentioned the white liberal, vegan, organic food angle, I could not help but look for Sarah Cunningham in the crowd. Having first met her in 2008, I knew she would admit that as a raw vegan, yoga-loving, infusion-drinking, astrology-obsessed white lady, she fit this stereotype. She and I were part of several overlapping social circles, some linked to the area universities we were affiliated with and other social circles that had grown organically. We were both part of a radical queer house party circuit with a multiracial group of queer and gender-nonconforming folks working to disrupt the norms of dominant hetero-patriarchal society in ways big and small. For a few years we regularly met up for morning walks at the Silver Lake Reservoir and chatted about life and her food justice work. I knew from our conversations that Sarah understood herself as ideologically aligned with Andrés's visions of liberation. She winced and shifted uncomfortably in her seat, but she held her gaze, intently listening to what Andrés had to say. I imagined that it hurt a little to hear this stereotype, but that this was a critical moment for Sarah to work on herself. Andrés continued:

> But for us, it was never really about a desert. We use the term "food apartheid" because we felt that the allocation of food, and healthy food, was a system by design that creates unequal access for communities that are flooded with death-selling businesses—alcohol outlets and fast food restaurants—while grocery stores and farmers markets and healthy restaurants are abandoned in other parts of the city.[10] We know that West LA has three times as many Ralphs [grocery stores] as South LA, even though West LA has fewer people.

Andrés underscored the importance of understanding food apartheid in context, mentioning some of the work his organization has focused on. Given that "our residents live next to underresourced schools, oil drilling sites, liquor stores, fast food restaurants, there's no surprise that we have the lowest life expectancy in the city," he said, emphasizing that "this is a result of historic and deliberate neglect, abuse and outright oppressive conditions in African American and Latino communities. So that's why we call it apartheid."

While the food desert concept was the most common way to understand the problem at the outset of my research, over the course of twelve years the term "food apartheid" became a counternarrative to characterize food retail inequality in settings across the United States.[11] Describing an essentially separate and unequal system of food distribution, with similar logic to Andrés, New York State–based activists Karen Washington and Leah Penniman, founders of Black Urban Growers (BUGs) and Soulfire Farm, respectively, have argued that "food apartheid" more accurately describes the intentional and systematic forms of racism and economic discrimination that have created the inequitable food system.[12] If a "food desert" is a landscape feature based on a moralized misunderstanding of ecology, "food apartheid" is a politically maintained state of affairs involving a politics of active neglect.

There was quiet laughter in the room when Andrés mentioned white liberals and vegan organic food. He was tapping into the genuine California wellness and health culture that moralized particular ways of eating and specific body types. He was poking fun at it, but this was also a real problem for the food justice movement, because it pulled focus toward these trends and away from the needs of the community.

A few people applauded when Andrés mentioned food apartheid. Many people in the audience seemed to nod their heads in agreement. Others just stared blankly forward. His comments were impactful to me, in part because since I started doing this work in 2008, I had not heard many people explicitly lay out the connections between historical and ongoing racial oppression and the food access inequality in South LA.

During a break I found Julian in the crowd. After catching up about his nonprofit organization's work in local schools, I asked what he thought of the comments. "It's interesting," he said, "something I hadn't really thought about. It'll be good to keep in mind." And he turned toward a table of snacks. I was puzzled by Julian's response. I had always seen him as a food justice activist who really wanted to know what the community thought and needed, but he did not seem to digest what I understood Andrés to be saying, brushing off his remarks. While there could have been many reasons for Julian's flippant response, at that moment I realized that many activists I had been studying had similarly disinterested responses to the links between racism and food access inequality. They seemed to rarely ask questions about the community, what residents needed or wanted, nor did they dwell on the many other problems that residents were dealing with, as Andrés had laid out.

While I pondered this disinterest in residents' perspectives, two women introduced themselves to me and initiated a conversation. Raimi and Hazel had recently completed master's degrees in architecture and urban planning, respectively, and both worked for local design firms interested in "breaking into" food justice work. Both women aspired to get advanced degrees after working for a while. Hazel, who presented as white and had a British accent, introduced herself first, asking me if I was from South LA. After I replied with a simple "no," Raimi, who presented as Black, stepped in, adding that she was from the East Coast and had gone to Ivy League schools for her undergraduate and graduate degrees. She told me that she and Hazel were working on a new food justice app. When I asked Raimi what it would do, she said, "We want to have an app that will help people find grocery stores or other places that sell food in South LA."

An older woman with graying hair who appeared to be Black overheard Raimi and asked the three of us, "Who would that be for? Everyone who lives here knows where we can get food." Raimi and Hazel did not respond. Filling the silence, Julian joined the conversation, offering an excited response, asking if Raimi and Hazel would be interested in collaborating as tech experts or designers for his school-to-community garden program. I viewed Julian as trying to interrupt an awkward moment and help the two young women save face. As I listened to their three-way conversation, I drifted off, my thoughts fixated on the casual comment of the older woman. She had indicated that she was a resident and would not find their intervention useful. I was really puzzled by the way Raimi, Hazel, and Julian did not seem to register the significance of her interjection, quickly pivoting out of an uncomfortable critique by praising one another and deepening their focus on quick-fix, technological interventions.

As I drove home, taking Central Ave. to the freeway, I thought about how people like Raimi, Hazel, and Julian had been able to design and implement so many interventions in South LA. At the same time, residents and community leaders like Andrés and the older woman from the community were cast aside by Raimi, Hazel, and Julian. I questioned why the movement highlighted and supported particular kinds of food justice projects in South LA while others were overlooked. I had heard from residents and food justice activists alike that early on residents had complained that there were not enough grocery stores for the population in the area and that the stores in the area were considerably older than those in other parts of the city. They questioned the quality of fresh meat and produce in the older stores, which tended to have older refrigeration units and slower turnover of meat, dairy, and produce. Given these specific and very real complaints, I wondered how we got to gardens planted by outsiders, cooking demonstrations in K–12 classrooms, and introducing fresh fruit and vegetables at local corner and liquor stores as the primary models for increasing access to fresh food in South LA.

I wanted to understand how particular narratives around food and justice shaped different types of actors and organizations, how they shaped the food justice movement as well as those whom they wanted to intervene upon in specific ways. Throughout this book I analyze systems of meaning, shifting and contested spheres of knowledge, claims of expertise, and ultimately who can intervene and to what ends. On one level this book is about food and food justice; it is also about the broader stakes of social justice and the possibility of multiracial coalitions that work toward better futures. I spent a lot of time with organizations and activists like Julian, who believe that it is essential to "give back" to the community and strive toward improving the systems and structures that are in place. These activists see the benefits of our society in their own lives and believe that others too can share in those benefits. They work toward this either through individual action or collective organizing. I also worked with individuals like Andrés, who believe that our status quo systems and institutions are the root problem. In an ideal world they would abolish those systems and build new ones that serve the communities they care about. However, many in this group see the impossibility of metaphorically burning it all down. Instead, they work to reform the status quo while still holding a practice of envisioning radically different future possibilities.

My anthropological training cued me to the importance of using ethnographic methods to understand the role of organizations and institutions in shaping various elements of society. This project could respond to anthropologists James Ferguson and Akhil Gupta's call for more "empirical work on what these organizations are really doing, and how they create both new dangers and new possibilities for political practice."[13] Once I tuned in to the research in that way, I started to see patterns across the different ways of thinking that create distinct groups of food justice actors. For instance, the first group tended toward organizations that had only been involved in food justice work since it exploded in popularity in the mid-2000s, often working on quick, tangible solutions to immediate problems. The other group tended to look toward a much longer, centuries-long timeline that works toward justice and liberation while simultaneously attending to the needs of the community.

In this context I understand liberation as an ongoing historical process focused on freeing individuals and communities from oppression, inequality, and injustice. Liberation involves challenging and dismantling the systems and structures of power that have enabled conditions of oppression in the first place. It is about slow, long-term fundamental change to those systems and structures. Often the first step to liberation is simply creating awareness of how these systems operate and continue to produce oppression. Liberation usually involves solidarity with adjacent social justice movements and understanding the interconnectedness of struggle. Ultimately liberation is about working toward self-determination and the ability to live a decent life as people define decency for themselves. That said, I am profoundly aware that the concept of liberation can be co-opted and used as a logic for various kinds of political movements, from fascism to neoliberalism.[14] For instance, President Donald Trump dubbed the day he unveiled widespread tariffs on all imports into the United States as "liberation day." Such uses of the term "liberation" are not what I am referring to in this book.

Through this longitudinal research with food justice activists, I found people like Sarah Cunningham, who fundamentally care about making the world a better place and move back and forth between these different positions over time. They can go through periods of thinking pragmatically within the existing institutional structures that benefit them in many ways and other times shift into dreaming radically for a better future and trying to enact that future vision in their everyday work. This kind of ebb and flow between positions seems natural, and logically it would fluctuate depending on other life circumstances. Differently positioned actors could wield the power to foreclose movement toward radical future possibilities, pulling other actors toward the approaches they are more comfortable with or understand as more valuable and pragmatic. I saw others try to pull the conversations back toward more radical visions like Andrés articulated at the food justice gathering.

I understood Andrés and others like him as trying to educate the nonresidents, imploring them to see the bigger picture and ask different questions that would hopefully yield better solutions. But, like Julian's flippant response, I saw many nonresidents ignore, eschew, or shut down these kinds of conversations in other ways. In the way that Julian mistook Nipsey Hussle for Kriss Kross, because of their lack of experience in the community, many outsiders misrecognized the problems and developed interventions that were ineffective. Many outsiders did not understand the history of South Central or the broader historical factors that yielded uneven access to food. This all led to wildly different framings of the problem and divergent approaches to solutions across different groups of people, all claiming to work toward "food justice." I saw this as a way of jockeying for power to shape approaches to social justice.

SOUTH CENTRAL LOS ANGELES

In addition to divergent visions for food justice, the activists I studied had divergent ways of understanding or imagining South LA/South Central.[15] All the organizations I studied shared the goal of improving access to "healthy food" in the area. Geographically and demographically, the area can appear to be just like any other low-income inner-city area in the United States. South Los Angeles—roughly the area just south of Downtown Los Angeles, to the west and east of 110—consists of twenty-six official LA neighborhoods and spans roughly sixteen square miles. Depending on how you draw the lines, the area is home to hundreds of thousands of Angelenos. The *Los Angeles Times*'s Mapping LA project reported a population of nearly eight hundred thousand in South LA in 2000.[16] By comparison, South LA is a small part of

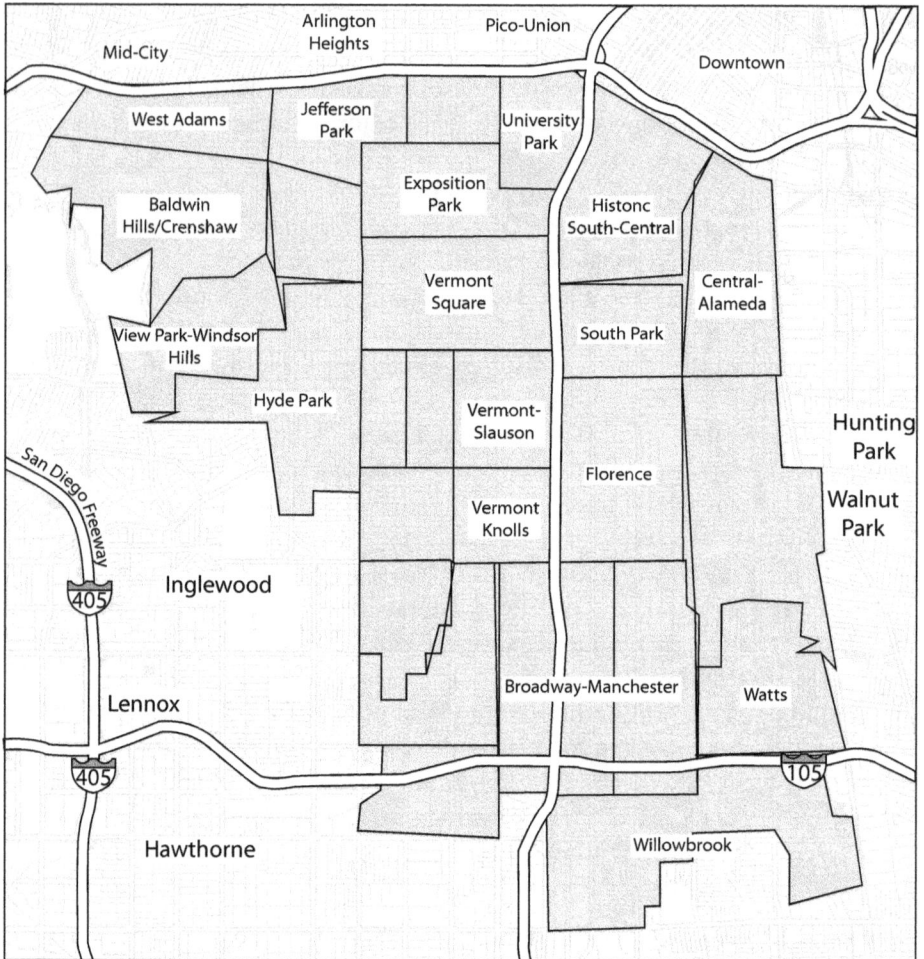

MAP 1. Map of South Los Angeles, including Watts. Creative Commons 3.0 Unported License.

the greater Los Angeles area, the largest metropolitan region in the United States by land area. While the City of Los Angeles has a population of 3.9 million living in 468 square miles, the area commonly conceived of as the Los Angeles metro area includes other cities, such as Beverly Hills and Santa Monica, and moves beyond LA county's bounds. Within this broader LA metro area, thirteen to nineteen million people live within 4,850 to 33,954 square miles, depending on how the boundaries are drawn.[17]

Beyond these official delineations, South LA is part of a particular racial and spatial imaginary, or what Black Studies scholar George Lipsitz has called the "racialization of space and the spatialization of race."[18] Portrayals of the area were popularized in rap music from artists like NWA in the late 1980s with their album *Straight Outta Compton* to Dr. Dre, Snoop Dogg, Eazy-E, Ice Cube, Ice-T, and, more recently, the late Nipsey Hussle.[19] These artists rap about South Central. Naming different streets and areas they would drive through, they reflected on the violence and difficulties of living there. Popular movies from *Boyz n the Hood* (1991) to *Friday* (1995) to the movie *Straight Outta Compton* (2015) extended the ways in which outsiders could imagine life in South LA as a place of poverty and violence but also music, family, and community.[20] The popularity of these portrayals made South LA the quintessential ghetto in many racialized imaginaries across the globe. Many people I met throughout this research who came from outside South Central felt that they knew what life was like in the area based on popular media. When I explained to my research participants that I tried to dedicate my Fridays to working on this project, many would laughingly reply, "Because it's Friday, you ain't got no job, and you ain't got shit to do"—perhaps the most famous line from the movie *Friday*. References to *Friday* or other television, film, and music lyrics about South LA were common and signaled how food justice activists understood their work in the community. Mainstream images were central to how they envisioned South LA's problems and their own possible interventions. In effect, they were oriented to the area through fiction rather than real experience.[21]

Although many of the activists that I worked with imagined South LA as a Black place, as of 2020, South LA is 56 percent Latinx and 38 percent Black.[22] Many residents made $20,000 or less per year and have less than a high school level of education. Only 8.2 percent of residents twenty-five years or older held a four-year degree. And 63 percent of South LA residents rented their homes.[23] Most residents held low-wage and temporary jobs, and the area had significant levels of unemployment.[24] These demographic realities are essential when assessing the problem of food access as well as initiatives to increase access to healthy food. While recent data paints a dire picture, I want to underscore that South Central is a Black and Brown community that once thrived. Residents had access to decent-paying jobs, could afford homes, and built a vibrant cultural hub. As I elaborate in chapter 1, decades of divestment and urban-suburban restructuring drained resources, reduced job

FIGURE 2. A street corner in South LA. Photo by the author.

opportunities, and diminished real wages and purchasing power. As a result, people living in South Central today are likely to live in poverty and unlikely to have access to decent-paying jobs. At the time of my research, residents faced high degrees of economic precarity and uncertainty. Food access was one problem among many, and as the residents I spoke with underscore, it must be understood within the context of broader conditions. A central point in this book is that the food justice activists from outside the area did not seem to understand the complexity of living in poverty. Instead, they wanted to bracket off poverty and other problems that they view as unrelated or too complex, keeping a narrow focus on food.[25]

FOOD ACCESS IN SOUTH LA

In popular media and scholarly work, South LA has been characterized as lacking full-service grocery stores with quality produce, fresh meat, and dairy but having an overabundance of liquor stores, corner stores, and fast-food restaurants. Data on the number of grocery stores in the area depend mainly on where the boundaries are drawn. Regardless,

FIGURE 3. A liquor store in South LA. Photo by the author.

South LA has fewer supermarkets per capita than more affluent areas.[26] The City of Compton, bordering on South LA, reports sixty full-service grocery stores in South LA, each serving approximately 22,000 residents.[27] Affluent West LA had fifty-seven full-service grocery stores serving 650,000 residents, each serving about 11,000.[28] The Los Angeles County Department of Public Health reports that the percentage of adults who consume five or more servings of fruit and vegetables per day is 12.7 percent in South LA, compared with 22.7 percent in West LA and 14.7 percent in LA County overall.[29] In South LA, 27.6 percent of adults rate the quality of the fresh fruits and vegetables where they shop as high, compared with 51.6 percent in West LA and 36 percent in LA County overall.[30] While these numbers reveal clear disparities, food justice activists use these statistics to conclude that people in South LA need to be told to eat more vegetables and taught to change how they cook and eat. The focus on changing individual behaviors—a phenomenon that is not specific to food justice activism or South LA—shifts interventions away from work that addresses structural inequities in the food system.[31]

Different parts of Los Angeles have different types of food retail with different prices and products. Some grocery companies are very targeted about their desired shopper. Trader Joe's, for example, honed in on the "overeducated and underpaid" of West LA who were willing to spend money on wine and cheese.[32] Compared to West LA, the markets in South LA tended to be older and smaller and were perceived as having lower-quality foods, specifically fresh produce, meat, and dairy.[33] I often heard both food justice activists and residents say that they wanted a Whole Foods Market in South LA, but when I asked residents if they would shop there, they said they would not because it was too expensive. Whole Foods Market, with its clean aesthetic and vast offerings of organic fresh produce and other "healthy food" options, served as a symbol of the idealized, healthy food store, bolstered by popular media denouncing the global industrial food system, "junk" foods, and imploring Americans to eat "real food." The Whole Foods dream described by my interlocutors was a direct response to the visible and visceral experience of food apartheid.

I understood the problems of food access in South Central as deeply entangled with broader systems of structural racism, where race-based discrimination and inequality have been or continue to be embedded within the legal system, public policies and programming, and the everyday operating principles of organizations within society. Following anthropologist Ashanté Reese, I operated from the position that geographies are not "race-neutral."[34] The conditions in South Central are derived from particular histories of residential and retail redlining as well as citywide developments that have built parts of the city in different ways depending on racial makeup and potential for profit.[35] To understand the problem of food access inequality, we need to theorize the ways that racism operates within food systems, including how governments and corporations have divested from Black communities.[36] Whether they recognize it or not, food justice organizations in Los Angeles work within a racially "contested landscape."[37] Within this space, garden projects, store improvements, or even the realization of the Whole Foods dream are not simply matters of improvement, they are divergent and shifting visions of justice across differently positioned actors.

THE RISE OF FOOD JUSTICE

The Los Angeles food justice movement grew out of a moment when a nexus of social factors came together to create an explosion of food-related media and content in popular US culture in the years just before I began this research. TV shows, films, books, and articles from various writers and producers, activists or not, were touting the US food system as broken. My own deep dive into mainstream foodie culture and the emerging critique of the American diet can be traced to Michael Pollan's 2006 book *The Omnivore's Dilemma*, a book my mother gifted me shortly after it was released. A wildly popular tour de force on how the modern food system influences what we eat, it was among the *New York Times*'s Top Ten Books that year. Pollan saw himself on a quest to answer the age-old question "What should I eat?" which he cast as the omnivore's dilemma. In short, his answer is "real food" and more of it—or, as others have put it, food that comes from the ground or had a mother. Pollan asserted, and I agreed with him on this point, that culture has guided us in responding to this question. He claimed that there has been a breakdown in this system of trusting our cultural knowledge to guide our eating decisions over the past century.[38]

Pollan concluded, and many agreed, that the broader global industrial food system had grown out of control and no longer produced the kinds of foods that most people understood as healthy or "real." The broad-scale attention to the food system and how we eat began with a sweeping critique that many people do not cook from scratch or sit down to family meals as we imagined Americans did a generation or two ago. Instead, we eat processed, microwavable, fast, convenient food, mainly because the average US household does not have the time to spend hours preparing and cooking meals. Although the focus of similar scholarship and journalism began as a critique of the middle-class household and the global industrialized food system, over time some researchers shifted their attention to low-income families living in urban areas like South LA. As attention moved away from the middle-class family dinner table toward the needs of low-income households with limited access to healthy food, the focus of the problem shifted too. The need for "justice" became more apparent, opening the space for well-meaning white, middle-class folks from other communities to work toward helping low-income people of color eat better.

Based on conversations with activists, I knew we were reading many of the same mainstream books and watching the same documentaries, which included, in addition to Pollan's book, Eric Schlosser's *Fast Food Nation*, Morgan Spurlock's documentary *Super Size Me*, and the film *Food, Inc.* Smaller subsets of food justice activists also read books like Vandana Shiva's *Soil Not Oil* and *Manifestos on the Future of Food and Seed* as well as Raj Patel's *Stuffed and Starved*. I read these popular books with my interlocutors while, as part of my scholarship, I was also reading longer histories of race and food charity including the move toward narratives of food sovereignty and justice.[39] Many of the activists I worked with tried to distance themselves from food charity, but they failed to recognize that the food justice movement was part of an extended history of food access projects, such as food pantries, soup kitchens, and, more recently, movements for food sovereignty. Charitable food assistance programs have a long history in the United States, and modern-day government-supported food programs can be traced back to the Great Depression.[40] Food pantries are still the most common form of emergency food assistance in the United States. Like most of my interlocutors, I understood food charity as part of a system of contemporary ideologies that stigmatized people needing food assistance. As sociologist Janet Poppendieck crucially pointed out in her landmark book *Sweet Charity*, the moralization to end hunger created a vast antihunger industry that benefited the givers more than the receivers. This is something I observed in the food justice movement too.

Over time, as the welfare state withered away, charities, nonprofits, and other programs have come to stand in for efforts to "end hunger" without robust, legal, government-based entitlement programs.[41] In a move to further distance the state from food welfare programs, the federal Supplemental Nutritional Assistance Program (SNAP), formerly known as Food Stamps, has been branded not as an entitlement program but as a "work support" program, which only provides assistance to those who have official employment.[42] At the same time, state-sponsored hunger relief programs were reconfigured through public-private partnerships and subcontracting processes with nonprofit organizations.[43] These programs worked to disentangle food security from state responsibility while perpetuating the liberal logics of hard work and individual personal responsibility as a central tenet of civic duty in the United States. Despite the fact that most welfare recipients are white, commonly held misconceptions that Black and Brown people are the main recipients of these programs have been part of a long-standing process of racializing welfare recipients. These misconceptions have been central to the US government's push to eliminate entitlement programs and strongly link state-based food assistance to work programs. The Trump administration seeks to further this trend by cutting funding for SNAP as well as the USDA benefits that many food banks and other food and agriculture organizations rely on.

As the US government's primary efforts to address food insecurity transitioned from food charity to a robust entitlement system to public-private partnerships, rising obesity rates emerged as an entangled problem. Obesity was described as an "epidemic" that "continues to threaten the public's health," as "a major driving force of health care costs," and an "economic burden."[44] In 2008 the UCLA Center for Health Policy Research released a policy brief titled "Obesity Among California's Low-income Teens Nearly Triple That of More Affluent Peers." Various sources pointed out that obesity rates were significantly higher in South LA than in other parts of the city.[45] The Los Angeles City Council used UCLA data to support a moratorium on new fast-food restaurants in South Los Angeles, using the obesity "epidemic" as justification.[46] By 2015 it was clear that the fast-food ban did not work, as obesity rates actually increased.[47] Funding for obesity prevention flowed from the federal and state levels as well as through private funders. In 2010 the Obama administration pledged $400 million to "bring grocery stores and other healthy food retailers to underserved urban and rural communities across America" with the goal to "eliminate food deserts across the country within seven years" and as a critical step in First Lady Michelle Obama's "goal to solve the challenge of childhood obesity within a generation."[48] Many food justice projects capitalized on obesity funding and justified doing so as a way to keep the lights on. This funding and the broader push to eradicate obesity were central in shaping today's food justice movement.

During the same time, it became clear that the food system was divided by class, race, and geography. The focus on the urban "food desert"—inner-city spaces devoid of full-service grocery stores but with high concentrations of fast food, liquor stores, and convenience stores—was slowly taken up by food writers and policymakers.[49] In a place like Los Angeles, where there is a food desert within a few miles of a food oasis, people were motivated to become involved with food justice initiatives.[50] Rallying behind the problem of food access inequality, a group of people sprang into action, coalescing around the concept of "food justice" because they wanted to rectify this situation. Los Angeles area scholars Robert Gottlieb and Anupama Joshi were among the first to publish a definition of "food justice" as a system that ensures "the benefits and risks of where, what, and how food is grown and produced, transported and distributed, and accessed and eaten are shared fairly."[51] Gottlieb and Joshi were central in promoting the connection between "food justice" and environmental organizing. Although this might not have been their intention, this academic turn erased the long histories of organizing around food, like the work of the Black Panther Party or other community-based groups or the care of the thousands of

FIGURE 4. Typical junk food display in a South LA corner store. Photo by the author.

Black teachers who made sure kids were fed every day. Many of the activists I knew were reading Gottlieb and Joshi; copies of their book were passed around electronically before it was even in print. Food justice as a branch of environmental justice shaped the direction of their interests. It gave them a historical narrative and justification for doing their work, which was divorced from the histories of organizing within communities like South Central.

As I was swimming in this literature and slowly piecing together the different branches and divides among the people I studied, an article by geographer Julie Guthman gave me language to describe what I observed. "Bringing good food to others" is exactly how people like Julian describe their work. Guthman, among other scholars, wrote about how working to bring fresh fruits and vegetables to places like South LA "under the banner of food justice" was built upon and continued to perpetuate "whitened cultural histories."[52] Guthman argued that much of this work served the "reproduction of whiteness" and was not allied with antiracist struggles or those that were fighting for liberation. Similarly, geographer Rachel Slocum published on the "whiteness problem" within the alternative and community food movements, which she critiqued as "slow to address the issues of white privilege." She attributed this to "the invisibility of whiteness as a racial category and the resistance within the movement to embrace an anti-racist practice for fear of offending allies."[53]

After digging into the literature linking whiteness and food justice, I asked Sarah Cunningham what she thought.[54] She had not read the articles I had, but after I explained this concept to her, she reflected: "I think that stuff is more about like agriculture and farmers markets and stuff. It's like more of a kind of foodie, wellness, healthy *blah blah blah* Northern California thing. It's not the same as what we are doing down here." I wondered if the fracturing of different categories or types of food activism facilitated shifting blame and abdicating responsibility in each corner of the movement. Although many activists and scholars would say that these problems are associated with other facets of the food movement, I saw that even within work understood as "food justice," the narratives that tied deservingness to a particular set of moral ideologies about health and appropriate lifestyles were embedded in a way that was heavily raced, classed, and gendered. Over time, I came to disagree with Sarah on this point. The same forms of whiteness theorized by Guthman and Slocum were cropping up in the food justice work I observed. I became interested in the relationship between whiteness and power, as power operated on both micro and macro levels and across multiple facets of the movement. This included forms of soft domination whereby one's own worldview, interests, needs, and desires are taken seriously and fulfilled through the dominant social and political apparatus, while others are not.

ROOTING CHANGE

After years of working with high-profile food justice organizations that I had found through snowball sampling (essentially asking each group which organization I should study next), I connected with Rooting Change. Like Food for All, Rooting Change approached food justice with a different foundation and orientation from most organizations I studied. Their mission was guided by "sovereignty," "well-being," "integrity," and "mutual respect." Founding executive director Jamarcus Green grew up in a low-income, food-insecure household in the area. His first-hand experience with struggling to access food was part of what motivated him to start Rooting Change—that is, to serve the community. This meant keeping in mind that the population Rooting Change served had a median income of $22,000 and lived with all kinds of shifting vulnerabilities. Jamarcus insisted that Rooting Change dedicate time and resources to understanding what their community needed at any given moment.

In part, Jamarcus could understand what community members might need because he was born and raised in (and is still part of) the community. He attended the many cookouts, birthdays, backyard BBQs, and other spaces where family and friends gather to share food and be together. He understood these gatherings as their own type of food justice created by and for the community, and he knew how these forms of commensality often extended to mutual aid within the community. Based on Jamarcus's deep-seated relationship with the community and through feedback from his staff, Rooting Change shifted from a community garden and community-supported agriculture model, which focused on selling locally grown produce to residents, to giving away free produce bags every Friday. Beyond the organization's ability to quickly pivot to serve its community, Rooting Change maintained a broader outlook that incorporated an understanding of the structural and historical conditions that gave rise to food apartheid. This view supported a hopeful vision of reclaiming the food system and uplifting Black and Brown ways of building community-driven forms of food justice.

Unlike many other food justice organizations, Rooting Change eventually deemphasized gardening because they realized it required land ownership, the ability to pay high water bills, safe outdoor spaces, and time and energy that working families do not often have. The organization realized that gardens were not the solution to food access that the community needed. Their work connected to residents' needs, staying grounded in the historical frameworks and forms of social relations that matter in the community. Working in this way better enabled organizers to "name the underlying racial capitalist logics of food apartheid—including the destruction of Black, Indigenous, and poor peoples' senses of place, and white supremacy culture's dehumanization of people who fall outside the norms of liberal individualism."[55] Although Rooting Change and similar organizations are more closely linked to the needs of residents, they still struggled with the impossibility of "getting outside" of systems of racial capitalism or white supremacy embedded in their funding streams, the various state structures they had to work within, and the required structures of the nonprofit world. Some of these organizations with more radical visions for justice and liberation kept fighting, while others acquiesced and shifted to more mainstream work. I became interested in the power struggles that these groups went through and what pushed them in particular directions.

JOCKEYING FOR POWER

This research took place in a context where racial geographies and racial projects collide in a multicultural, progressive social movement that far too often served to reconscript the very system it claimed to be eradicating.[56] Some organizations claiming to do food justice work were also part of a form of late liberal statecraft that sought to "change," "fix," and "help" people of color and (intentionally or not) ultimately worked to make people in these communities into idealized healthy, productive citizens grounded in upper-middle-class white norms, while maintaining status quo racializing hierarchies. Such organizations assumed that people within the community did not know what was best for them and that they needed outsiders to help. These groups assumed that the same systems—legal, political, social, and structural—that worked to improve the lives of white middle-class Angelenos would work to improve the lives of Black and Brown folks in South LA. Outsiders who worked within these organizations had the power to retain false ideas about the community's lack of knowledge or skills while simultaneously crafting interventions around systems familiar to them as outsiders, thus ignoring the advice of local residents. This phenomenon, replicated across many different organizations under the banner of food justice, was a central reason why projects failed. When projects failed, however, these outsiders often blamed South LA residents rather than their own inability to understand the problem or design interventions that might have been useful to the community.

Throughout this book I build upon these introductory ethnographic encounters to show how diverse actors organizing around food access in South LA work from antithetical understandings of the problem and the best solutions: Food justice versus food apartheid. Individual behavior change versus abolishing systems and structures. White racial projects versus the racial projects of Black and Brown people. The food justice movement has the potential for radical change as an emergent space articulated through the messiness of different understandings of problems and solutions, where these divergent understandings bump up against each other, join together, or push apart. While organizing for better food access, different sets of actors articulated competing accounts of what "good food" and "justice" means. I observed individuals and organizations jockeying for visibility, power, money, and material resources. As I witnessed these groups attempt to push and pull the movement in particular directions using the forms of power available to them, I could see food justice as a space where "community interest and cultural value are negotiated" and part of a more extensive struggle for the power to shape the movement.[57]

I am specifically interested in forms of power that have immediate effects on the lives of people or the operations of organizations and how such forms of power determine future courses of action with directly productive or destructive roles. Examples of tangible forms of power include how one or two comments in a room could shut down a whole conversation on race and inequality, or how fear of job loss might pressure a resident working for an organization to present the work of food justice in ways that their bosses wanted even if they did not agree. I looked for the critical junctures where tangible forms of power are acquired, seized, or shared at relatively small scales, and I analyzed how the multiplicity of these forms of small-scale power could shape a social movement.

Some food justice activists, including individuals and small groups, had the power to shape the narrative about what food justice encompasses and what is achievable through food justice work. This had a stifling effect on more radical approaches to food justice and broader dreams of liberation. At the food justice gathering in 2017, I saw Julian's disregard for Andrés or how Raimi and Hazel ignored direct feedback from a community elder as examples of how forms of power limited the imagined horizons of food justice. That organizing space had great potential to build radical change, but people with power limited that potential.[58] That was just one case among many that I observed where small subtleties in communication or action opened or closed doors for discussion and opportunity. The boundaries of food justice were shaped in team meetings, breakout groups, and board rooms where collective visions were articulated and interventions planned. Whereas residents might be concerned with their struggles to survive and eat well enough, food justice activists, seemingly unaware of local concerns, directed their attention toward "doable" tasks such as cooking demonstrations, healthy eating workshops, gardening lessons, and K–12 interventions to teach "healthy" eating practices.[59]

I often observed food justice activists argue for projects they understood as conceivable, "doable," and close enough to the status quo to be acceptable to those in more powerful political positions—that is, elected officials, nonprofit board members, and donors. The more grassroots radical organizations in South Central are attempting to challenge existing visions, "undoing discipline," and create what scholars Katherine McKittrick and Carole Boyce Davies have called "freedom spaces."[60] I was seeing two radically different ways of addressing the problem— one focused on quick solutions, the other on long-term change. As critical geographer Julie Guthman has noted, the problem with these quick solutions is that they are shaped by an approach to problem-solving that actually constrains the possibility of broader, systemic change.[61] In my mind a justice approach would necessitate a constant iterative process of learning, adjusting, shifting, implementing, and tacking back and forth as needed, giving constant attention to how the problem is constructed and who the interventions are serving. However, I found many working under the banner of food justice to be much more focused on quick fixes to a narrowly defined problem, with the complexities of broader structures bracketed off in the interest of developing short-term, easily quantifiable outcomes. These different ways of understanding the problem and its solutions fomented conflicting visions of justice in the food movement. I became very interested in how power structures pushed and pulled the movement in different directions across these divergent visions.

In analyzing these conflicting visions of justice, I am building on anthropologist Elizabeth Povinelli's questions regarding "what social practices and forms of social power are used to commensurate disparate ethical and epistemological systems." Within food justice the tactics of jockeying for power are central to the work of making these disparate things seem commensurate. The ways in which food justice activists deploy empty signifiers like "healthy food" and "justice" can create a tricky sense of commensurability among both residents and outsiders who on the surface agree that "healthy food" and "justice" are both good and much needed. These signifiers and their uses show "the power of a particular form of communication to commensurate morally and epistemologically divergent social groups."[62] Building on the ideas of anthropologist Michel-Rolph Trouillot, I analyze "the reworking of processes and relations of power so as to create new spaces for the deployment of power."[63] Jockeying for power in this way is not just about well-intentioned people who produce bad outcomes, but it is also implicitly debating broader questions of who determines what Others need and when it is sufficient or adequate. Each actor or set of actors pulls threads from different parts of the assemblages of power surrounding food organizing spaces. In the end those coming from outside of South LA tended to have the power to leverage specific narratives to sculpt possibilities within food justice organizing spaces. I analyze the structures of power that facilitate how and why this phenomenon transpires.

So what is at stake? Beyond food access, this book explores the stakes of social change and whether disparate groups of people can come together, build coalitions, listen to one another, and work toward positive change that benefits the most vulnerable.[64] At stake are questions of how to be an ally or an accomplice and whether well-meaning people can actually support the political projects of others even when their approaches to social change have many elements that are incommensurate. This book offers insights into how and why things go wrong. The question of how to do this well remains at large. The book's title, *Food Justice Undone*, refers to the various ways in which the kinds of interventions detailed here, purported social justice work, actually undermine the meaning of "justice" and the potential for equity or radical change more broadly. The radical possibilities of food justice were undone by the multiple ways outsiders took over the movement and crafted programs and interventions without regard for residents' everyday lives or desires. At the same time, even more radical, grassroots visions of justice were thwarted by the structures of nonprofit and governmental funding opportunities, which undermined more radical projects.

The food justice interventions detailed throughout this book were built from processes and logics that organizers learned through education and prior work experience. They were simply working within paradigms they knew and lacked the capacity to fully understand and undertake different approaches to understanding the problem and envisioning solutions. Instead, outside organizers leaned on status quo power dynamics, unconsciously engaging whiteness, narratives of health and justice, and concepts of what kinds of behavior are "good" versus those that are "bad" in ways that foreclosed the potential for radical change. In spaces of multiracial organizing without critical attention to existing power asymmetries within a group of activists, status quo power hierarchies remain in place. With sustained ethnographic analysis of those who leaned on various forms of power to shape the food justice movement, this book reveals the inevitable pitfalls of any purported social justice project initiated and sustained from outside the community being intervened upon. My analysis reveals how the plans conceived by the community and more grassroots organizations were unable to enact radical visions because of the nature of the various systems and structures within which they operated.

This book shows how justice is undone. "Undone" in that these projects did not shift the everyday realities of healthy food access for

South Central residents. On a more profound register, justice was undone in the sense that the liberatory potential of this movement was foreclosed, and nascent forms of trust and collaboration that blossomed in some food justice work were inevitably unraveled as outsiders took over within movement spaces that had potential for radical change, instead undermining the desires of residents. Justice was also undone in the sense that it is not a finished project.

Journee

One mid-August afternoon, while volunteering at Produce Power's urban garden in South Central Los Angeles, I sat with a group of youth summer interns under a small grapevine shade canopy. We sat in a circle of benches and tree stumps, planting seedlings for a winter garden. I sat next to Journee, a young woman from South Central who had spent the summer interning with this local gardening-based food justice organization. She and six other interns had learned how to plant seedlings, prepare garden beds, and amend the soil. They learned how to compost and transfer seedlings, slowly hardening the plants to the harsh summer sun.

From the street to someone like Julian this garden might have appeared to be an abandoned lot. Along the chain link fence that separated the garden from the street grew thick bunches of banana and plantain plants, a gnarly lemon tree, passion fruit vines, and a variety of Peruvian corn that the organization's garden manager had slowly adjusted to the Southern California climate. Along the other edge were steaming compost piles; a haphazard jumble of shovels, wheelbarrows, and other garden tools; and a collection of buckets, plastic crates, and planting containers. Within this unsuspecting plot, the interns harvested fruits and vegetables and made salads, juices, jams, teas—anything they could create within the garden's limited cooking space. The organization was attempting to empower young people like Journee, instilling the idea that growing their own food could be a solution to the area's relative lack of full-service grocery stores. The hope was that growing food might inspire healthier eating to stave off the chronic illnesses that were all too common in this area.

As Journee and I sat together in the cool respite from the hot afternoon sun, we spoke about our prior experiences with gardening. I told her of my grandmothers' gardens, my mother's garden, my struggle to find space to garden while living in an apartment in LA, and my vision of having the space to cultivate a large enough garden to produce significant amounts of food for the future family I dreamed of. Journee could relate. She pointed up the street and said, "Yeah, my grandma lives just up the street from here, she has a whole yard full of plants and fruit trees and all that." She was quiet for a while, filling the cells of a seedling start tray and carefully picking out one or two of the tiny black seeds from the bowl we all pulled from.

I asked Journee if her work with Produce Power had influenced her plans for the future. She sighed deeply. "At the beginning of the summer I thought I might want to do some kind of community work," she said. "Like, that is why I did this internship. I mean, there were times it was fun, but it was also really hard being out here all day every day. It is hot, it is dirty. And also, I am not really sure about what we are doin'." She explained that throughout the internship, she had gathered that the organization's goal was to train her and others to teach area youth and adults about gardening and growing their own food. Produce Power was trying to mold the interns into a particular type of community leader, shaping their vision of food justice in specific ways. On some level Journee could see through that, which raised questions for her. "Like, I realized that, like, my grandma who lives just up the street from here, she takes care of her garden and, you know, we eat everything she grows in it. But like we also shop at the store because you can't grow everything you eat or nothin' like that. And, like, I realized that I have always known how to grow my own food, been doin' it with my grandma since I was born."

We pushed tiny black seeds into the dirt cells in silent reflection. Eventually, Journee added, she realized that she saw the problem and its solutions differently from the food justice organization. "Like, for me right now," she explained, "I live in an apartment with my mom, and we don't have a space to grow things—kinda like you were saying with your apartment. My grandma does because she owns her own place, and we can go there and use her space. But, like, the problem for most people is that there isn't anywhere to grow, and there's no time to be doing all this when folks are working two, three jobs to pay rent and bills and all that. So, like I said, I am just not sure what we are doin' here."

"Yeah," I replied, "the problem is structural." Journee brushed the dirt off her hands and, as she got up to walk away, she said, "I don't know what that means, but I think what I learned is that I gotta figure out a way to make good money or figure something out so that I can live somewhere where I can do all those things my grandma taught me, you know?" I thought about how different food justice interventions I had been observing would be if organizations prioritized Black residents' lived experiences, knowledge, and experience as much as Journee was as she reflected on the practices of her grandmother.

1

History

One evening, as I was leaving fieldwork to head home for the night, I needed to grab something to eat before sitting on the 110 freeway for forty-five minutes driving at 5 to 10 miles per hour. Quickly grabbing food, especially healthy food, was not simple in South Central, but I knew from my research that I was near a grocery store—the Numero Uno Market at Ninety-First and Figueroa.[1] As I made my way into the parking lot, I saw the Carnitas Estilo Michoacan Primo food truck parked out front. I opted to order tacos. I stood on the sidewalk leaning against the iron gates that surrounded the parking lot. As I looked at the building and thought about what kinds of food retail existed in South Central, I took note of the elongated shadows of utility poles hauntingly stretched over the cars that filled the lot.

A young man sat in a car, windows down, eating tacos and blasting a popular Norteño song, "La Maria" by Julión Álvarez y Su Norteño Banda, which I only recognized because my elderly neighbor in Silver Lake had taken to blasting the song every morning at dawn just after his roosters woke up the neighborhood. Further in the distance someone else was blasting The Game's "The City." The cacophony of South Central sounds pulled me out of my head and into the moment. Three other street food vendors set up along the side of the grocery store turned on their lights for the evening as customers gathered under their folding tents. The day's last rays of sunshine reflected off the sequined bikini and stilettos worn by a young woman standing on the corner with a group of women. The Number 81 bus stop was nearby. As loads of passengers departed, several stopped for tacos or headed into Numero Uno for groceries. The 81 originated in the Eagle Rock area, not far from where I lived in Silver Lake, and moved through gentrifying areas like Highland Park. I imagined that some of the bus passengers might be people who cleaned houses, provided childcare or eldercare, or worked in service jobs that kept other parts of the city going.

When my order was ready, I added fresh salsa, diced onions, cilantro, and a squeeze of lime to my tacos. I ate on the sidewalk and washed my meal down with an orange Jarritos soda before getting into my car and tuning into NPR for the ride home. Only later did I realize that I had been standing, eating tacos and drinking an orange soda, at the former location of Empire Liquor Market Deli, where on March 16, 1991, Latasha Harlins, a fifteen-year-old Black girl from South Central, attempted to buy a $1.79 bottle of orange juice. Harlins got into an argument with the owner, Soon Ja Du, about whether she was attempting to steal or pay for the drink. Video footage captured the heated argument and intense physical altercation. As Harlins was leaving the convenience store, Du reached under the counter, pulled out a gun, and fatally shot Harlins in the back of the head. After claiming self-defense, Du was given five years' probation, four hundred hours of community service, and a $500 fine; she was also required to pay Harlins's funeral costs.[2] The sentencing enraged folks throughout the city, and hundreds protested in the streets. This happened less than two weeks after the release of the damning footage of Rodney King's brutal beating by California Highway Patrol officers Tim Singer and Melanie Singer, LAPD sergeant Stacey Koon, and LAPD officers Laurence Powell, Timothy Wind, Theodore Briseno, and Rolando Solano.

Under the tensions of that footage circulating through the city, Harlins's racially charged murder was cited by many Black residents of South Central as a tipping point. The racial tensions and animosity in the area would soon boil over into the 1992 uprisings after the King trial's verdict, which acquitted all four police officers who were filmed of assault and acquitted three of the four of using excessive force.[3] Harlins was a straight-A student at the nearby Westchester High who aspired to be a lawyer.[4] I wondered if she wanted to be a lawyer because of everything she and her family had been through, or if she cared about justice from a young age. I imagined that Harlins was not unlike Journee. They might have been friends if Harlins had lived there at the same time as Journee. They might have both been involved in food justice programs through their school and community organizations. I wondered if, even then, Harlins could see the problems with the multi-faceted layers of the racialized food system. By the early 1990s shopping for food staples like orange juice at a liquor store was increasingly common in South Central.

Harlins's story, and its connection to race, food retail, and crucially to the 1992 uprisings, was not commonly known or understood by the food justice activists I had been following. Most of them were aware of food retail divestment in South LA, which increased following the 1965 Watts Rebellion and peaked after the 1992 uprisings. Without knowing stories like Harlins's, it was hard for those unfamiliar with the area and its history to fully grasp the links between racialized state violence and food retail inequality. It was also hard for them to see the food sources that do remain in place in South LA, or to imagine the myriad ways that residents can and do access various types of food within and beyond the bounds of South LA, such as tacos with freshly cooked protein, fresh salsa, diced onions, cilantro, and lime available at local taco trucks or the *fruteros* selling fresh cut fruit. Food retail inequality was a central part of everyday life in South Central. However, that did not mean, as many food justice activists presumed, that there was no food in South LA.

To understand these different ways of seeing the problem, I turned to history to understand the contemporary logics that framed food justice. The history would help me understand why Latasha Harlins was buying food at a corner store in the first place. I needed to unpack the historical and structural factors that led to South Central becoming a place with fewer full-service grocery stores per capita than other parts of the city. A series of factors have led the idealized suburban superstore to stand in for "good" food, and the myriad other ways of acquiring food have been cast as unfit or "bad." This racialized history of "good" and "bad" food retail is part of a broader system that associates whiteness with "good" food and "good" health, which often forms the foundational frameworks through which contemporary food justice activists define food access in South LA as a problem. The historical conditions that gave rise to food retail inequality in South Central are part of a broader story of Los Angeles and California.

A BRIEF HISTORY OF SOUTH LOS ANGELES

Mike Davis, the city's famous cultural critic, has argued that Los Angeles represents capitalism itself as the city straddles the imaginaries of "utopia and dystopia for advanced capitalism."[5] Between the nearly perpetual sunshine, moderate temperatures, ocean views, and Hollywood dreams, the Los Angeles imaginary of luxury, glamor, and fame is world-renowned. Nestled within and between these dreams of stardom across the city are the realities of slow violence witnessed in the underpasses and alleyways and behind buildings, as the city cannot sustain decent living, let alone luxury, for everyone. This is connected to an enduring slow violence sustained by systemic practices of underemployment, low pay, education inequality, food and housing insecurity, as well as anti-Black and -Brown state violence. Los Angeles is a place deeply entangled with histories of racial terror that have sedimented and maintained spatial boundaries of Blackness as separate from extreme forms of wealth, power, and privilege in the city. Here, racial capitalism has long functioned as an apparatus to support privilege and power among elites through the underpaid labor of deeply impoverished racialized Others.[6]

Originally inhabited by the Gabrieliño-Tongva people, in the late 1700s, Spanish colonizers established twenty-one missions along the Southern California coast. Mythical narratives of the missions painted the picture of docile, peaceful Indigenous people who welcomed the white settlers. The forced labor of the Gabrieliño-Tongva and other Indigenous people built the missions and sustained settler life in the region.[7] Local Indigenous people continue to fight for their community and rights to their land today.[8] The area also consists of people who migrated north from what is today Mexico and Central America. Spanish-descended settlers, called Los Californios in the region, were among the first to colonize the area, endowing towns, regions, streets, and mountains with Spanish-origin names. The earliest documented migrations of Black people to the region began in the 1700s with at least ten Black people.[9] Most of these early migrants were people of mixed ancestry migrating from other parts of the Spanish colonial world. In 1781 twenty-six of the forty-four people who settled in El Pueblo de Nuestra Señora la Reina de los Angeles del Rio Porciuncula, which would become shortened to "Los Angeles," were of African origin.[10] After the Treaty of Guadalupe Hidalgo in 1848, Mexico ceded California to the United States, and California was granted US statehood in 1850. During this time Mexican Angelenos started to migrate east of downtown toward what is now East LA.[11]

In the late 1800s, according to Davis, Los Angeles was a "back country town, tributary to imperial San Francisco, with little water or capital, and no coal or port."[12] He writes of early Angelenos Charles Lummis and Colonel Harrison Gray Otis, who set the tone of the Southern California region as a place of fun in the sun, ready to be developed and sold to anyone with the cash to migrate and buy land.[13] LA was billed as a healthy oasis, with ocean breezes and pure water flowing down from the mountains.[14] It was an invented dream, a settler-colonial fantasy, established through the "racial terrorism and lynchings that made early Anglo-ruled Los Angeles the most violent town in the West during the 1860s and 1870s."[15] Given the centrality of glamour, modernity, and health to the primary image of Los Angeles, threats to this image by way of poverty, squalor, or disease needed to be quickly eradicated. These threats were tied to racialized Others from very early on.[16] Historian Natalia Molina has argued that Los Angeles's "public health officials' early commitment to making Los Angeles a 'modern' (meaning sanitary and healthful) metropolis influenced the way they perceived and treated the city's nonwhite residents."[17]

These racialized notions of health also impacted regulations of food distribution in Los Angeles in the early 1900s. During this period many fruits and vegetables peddled by white vendors were sold at the Los Angeles City Market at Sixth and Alameda and the City Market of Los Angeles at Ninth and San Pedro Street, both located downtown.[18] By contrast, Chinese food vendors sold fruits and vegetables at small stands on the street or door to door. Los Angeles public health officials warned Angelenos not to purchase foods from "foreigners" and labeled Chinese vendors unsanitary.[19] These race- and place-based regulations were among the central ways that Los Angeles's long-standing separate and unequal food system was established and maintained. In other words the racist underpinnings of equating food vending by racialized Others or within places populated by racialized Others as "bad" or "unhealthy" food persists today in the ways that Angelenos evaluate food retail. The logics underlying the racialized processes of ensuring a modern, clean, healthy Los Angeles are historically and ideologically structured and have an ongoing influence on food justice interventions today.

Starting as a landscape of ranches and farmlands, by the early twentieth century the South Central area was made up of mostly white residents, with small enclaves of Japanese and Black people mainly residing in the Watts area.[20] Beginning in the 1910s, millions of Black Americans fled the Jim Crow South, looking for work and better lives.[21] Often referred to as the Great Migration, this exodus reshaped American cities throughout the country. Between 1910 and 1920 the Black population in Los Angeles doubled from nine thousand to eighteen thousand; by 1930

FIGURE 5. Wagons loaded with food at the Old City Market at Third Street and Central Avenue, Los Angeles, ca. 1910. Photo in the public domain.

it had more than doubled again.[22] In cities across the United States social and cultural revival was common in Black communities formed after the Great Migration. From 1920 to the mid-1950s, Central Avenue (running north-south from downtown LA) was a vibrant social and cultural hub for Black residents. During this period racial housing covenants limited where Black Americans could buy or rent homes. These covenants did not cover property in the heart of South Central. This meant that for many Black people this area was the only place they could live. Racial redlining extended not only to residential property but to retail as well. Even after these covenants were deemed unconstitutional in 1948, banks and insurance companies helped maintain segregation by denying loans and insurance policies for Black home and business owners.

World War II brought more waves of Black people to Los Angeles in search of work. During these years South Central was a significant locus of Black culture, even though it was not majority Black in population yet. At that time the area was racially mixed with Black, Mexican, Filipino, Japanese, and Italian Angelenos.[23] Wartime manufacturing jobs in the region flourished, bringing more Black migrants from the South to Los Angeles, though laborers were still segregated by race. By 1960, as much as a quarter of Black men and 18 percent of Black women in LA worked in the city's relatively stable, decent-paying manufacturing industry.[24] Companies like General Motors, Goodyear, Firestone, and Bethlehem Steel were located in or near South Central. The growth of the Black population further created opportunities for Black women to find stable jobs as teachers in local schools.[25] As the Black middle-class grew, white flight gave rise to white residents moving out of South Central throughout the 1950s and 1960s at high rates, eventually creating an area that was more than 80 percent Black. South Central had become a vibrant, well-developed Black cultural hub, where residents could find decent, single-family homes and good jobs with benefits; it was a very livable place for Black folks.[26]

South Central demographics continued to shift in the late twentieth century. Latinx migrants from Mexico, Central America, or other parts of Los Angeles and the United States began moving to South Central in search of lower rents, more space, and a better life. By the early 1970s, amid changing migration patterns, the Latinx population increased to about 10 percent, doubling again in the 1980s to 20 percent.[27] By 2014 census data indicated that 61 percent of South Central residents were "Hispanic" or "Latino" and only 28.7 percent were African American.[28] Some Black residents left the area, fleeing increasing violence and overpolicing, but many remained within this newly multiethnic area that had both racial tensions and newfound alliances.[29] In 1980 nearly half of LA County's Black population lived in South Central; by 2016 it was only 28 percent.[30]

Beyond notable demographics, South Central has a particular look and feel. Much of the area is characterized by blocks divided by small lots with bungalow homes. Even today you can find the ubiquitous palm tree–lined residential streets. Small retailers intermix within residential areas, and large intersections commonly have shopping plazas and grocery stores with parking lots. The northern part of South Central is home to University of Southern California, the LA Coliseum, and Exposition Park, which hosted the 1932 and 1984 Olympics. Residents walk, bike, drive, and take buses to traverse the city for work, school, and recreation. Although South Central is a low-income area suffering from years of divestment, it is a deeply Black and Brown place and there is still a vibrant pulse in the area. Popular imaginaries of Los Angeles often depict the city as a white settler-colonial oasis of health, glamour, and fun, but the region has always been filled with nonwhite people. And, in part because of this, it has always been a place of racialized conflict. Understanding race relations in a historical context is essential for attempting to solve problems within the city today.

FIGURE 6. 27th St. Bakery Shop, South LA. Photo by Joey Zanotti. Creative Commons Attribution 2.0 Generic.

RACIALIZED FOOD RETAIL

Deindustrialization and declining real wages were part of a broader process of retail decline in places like South Central. The 1970s and 1980s marked a period of rapid economic decline in South Central as it did for cities across the United States. As manufacturing and other industries increasingly sought labor forces abroad, job opportunities in South Central and surrounding areas diminished. In the 1980s the Reagan presidency brought sweeping assaults on social welfare programs and decimated the safety nets of the Johnson administration's War on Poverty and Great Society programs of the 1960s.[31] The welfare rollbacks were met with declining wages. In anthropologist João H. Costa Vargas's analysis, every demographic of workers saw a reduction in the real value of their wages in the 1980s, but people of color were most affected. During this time the racial wealth gap worsened, and in general, Black families made less money, held fewer assets, and had fewer opportunities than white families.[32]

By 1990 the poverty rate for families in South Central Los Angeles was twice that of the city overall, nearly three times the national poverty rate of 11 percent.[33] As consumer buying power was reduced, retail spaces closed.[34] Relatedly, as white, middle-class populations moved out to the suburbs, the grocery industry shifted its model toward larger supermarkets, with ample parking lots accessible by car. The move to the suburbs also drove the expansion of the highway system. Perhaps ironically, just as white populations were leaving South Central, Interstate 110 was being expanded southward toward the port community, San Pedro, effectively cutting South Central in half. The expansion of Interstate 10 also cut off the community from areas to the immediate north. Suburbanization meant changes in distribution and contracts with larger suppliers. The links between white flight to the suburbs, grocery expansion into suburban markets, and the shift toward large-footprint supermarkets strengthened ties between racialized places such as the US suburbs and food retail. As the grocery industry heavily focused on suburban expansion and could not afford to continue investing in other markets, this meant a broad and systematic turn away from food retail development in urban areas.

The US grocery industry in the 1980s and 1990s was characterized by corporate mergers and leveraged buyouts, ultimately benefiting shareholders.[35] Larger supermarkets owned by fewer and fewer chains became the norm. Walmart grew as a grocery competitor, building supercenters across US suburbs. During this time fifteen of the top twenty supermarket chains merged or underwent buyouts, which meant they were saddled with debt and needed new ways to reduce costs and increase prices.[36] By the 1990s the major US supermarket chains were Kroger, Safeway, and Albertsons. These mergers and leveraged buyouts consequently led to the loss of small, locally owned full-service grocery stores in many settings across the country. The grocery industry has been a profit-driven industry basically since its inception. The first self-service grocery store, Piggly Wiggly, was a publicly traded company.

Since the 1920s the grocery industry has been entangled with Wall Street. In fact, as corporations these grocery companies actually have a legal obligation—a fiduciary duty—to act in the best interest of the shareholders, and not necessarily the consumer.

In addition to the three major national chains in Southern California, other regional stores were prominent players in more affluent areas. Kroger-owned Ralphs stores were found throughout the region, along with Vons, a California-based chain founded in 1906 and acquired by Safeway Inc. in 1997.[37] Trader Joe's has been a ubiquitous California chain since Joe Coulombe opened the first location in Pasadena in 1967.[38] Coulombe explicitly sought to create stores that appealed to a specific group of "overeducated" well-traveled consumers, of which he determined many were in places like Pasadena. Later, he intentionally expanded his brand to target the growing group of consumers who cared deeply about health and the environment.[39] In the early 1990s, John Mackey's Whole Foods Market chain expanded into California and became a publicly traded company. Big grocery players like Ralphs, Vons, and Albertsons shared the field with more niche chains like Trader Joe's, Whole Foods, Bristol Farms, and Gelson's stores. Based on my observation among food justice activists and South Central residents, these big grocery players have each crafted distinct retail brands that broadly signal high-quality, fresh, modern, and healthy food as part of their marketing. The link between "healthy food" and the reputation of a grocery store is deeply entangled with these top grocery retailers and their store aesthetics.

As grocery stores expanded into the suburban market and shifted toward large-footprint supermarkets, their stores declined in urban centers, where existing stores either closed or were not updated. There was little to no incentive for large chains to build new stores. However, despite these trends, some smaller supermarkets have persisted or emerged. Other stores that catered to Latinx and Asian customers, such as Northgate Gonzales Markets and 99 Ranch Market, spread throughout the region, along with a few smaller independently owned markets. In 1981, Superior Grocers opened its first store in Covina and expanded to forty-seven locations throughout Southern California. Superior was founded by Mimi Song, an immigrant from South Korea, in 1977. She started as a cashier at a local Korean market.[40] In 1982 the Numero Uno market first opened in the area, growing to eight store locations. Managing partner Luis Nogales said in 2009, "Numero Uno has a strong presence in Los Angeles and is well positioned to capitalize on the growth in the Southern California Hispanic consumer market."[41] Although now owned by a Korean proprietor, Numero Uno stores cater to a Latinx clientele.

During the 1990s large supermarkets had moved out of South Central and grocery corporations did not have a vested interest in establishing new markets there. By 1991, Vons, then the largest supermarket operator in the region, had closed most of its stores in South Central, and only two remained.[42] Smaller grocers stayed in South Central, but many could not compete with the lower prices of suburban supermarkets because they could not make large volume purchases due to their limited footprint. They could not turn over products as quickly, meaning food stayed on the shelves longer, contributing to a perception that they stocked lower-quality foods compared with markets in more affluent areas. Furthermore, retail redlining prevented existing and new businesses from obtaining loans to improve or develop food retail in the area.

RACIAL TENSIONS AND FOOD RETAIL

Racial tensions between Korean store owners in South Central and African American clients came to a head in 1991 after the murder of Latasha Harlins, though racial animosity had been brewing well before that incident. Although retail redlining and discrimination prevented Black Angelenos from opening businesses, Korean and other Asian Americans had access to loans and credits through Korean banks and mutual aid.[43] Because of this, there was a broad impression that Koreans could buy Black store owners out of area grocery and corner stores. Korean-owned businesses in Los Angeles increased from four hundred in 1972 to seventeen thousand in 1990.[44] About one-third of the corner and liquor stores in South Central were Korean-owned and operated.

In addition, compared to Black and Latinx independent grocery store owners, some residents felt that Korean business owners were more profit-driven and less community-oriented or sentimental about their businesses, which they interpreted to mean that Korean store owners were less likely to offer discounted goods or store credit to clients. Many residents believed this translated into higher profits for Korean store owners compared to Black or Latinx store owners.[45] To give an example from my research, one Latinx South Central corner store owner went out of his way to stock Shasta sodas and Great Value bottled waters. By personally procuring these discounted brands, he could resell them at a lower price than the major brands delivered directly to his store by company vendors. He believed his extra effort kept many regular customers loyal to his store over others in the area. While this is a small example, it illustrates rising tensions and an emerging belief that Korean stores were not serving the needs of their Black and Latinx clientele.[46] Tensions between Korean store owners and managers boiled over into the 1992 uprisings, some residents boycotted Korean-owned stores, others vandalized those stores. These tensions continue to impact South Central and the highly racialized perceptions of grocery and corner stores today.

In the late 1990s demographic shifts in South Central generated a demand for new supermarkets that served Latinx customers, changing the grocery landscape. In 1997 the El Super grocery store opened in South Gate, just east of South Central and close to the 710 freeway. El Super is a subsidiary of Grupo Commercial Chedraui, the third-largest retailer in Mexico, and prides itself on having "a clean, modern, and welcoming atmosphere for our customers" and making customers "feel at home among the vast selection of grocery products from Latin America as well as local favorites, with delicious scents and flavors coming from our in-store bakery with freshly made bread and tortillas."[47] The store's branding and slogan "El Super is at the heart of your *cocina*" signaled to locals that the stores catered to Latinx shoppers.

The state of the grocery industry in the mid- to late 1990s offers a window into the ways a profit-driven industry operating within unfettered capitalist markets can expand and contract along racialized lines. From the vantage point of big business, the corporate mergers and leveraged grocery buyouts of the 1990s positively impacted shareholders. The mergers and buyouts streamlined supply chains and distribution processes, established purchasing structures that drove retail prices down, and worked in tandem with real estate development to establish and maintain a new market of suburban consumers. From the perspective of suburban consumers, this shift toward large supermarkets near their homes with lower food costs was an overall positive gain. However, for those left living in city centers and urban cores, the fact that food retail was so fully invested in suburban markets meant that they were almost wholly divested from urban areas. When we account for the racialized dynamics of demographic shifts and population movement, the changes in food retail development and divestment were (and continue to be) a part of a process of structural violence, divesting from low-income communities of color and investing in new majority-white suburban areas.

FIGURE 7. El Super grocery store in South Central LA in 2022. Photo by the author.

VIOLENCE, UPRISINGS, AND THE ROAD TO DIVESTMENT IN SOUTH LA

Although food access is one of many indicators of how structural violence has plagued South LA, physical violence is a common concern in the area that comes up repeatedly in food justice conversations as people think through why food apartheid exists and how to resolve it. In *Catching Hell in the City of Angels*, anthropologist João H. Costa Vargas carefully elaborates both the causes and consequences of violence as it is associated with the drug trade and gangs in South LA.[48] Violent crime in South LA is often associated with gangs, and gun violence is prevalent in South LA. In July 2022, Los Angeles ABC7 reported that there had been 181 murders in LA, and homicides had reached their highest level in fifteen years.[49] That said, in comparison to other US cities, the gun injury death rate in the area is relatively low. California does not even figure into the top ten states for gun-related deaths. In 2021 the gun death rate for the entire state was only 8.5 per 100,000, which was the forty-fourth lowest in the nation.[50] In 2019, Los Angeles's overall murder rate was 6.5 per 100,000 people, rising to 9.0 in 2020. By comparison, this rate is low. Saint Louis registered the highest murder rate in 2019, with 64.5 murders per 100,000 people. At the city level, Los Angeles did not rank in the top sixty-five deadliest cities in the United States in 2022.[51]

Even though gun violence and homicide rates are relatively low in Los Angeles compared with other US cities, both news and popular media perpetuate the idea that South LA is a violent place. To use an example of crowdsourced information that reflects public perceptions, as of 2022 the Wikipedia page on "Crime in Los Angeles" referred to South LA as "a notoriously dangerous region of the City of Los Angeles which has had an extensive history of gang violence." This is an example of a commonly held belief, despite the fact that gang activity and crime rapidly declined in South LA from the late 2000s through the early 2010s.[52] Further linking actual rates of violence to fictional accounts of crime, the Wikipedia page cites a series of movies as perpetuating South LA's "bad reputation," including *Colors, South Central, Menace II Society, Poetic Justice, Friday, Training Day, Baby Boy, Dirty, Gridiron Gang, Waist Deep, Street Kinds, End of Watch*, and "in particular South Central native John Singleton's *Boyz n the Hood.*"[53] These films perpetuate violent stereotypes that influence not only outsiders but also those who live within South LA. The genre feeds on an audience's desire to imagine Blackness in particular ways, depicted as "raw" and "real," offering voyeuristic views into exaggerated forms of violence within Black and Brown communities. The genre thrives because it reinforces stereotypes while offering glimpses into the seemingly inaccessible lives of the Other. In turn, these films perpetuate forms of structural violence because they can impact residential and retail redlining practices, make it difficult to access affordable insurance policies, or pave the way for projects of gentrification and displacement.

Images of South LA as a violent place should also be contextualized within the greater Los Angeles area. In the gentrified area where I lived during my research, Silver Lake, there were countless reports of theft and assault. Homicides were regularly reported in the area, particularly within Griffith Park. Shortly after I moved into my house, I was writing at home one afternoon when I looked up to find officers in riot gear in my front yard. The US Drug Enforcement Administration (DEA) was raiding the business two doors down on suspicion of human and drug trafficking. On July 21, 2018, a friend was picking up a few items at my neighborhood Trader Joe's on Hyperion Avenue when a car crashed into a nearby utility pole during a high-speed police chase. The armed suspect fled into the Trader Joe's holding my friend and the other patrons hostage for several hours. As the LAPD attempted to negotiate with the suspect, descending upon the store in riot gear, two officers fired their guns, fatally shooting beloved store employee Melyda Corado. Many of the food justice activists that I worked with also lived in Silver Lake. Within my social circle the Trader Joe's shooting was written off as an exceptional event that did not stigmatize the store as a violent place. It's hard to imagine that a shooting in a grocery store in South LA would be perceived the same way.

THE WATTS REBELLION

The belief that South LA is a violent place has a long history that pre-dates contemporary ideas about the area and dates back to the 1960s, during a time when the area's Black middle class flourished. A series of uprisings impacted the people living in the area and directly led to a pattern of migration out of South Los Angeles. On August 11, 1965, the Watts area of South Los Angeles erupted into an urban rebellion. A Black motorist had been brutalized by police following a "routine" traffic stop. In response, the community erupted into six days of protest, which took the form of arson and looting and resulted in thirty-four deaths. The National Guard was brought in to quell the situation. Four thousand people were arrested, and there was an estimated $40 million in property damage. The Watts Rebellion was the largest and most costly uprising of the Civil Rights era.

In the aftermath local businesses closed, and many never reopened. Historian Gerald Horne has argued that the Watts Rebellion marked the end of the Civil Rights era and the dawn of Black Power.[54] It also marked the beginning of a massive exodus of white residents from the area, and South LA rapidly became understood by many nonresidents after 1965 as a "black ghetto."[55] Although often portrayed as a violent riot, scholar and political commentator Keeanga-Yamahtta Taylor analyzes the Watts Rebellion as a "hastening of the radicalization of all African Americans," noting that there were "cries of Selma" during the rebellion.[56] For Taylor these events were an "unprecedented rebellion against the effects of racial discrimination, including police brutality and housing discrimination." The sustained efforts of the rebellion were "evidence of a developing Black radicalization rooted in the incongruence between America trumpeting its rich abundance as proof of the superiority of free enterprise and Black people suffering the indignities of poverty."[57] Grassroots organizers and author Mariame Kaba marked the Watts Rebellion, along with other Black uprisings of the 1960s, as a moment that solidified the image of urban disorder and unrest that would equate Blackness and crime ever since.[58] Concerning food retail, during the Watts Rebellion, thirty-seven markets and thirty-five liquor stores were destroyed by fire.[59] In addition to promoting the idea that there was a link between crime and Black spaces, there was a massive loss of local retail and jobs in the wake of the rebellion.

THE YEAR 1992 AND RODNEY KING

The 1992 Los Angeles uprising was pivotal in the city's history and particularly impactful for South LA. The uprising began on April 29 and lasted six days after a jury acquitted four LAPD officers who were caught on videotape beating Rodney King, a Black Angeleno. The Army National Guard and the Marines were brought in to stop the situation. Sixty-three people were killed, over two thousand people injured, more than a thousand buildings were burned, and an estimated $1 billion in property damage was concentrated in South Central Los Angeles.[60] Over ten thousand people were arrested.[61] The devastating economic impact is ongoing. The uprising resulted in an estimated "$4.9 billion in foregone sales and $171 million in lost City revenues through to 2002."[62] The 1992 uprisings also marked a moment heightening police efforts to discipline and control communities in South LA. In addition to retail and residential property loss, more than one hundred thousand local jobs were lost between 1991 and 1992.[63]

Beyond the more tangible economic effects, the 1992 uprising drew negative international attention to Los Angeles. People all over the world were made aware of the stark inequalities between the Los Angeles they saw on TV and the Los Angeles where real people lived. The public eye on these disparities yielded some good—for example, organizations and money began to go toward thinking through how to improve the conditions in South LA. According to sociologist Darnell Hunt, this attention is "a gaze invested in focusing on symptoms rather than underlying causes—particularly those causes that might challenge the efficacy of the neoliberal, market-based logics routinely invoked by elites to justify the contemporary status quo" and "the kinds of sentiments corporate media associated with the 'senseless rioting' of problem minorities in 1992 [that] are expressed today by white Americans, young and old, who see no viable future for themselves in the status quo."[64] Living through the aftermath of the uprising, the desire for

FIGURE 8. Los Angeles, April 1992. Photo by Glenn Gilbert. Creative Commons Attribution 2.0 Generic.

South Central residents to rebuild the area must be understood within a historical moment where "the economy is no longer a source of growth or optimism" and "our jobs" either do not exist or could be lost at any moment.[65] These structural factors continue to be overlooked by those who want to intervene in South LA. The 1992 uprising marks a moment when stereotypes about South LA are solidified along with ideas that it is a place that needs help from outsiders because the people who live there are incapable of taking care of themselves.

The 1992 uprising left massive property destruction in its wake; 94 percent of the buildings damaged were commercial buildings, and 40 percent of the damaged businesses had to close permanently, partly because many area businesses were uninsured or underinsured.[66] In all, 31 of 366 area liquor stores closed.[67] The grocery industry was hit hard: 46 of the 714 grocery stores in South LA and Koreatown combined closed their doors.[68] Food 4 Less (affiliated with Boys, ABC, and Viva Markets) had forty-four stores damaged, with an estimated cost of $42 million.[69] Korean Americans owned the majority of destroyed stores; many people speculate that certain retail establishments were targeted due to resentment over price gouging and racial conflict in the area.[70]

PAST EFFORTS TO REBUILD SOUTH LA: LESSONS LEARNED?

Formal efforts to rebuild grocery stores after 1992 were only marginally successful. For instance, after the uprising, the city created a campaign called Rebuild LA (RLA) to spearhead the redevelopment of South LA. RLA was announced on the heels of an unprecedented gang truce that led to the creation of the Crips' and the Bloods' "Plan for the Reconstruction of Los Angeles."[71] RLA promised to raise $6 billion and create more than seventy thousand jobs, and pledged to require employers to only hire within the affected areas. The cornerstone of the project was a promise that Vons would build twelve new grocery stores throughout South LA, creating thousands of local jobs. Peter Ueberroth, a Coca-Cola executive, former major league baseball commissioner, and the main organizer of the 1984 LA Summer Olympics project, was appointed by Mayor Tom Bradley to lead the project.[72] The '84 Olympics were famous for being the first privately funded Olympics in history. Ueberroth had raised $250 million for the project and was named *Time* magazine's "Man of the Year." Like Ueberroth's other projects, RLA was to be an example of public and private partnerships.[73] RLA partnered with Shell, GM, Coca-Cola, IBM, Toyota, Hyundai, Exxon, Occidental Petroleum, and the New York Stock Exchange.[74] Although Ueberroth named several companies that planned to invest in RLA, about one-quarter of those named denied that they ever promised to invest.[75]

Beyond this short-lived success, there were many severe problems with RLA. Among the biggest was that RLA seemed to operate under the assumption that people living in South LA were incapable of caring for themselves and overreliant on public assistance.[76] RLA worked closely with a program called Community Resources Against Street Hoodlums (CRASH) and the LAPD. RLA's projects were conceived as development, crime prevention, and social control. RLA focused on privatized investment and redevelopment in conjunction with programs to support the LAPD.[77] In 1997, RLA was dissolved, and all its assets and databases were turned over to the Los Angeles Community College District (LACCD).[78] In her exposé for *Curbed LA*, journalist Melissa Chadburn summarized the fiasco: "[A] wholly unaccountable organization that had the means to funnel money and influence wherever they wanted. How else would a Coca-Cola executive find himself designing policies and revitalization programs for the city of Los Angeles?"[79] Other than bolstering the careers of the organizers, RLA had little to no impact on the residents of South Central despite hundreds of millions of dollars spent. This 1990s nefarious attempt to improve South Central by outsiders should offer important lessons for those engaging in food justice in the area today.[80]

FOOD RETAIL IN SOUTH LA TODAY

Although the notion of the food desert conjures images of a barren wasteland with nothing edible in sight, there is in fact a great deal of food for sale in South Central. The food retail that does exist there is understudied and widely misunderstood. I worked with undergraduate and graduate student research assistants to map and analyze the existing grocery stores in the area. Unlike the food access app developers I mentioned in the book's introduction, I created these maps so that I would understand the food retail landscape of South Central; these maps served as proof to myself and others that the many people who said there was no food in South LA were wrong. Although there are periodic store closures and occasional new stores in the area, as of 2022 my research assistants and I have visited or driven by eighty-six full-service grocery stores that are either within the boundaries of South LA or within a reasonable distance and utilized by residents of South LA. The most common store chains were Superior Grocers, El Super, Food 4 Less, Numero Uno Market, Northgate Market, Smart and Final, Grocery Outlet Bargain Market, and Ralphs. Stores in the surrounding areas or with only one location in South LA included Albertsons, Vons, Trader Joe's, Target, Amazon Fresh, Whole Foods, Walmart, Costco, Sprouts, and Aldi (Map 2).

In addition to these eighty-six full-service chains, many smaller grocers are in the area (Map 3). It is difficult to categorize these types of stores objectively. Some might be considered corner stores or convenience stores, while others could be called small independent grocery stores.[81] As a third category for food access, there are several types of stores that residents use to purchase food, which may be overlooked by other researchers who do not understand these to be grocery stores. Such stores include Target, Dollar Tree, 99 Cents Only Stores, Mother's Nutritional Center, and local fish markets (Map 4).[82] Many dollar stores in LA have a relatively large selection of fresh produce. Most include, at a minimum, milk, eggs, deli meat, carrots, celery, bell peppers, onions, apples, oranges, and bananas. The stores almost always carry bread, tortillas, and rolls as well as a wide selection of canned and boxed foods and a small selection of frozen and refrigerated foods.

MAP 2. Map of full-service grocery stores in South LA and immediate surrounding area as of August 2022. These include store chains Superior Grocers, El Super, Food 4 Less, Numero Uno Market, Northgate Market, Smart and Final, Grocery Outlet Bargain Market, and Ralphs. Stores with only one location in the area include Albertsons, Vons, Trader Joe's, Target, Amazon Fresh, Whole Foods, Walmart, Costco, Sprouts, and Aldi. Source: Google Maps, created by the author.

More produce—including fresh strawberries, blueberries, bagged spinach, and lettuce—is regularly available at specific locations. South Central also has several fish markets, where fresh fish and seafood can be sold raw or prepared to the customer's taste on location. Many South Central households habitually buy fish at these local markets rather than at full-service grocery stores. There is a general impression that the seafood at these markets is fresher than at grocery stores, and there is a cultural and generational preference, particularly among immigrants, for buying from these markets.

Finally, the area also has several Mother's Nutritional Center stores carrying food for customers receiving the Special Supplemental Nutri-

MAP 3. Map of small full-service stores selling dairy, meat, dry goods, and fresh produce, as of August 2022. These are corner stores, convenience stores, and small independent grocery stores. Source: Google Maps, created by the author.

tion Program (SNAP) for Women, Infants, and Children (WIC). WIC provides federal grants to states for supplemental foods, health-care referrals, and nutrition education for low-income pregnant, breastfeeding, and non-breastfeeding postpartum women and to infants and children up to age five who are found to be at nutritional risk. These stores carry items covered by SNAP and WIC, including fresh dairy, eggs, formula, baby food, and a wide variety of fresh produce.

During the summer of 2018, as part of visiting and assessing South LA food retail, I worked with a research assistant, Jorge, who had been living in Orange County. He visited and visually documented various markets across South LA, including El Super, Superior Grocers, and a

MAP 4. Map of other commonly used retail locations for food purchases, as of August 2022. Such stores include Target, Dollar Tree, 99 Cents Only Stores, Mother's Nutritional Center, and local fish markets. Source: Google Maps, created by the author.

smaller corner store in the immediate area at the corner of Vermont and Slauson. As Jorge entered each of these markets, he inhaled deeply to take in the stores' smells and breathed out a blissful sigh. He said he could smell his grandmother; he could smell home. This was the smell of freshly baked bread, ripe fruit—guava, melons—other produce that reminded him of "home," which could have meant any number of places that gave Jorge a sense of comfort and belonging. He noted that he had not realized how much he missed shopping in Latinx markets since moving to a predominantly white area of Orange County to attend college. Jorge delighted in passing through the produce section. "Look, even the sign says 'Frutas y Verduras,'" he said, "like they are saying

FIGURE 9. Produce section at a small independent market in Los Angeles. Photo by the author.

this market is for Latinos." In Superior Grocers he noted the photo of "una AfroLatina" eating fruit and smiling, positioned in the wall behind a row of piñatas placed above bins of "Red Tag Special" produce, including a bin of red radishes, which he called "totally Latino." Although the signs at Superior were in English, Jorge felt it was a decidedly Latinx store, pointing out that they sell Peruvian beans as supporting evidence.

Jorge's feeling that El Super, Superior Grocers, and Numero Uno market were *for* the Latinx community was also felt by the Black residents of South Central that I spoke with, who usually referred to these stores as the "Latin Markets" along with other smaller stores that explicitly used the label "Mercado Latino" to signal that they carried a mix of products catering to a generic Latinx clientele. Black residents were more likely to mention Ralphs, Food for Less, smaller chains like Grocery Outlet Bargain Market, or Smart and Final as "for Black folks," although many residents would shop at "Latin Markets" if it were more convenient.

PERCEIVED LACK OF QUALITY

In contrast to Jorge's feelings about South LA markets, I met a variety of residents who either did not shop for food in South Central or did so begrudgingly because of what they perceived to be a lack of quality. Several residents complained about how cramped South Central stores were, that it was too difficult to park, that too many people were trying to shop, and that too much stuff was packed into the stores. Others complained that the produce and meat were less fresh and lower-quality items than those they sourced at markets in other parts of the city. Some residents complained that the stores were dirty and smelled bad due to older refrigeration units. Others shopped elsewhere in search of specific food items that South Central stores did not usually carry. One resident, Ms. Judy, shopped on the westside because she ate a particular kind of wild-caught sockeye salmon every week. Since she could not find that one product in South Central, she did all of her shopping at the West LA stores that carried it. Other residents who sought plant-based milk due to lactose intolerance shopped outside of South Central for similar reasons.

Although some people lamented the quality of food available at local markets, particularly fresh meat and produce, others told me that they valued the ability to buy ingredients for traditional cultural dishes—both Black and Latinx—at local markets, which are not available in other parts of the city. One resident, Ms. Corrinne, told me that during her four years of college in a suburb of Los Angeles, she came home to South Central to grocery shop every weekend because she could only find many of her favorite ingredients at South Central stores. I observed a wide variety of shopping preferences, and I found that visual representation and subjective perceptions of grocery retail spaces matter deeply for individual and collective assessments of whether the space is sanitary and whether it can feasibly house fresh and safe food.[83]

While evaluations of quality by residents vary, my research suggests that local stores were commonly racialized, so quality assessments were entangled with the racial or ethnic identity of the store. Residents stressed that some markets cater to Latinx clients and others cater to Black clients, and for some people crossing this racial divide as a shopper can invite unwelcome discrimination and overt racism.[84] These various forms of dissatisfaction with existing South Central retail were central to residents' outcries about the food retail inequities they experienced, which also fueled the food justice movement. Overall, I found a wide range of feelings about local grocery retail, and it was not easy to characterize a singular sentiment.

FOOD JUSTICE COMES TO SOUTH LA

This problem of food access inequality, coupled with the early to mid-2000s explosion of popular media that brought the food system problems into broader public consciousness, gave rise to the food justice movement in Los Angeles. Popular media implored household cooks to eat "real food," which meant cooking at home, making as much as possible from scratch, buying locally produced food, or even growing your own food. In the context of South LA, the 2008 Academy Award–nominated documentary *The Garden* was a pivotal film that drew a lot of public attention to the area and the problems. The film featured the South Central Farm or the South Central Community Garden. When I talked about this research with Angelenos who were not involved in the food movement, they often mentioned the South Central Farm as their point of reference for food justice in LA. Operational from 1992, which was the year of the Rodney King uprising, until 2006, the South Central Farm was both a symbol of community-based food justice efforts and a real source of fresh produce in the heart of South LA.

At fourteen acres the South Central Farm was considered to be the largest community garden in the United States. After a series of complex disputes about ownership and use of the land, the farmers were eventually evicted from the land. The farm was developed on land that was supposed to become a sizable waste-to-energy incinerator project known as the Los Angeles City Energy Recovery Project (LANCER). In 1986 the City of Los Angeles seized the land by eminent domain for the project. South Los Angeles and the South Bay have been common sites for these kinds of hazardous environmental projects that would not be politically feasible in the city's more affluent, white areas. There has also been strong resistance to this kind of environmental racism from the residents. In the case of the LANCER project, a group called the

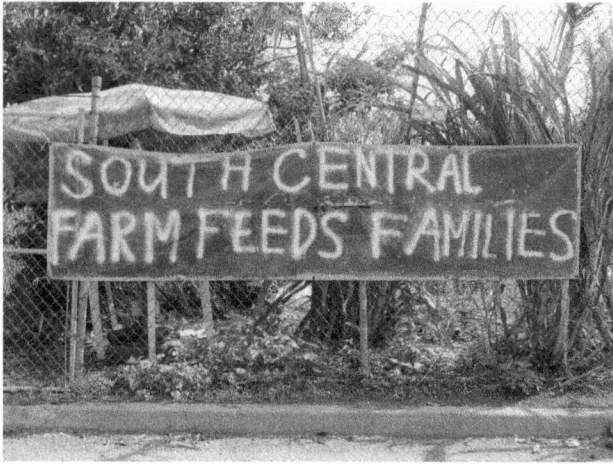

FIGURE 10. South Central Farm. Photo by Jonathan McIntosh. Creative Commons 2.5.

Concerned Citizens of South-Central Los Angeles was able to collectively organize to shut down the project. The City of Los Angeles then sold the land to the LA Harbor Project in 1994, which granted a permit to use the land as a community garden to the LA Regional Food Bank, a nonprofit located across the street from the site.

One of the original owners of the land, Ralph Horowitz, sued the city in 2001 for breach of contract. In 2003 the city settled with Horowitz, selling the land back to him for just over what the city had paid to seize it. Horowitz agreed to donate 2.6 acres for a public soccer field. He issued a notice to the gardeners, setting February 29, 2004, as the eviction date and end of the community garden. In response, the farmers organized themselves into the South Central Farmers Feeding Families, obtained legal counsel, and filed a lawsuit, halting the eviction. An injunction halted the eviction and development of the property until the suit was settled. The farmers inspired the community and people throughout Los Angeles; they were an example of genuine grassroots organizing from the ground up. The farmers protested and refused to be evicted by Horowitz. However, on June 13, 2006, the Los Angeles Police Department arrived in riot gear to remove the farmers and protestors. Celebrity involvement in the protests drew additional media coverage.[85] Over forty people were arrested, including actress Daryl Hannah.[86] On July 5, 2006, as the farm was bulldozed to the ground, another protestor chained himself to a bulldozer. He and ten others

FIGURE 11. New warehouse buildings in 2022 on the previous land of the South Central Farm. Photo by the author.

were arrested that day. The South Central Farmers continued organizing and tried to reclaim the land and other green space in South LA. The farmers have continued to grow food in different parts of LA, and they still operate a CSA (community-supported agriculture) program with pick-up and home delivery. This was an early example of a food justice project initiated and sustained by the community while being supported by outsiders.

Jamie Oliver's Food Revolution was particularly important for the Los Angeles food justice movement. The show was wildly successful, winning the 2010 Emmy for Best Reality Show. Oliver, a Gen X white British chef, exuded masculine confidence and privilege, and he took that vibe into a mission to "revolutionize US school lunch programs and help US residents fight obesity." Oliver wanted people in general and school lunch ladies specifically to make meals "with love, from scratch." *Food Revolution* positioned Oliver as the "expert" who came in from the outside to tell folks what they were doing wrong and how they should change. In one episode Oliver learns that the USDA counts ketchup as a vegetable, and in another he does a demonstration of the shocking "pink slime" that school lunch chicken nuggets are made of.[87] The show's second season was meant to feature the Los Angeles Unified School District (LAUSD), the second largest district in the country. However, a few weeks into filming the second season, LAUSD had the filming permit revoked.[88]

In addition to the uptick in media critiquing the food system and the way many Americans ate, the concept of "food desert" became more widely known during the early 2000s. The 2008 Farm Bill was the first to use the term "food desert" explicitly. In 2010, shortly after unveiling Michelle Obama's Let's Move campaign to combat childhood obesity, the Obama administration provided more than $400 million to fund the Healthy Food Financing Initiative, which sought to bring grocery stores and "other healthy food retailers to underserved urban and rural communities across America."[89] In May 2011 the USDA created an interactive mapping database of grocery stores across the country, calling it a "food desert locator."[90] Developed by USDA's Economic Research Service, the Food Desert Locator defined "food desert" as "a low-income tract where a substantial number or substantial share of residents does not have easy *access* to a supermarket or large grocery store."[91] If the concept of the food desert was not already understood, this official USDA mapping tool launched the understanding of food deserts onto the national and international scene. The USDA tool also enabled the expansion of Geographic Information Systems (GIS) research to locate food deserts and quantify food access information based on distance between supermarkets, population density, transportation, and data on income levels.[92] Increased awareness of food access inequality combined with GIS data allowing for the precise location of "food deserts" led to focused attention on these areas, which were often urban, low-income, and majority Black and Latinx. They quickly became the focus of food justice interventions.[93]

Organizations and individuals working under the umbrella of food justice are diverse and have wide-ranging interests. Some have been doing this work for more than fifty years, and others are new to the scene. Grassroots organizing by concerned residents drive some initiatives and not others. Hundreds of organizations are doing food justice work in the greater Los Angeles area—focusing on wide-ranging issues and areas within the food system. Among other types of food justice projects, there are projects that focus on community gardens, school gardens, the legalization of parkway gardens, community-supported agriculture programs, K–12 educational interventions, pregnancy and pre-K interventions, college campus programs, agricultural workers' rights, fast-food workers' rights, animal rights, the legalization of street food vending, farmers markets, supporting and expanding local small food businesses, expansion of EBT/food stamp benefit use at farmers markets, composting and food waste interventions, and food as medicine. An ever-greater range of projects are initiated under the umbrella of food justice.

CONCLUSION

South Central residents still face a persistent situation of food retail inequality. Returning to Latasha Harlins's life and the events surrounding her death, food retail problems in the area operate alongside many other issues faced by South Central families, including job insecurity, declining wages, and police violence. South Central continues to suffer from race-based marginalization and underdevelopment. In 2021, 27 percent of South Central households were living below the poverty line, and roughly 40 percent of residents never graduated from high school— one of the lowest rates of school completion in the country.[94] There are indeed fewer stores per capita in South Central than in other parts of LA. Stores in the area are often older, smaller, and are not maintained the way that they are in other communities. They often rely on older refrigerator and freezer cases, which can impact food safety and the ability to stock fresh foods requiring refrigeration. That said, with increasingly narrow profit margins, small stores might struggle to remain solvent if they did invest in infrastructural improvements.

Residents see commercial differences as they visit stores in other parts of the city and respond to this problem in different ways. Like my research assistant Jorge, some residents revel in the fact that South Central stores carry the ingredients they need to make culturally meaningful foods. Others drive out of the area to shop because they need specific items not readily available in South Central. Some residents who understand South Central food retail within the broader landscape of Los Angeles perceive food retail inequality as linked to a wider system of institutionalized inequities. They question why their area does not have newer, nicer stores like those they drive to in other parts of the city. Some residents see this as part of a broader racialized history that involves what historian George Lipsitz called "progressive investment in whiteness" and in turn divestment from places like South LA.[95] Those residents have called this out as a racialized injustice that they would like to see rectified. While this is the most common story I heard from residents, other people, like food justice activist Ron Finley, painted a somewhat different picture. Finley, who calls himself a "gangsta gardener," opened his 2013 TED Talk by saying, "I live in South Central. This is South Central. Liquor stores. Fast food. Vacant lots." Like many food justice activists, his characterization paints South LA as if there is nothing there at all. That is to say, although Finley is a resident, his work can promulgate stereotypes and invite more misguided superficial interventions.

I saw how food justice activists, particularly those from outside the community, could make the logical leap, based on exaggerated or oversimplified depictions of the food retail landscape in South Central, that there was nothing to eat in South LA. Following anthropologist James Ferguson, I understood it as essentially a "fallacy of equivocation," where the definition of the problem is vague, ambiguous, or simply incorrect, but people incorrectly assume they understand the meaning and therefore operate from an invalid position.[96] In other words, through the same historical frameworks detailed in this chapter, I could see how contemporary activists and planners followed a fundamental logic that oversimplified a complex set of problems: All food sold in South LA is "bad food," therefore no healthy or "real" food exists in the area, thus food justice activists must create interventions to fill the void. By their own logic, which presents a limited understanding of what is available and a limited framework for intervention, activists circumvent the need to address deep-seated structural issues that have created the problem in the first place. This type of food justice activism assumes that the people of South LA urgently need good, healthy food; "hard-working" outsiders are equipped to address this particular crisis; and structural matters can wait.

These different vantage points on the nature of the problem help facilitate the production of a particular narrative of South LA as a place of lack and need. Whether influenced by popular media or scholarship of the time, organizations I worked with all shared an understanding that South LA was a food desert with an abundance of liquor stores, corner stores, and fast-food chains and that it was a place where residents could not access healthy fresh fruits and vegetables. Food justice organizations tended to assume that South LA residents would buy fresh fruit and vegetables if availability were increased.[97] Or they believed that residents did not know that they should eat fresh fruits and vegetables or did not know how to cook. The idea that adults in South LA are incapable of being healthy eaters without the help of well-meaning outsiders was leveraged to produce a sense of urgency and bolster the power to intervene in local schools. These approaches to food justice can reinforce the racist history of associating Black and Brown communities with "dirt, disease, and disorder."[98] These approaches moralized particular kinds of practices, such as how to parent and nourish children, promoting a "healthy" and virtuous lifestyle that was out of reach for residents due to structural factors.

Many outsider activists held the belief that far-reaching media attention could support their projects and increase awareness of the problem and the solutions they created. As scholars have argued, "those in nonprofit food activism are constantly encouraged to construct such heroic narratives to justify their projects."[99] The organizations I observed that were most focused on self-promotion and media tended to skew the picture of food justice toward the concerns of outsider activists. This was unlike the food justice projects of residents or more grassroots-leaning organizations. I understood this as the ability of certain groups to leverage power to build a specific kind of food justice narrative. Although the initial impetus for this work may have begun with the outcries of residents, at some point the movement bifurcated along different approaches ranging from outsider intervention to more radical liberatory approaches. At the beginning of my research, I was mainly focused on outsiders intervening to bring justice to South LA, in part because I wanted to understand how they use their power to shape the meaning and public understanding of food justice. Their power allowed them to characterize any evidence contrary to their own portrait of South LA as exceptional and unrelated to the work of food justice.[100]

Thinking back to Harlins, I am reminded of Tupac Shakur's "Keep Ya Head Up," a song dedicated to her, and his lyrics in *Something 2 Die 4*: "Latasha Harlins, remember that name, cuz a bottle of juice is not something to die for." Thinking beyond grocery stores, gardens, cooking workshops, and corner store conversions, Shakur's calls for justice require a much more complex understanding of the conditions of structural violence in South Central, which requires a holistic approach to food justice. Many of the activists I worked with could not imagine such an approach.

Wendy

Wendy shopped for groceries every two weeks, never more often, never less often. On a midsummer day in 2022, I joined her on a grocery shopping trip. We met at her house in South Central and rode together in her nearly new white Toyota Corolla. "I bought that with my own money," she said, pointing to the car. "I'm proud of that." I could tell Wendy washed it often because even though she had to park it on the street, the car did not have the signature Southern California smog dust caked on it.

As we rolled through South Central, we passed a Food for Less and a Ralphs. I asked Wendy why she was not going to stop at either of those stores. "Well, it's a few things," she explained. "One, I just don't like going to them. It does feel like the food is not as fresh. I don't think a lot of people in our neighborhood actually buy their vegetables and meat at those places, so it just kind of sits too long." She merged the car onto the 110 South. I was surprised we were going southbound. She smiled and nodded. "Don't worry," she said. "You'll see what I'm doing. The other thing is that I like to shop where my parents sometimes shopped. Like, they knew where the good meat markets were, and the good produce. It's a balance to find what we want, things like collards but also fresh, you know?" I had my own experiences with not being able to find certain produce at the grocery stores in my area that were known to be "better" than those in South Central. I had found myself driving out of my neighborhood into areas that might be called food deserts to find things like green plantains or oxtails.

As Wendy merged off the 110 onto the 105 westbound, she said, "So I also am lactose intolerant, and I like certain types of plant-based milk that they don't carry at the stores near us, so that has always pulled me out of the area to shop. I need it for my coffee." She merged onto the 405 and headed south. I gave her a look of confusion. She smiled again and said, "You'll see." The final reason for driving such a distance for food shopping, she explained, is that "it's my system for saving money. I go around to a lot of places to get the best prices on different things at different places. I also only shop every other week and never stop at the store to pick up random things. That's how I feed a family of four on a couple hundred dollars a month."

Wendy was right; as soon as we pulled into the Walmart parking lot, I nodded and said, "Ohhhhh." We both knew that Walmart consistently had the lowest grocery prices in the United States. As Wendy put the car in park, she said, "To me, the biggest injustice to our community was the closure of the Crenshaw Walmart. My life was much easier back then, but I don't care. I am still gonna go to Walmart." That day Wendy bought mainly dry goods and basic staples like eggs, milk, and bread for her family at the lowest prices she could find in the area. After Walmart we got back in the car and drove down Rosecrans to the intersection with Crenshaw, where she did the rest of her shopping at Dat Moi Market, which billed itself as "your source for African, Asian, Caribbean, Hispanic & Polynesian products." There, Wendy bought fresh produce, fresh fish, chicken, and some ground beef. She and her family don't eat pork. As we left Dat Moi, she smiled and said, "Bet you didn't know how great that place is. I call it my little hidden gem. My mom used to shop there when I was a kid. I trust her decisions about what to feed us, and that will work for what I feed my kids."

As we drove back to Wendy's to unload the groceries, I wondered if greater understanding of how people like her shop for food, and why they do so, would have reshaped the food justice movement in beneficial ways.

2

Justice

The Los Angeles Food Policy Council (LAFPC) hosts an annual Food Day at City Hall and the neighboring grounds in downtown Los Angeles.[1] The event is held in late October as part of national celebrations of Food Day. I attended this event several times over the years, inviting student researchers to attend as well. In 2019, after observing the Food Day discussion in the City Hall chambers—listening to discussions on city policies, laws, and programs relating to food—I made my way outside to see the tables and displays set up by various food organizations in the area. As in past years there was very little food served at the event—a disappointing reality of Food Day is that it is all about city policy. One group passed out apples, and another was frantically and belatedly preparing Thai street food for a growing and hungry crowd. Like every year, I visited each booth and spoke with the people representing the different organizations, including someone from the University of California Agriculture and Natural Resources Cooperative Extension as well as a woman who had converted a van into a mobile sliding-scale produce stand that she alternately parked in South LA or the West Side.

In previous years I spoke with organizations trying to "revolutionize" school lunches, a "health doula" offering individualized health advice and nutrition planning with daily check-ins and meal preparation at additional cost, a group of "master food preservers," and representatives from Oxfam, the Garden School Foundation, Volunteer Los

FIGURE 12. Food Day LA, sponsored by the Los Angeles Food Policy Council. Photo by the author.

Angeles, and the Food Chain Workers Alliance. I met a nutritionist trying to teach people to eat according to the food pyramid/MyPlate and an organization selling health-care plans for restaurant workers. City farmers markets were trying to recruit new vendors and inform people about EBT programs at farmers markets. One year, council members and leaders of local organizations participated as judges in a kimchi-making contest. Each year, a wide variety of organizations participated in Food Day. For most of them, the objective was to inform "the public" and potential users of their programs and services.

In 2019, I spoke with a few other attendees as we waited for Mayor Eric Garcetti to speak. I talked to a graduate student studying food policy, two women dressed in business attire who were attending the event as part of their job at the Department of Public Health, and two retirees who had gathered pamphlets from each booth because they were "interested in food." The other people gathered were members of the press, photographers, or councilmembers' staff. From my perspective, after many years of attending and reflecting on Food Day as an observer rather than a participant, one problem with the event was that there tended to be very few attendees from "the public." Instead, Food Day catered to a narrow set of people within the food movement. There was unrealized potential to facilitate dialogue across organizations in the food justice movement and open a space for connecting across differences. Food Day and the various kinds of food justice planning meetings that I analyze in this chapter had the potential to become the kinds of organizing spaces where radical change was possible. However, these spaces did not cultivate the kind of organizing and conversations that could result in truly remaking the status quo. I tried to dig deeper to understand why.

Once the meeting in City Hall chambers finished, a large group of people poured out of the doors and joined the small crowd that gathered on the grounds. I recognized several people who worked for and led various food justice organizations across the city as well as several council members and their staff. As they moved down the stairs toward the yard, many were stopped by the photographers for quick photo ops. Councilmember Mitch O'Farrell took to the podium and announced that the program would begin soon. Mayor Eric Garcetti and councilmembers gathered for more formal photographs with the attendees and members of the organizations that were honored that year; each district in the city can award one person or group as a "Good Food Champion." Garcetti took the stage, waving with both hands above, held out high like a politician, and saying, "Thank you! Gracias!" As he took the mic, he asked, "What's the best place in the world to eat food?" The crowd yelled back, "Los Angeles!" The mayor responded: "It's LA because, literally you see the face of the world in the streets of LA. You see—by the way—the face of this nation *tomorrow* in the streets of LA. We are the future. We are about belonging. We are about freedom. And at a moment where everyone is seeking to divide us, we—not only through food but through culture—unite ourselves and unite this world. Give yourselves a hand, Los Angeles!" Garcetti thanked Councilman Ryu, whom he noted was his own councilman because he lived in Ryu's district.[2]

Los Angeles is organized into fifteen city council districts, with residents organized into smaller neighborhood council units billed by the city as grassroots-level political organizations through which anyone can become involved. At the time I was involved in both my neighborhood council and residents' association, through which I had several opportunities to speak directly to city council members. This gave me a feeling that I was part of local politics and the ability to make a difference in very local-level issues. Like Garcetti, I also lived in Ryu's district—an oddly shaped area that includes Koreatown, Hancock Park,

Silver Lake, Los Feliz, Griffith Park, Mid-Wilshire, Miracle Mile, the Fairfax District, Hollywood Hills, Sherman Oaks, Cahuenga Pass, and North Hollywood. The district includes some of the most iconic markers of Los Angeles as well as some of the wealthiest areas in the city. After positioning himself in this way, Garcetti went on to say:

> When I was on the Council, I started getting involved in food policy. My wife and I serve on a number of different boards that help us get community gardens, more green space, and connect people with the idea of *food justice* [Garcetti's emphasis]. Because food is not *just* for *us* [Garcetti's emphasis], it has to be about food justice for everyone. Especially those who don't have healthy food, those who don't have nutritious food, those who don't have access to food. And that's why I am very, very proud . . . this isn't just a moment; this is a movement.

Eric Garcetti, who identifies as Mexican and Jewish, is the son of Gil Garcetti, the former Los Angeles County district attorney who famously prosecuted O.J. Simpson. Garcetti is an Angeleno through and through, having attended elementary school at the prestigious UCLA Lab School and one of LA's most famous private schools, Harvard-Westlake, for middle and high school. Throughout his remarks the mayor discursively twists himself between "us" and "them." Locating himself within one of the city's wealthiest and most iconic districts, he delineates as "us" those who have food, healthy food, nutritious food, and a "them" who lack access to food. His comments indicate that it is through his work—"serving" on boards, "connecting people with ideas," and the "movement"—that is the "justice" "they" need. In other words, through the help, service, work, and offerings of those with food access, those without will have "food justice."

One week later I was at an event with Lindsay Adams, a program manager at Food for All, the food justice organization I had been working with the longest, where I had first volunteered back in 2008 when I shoveled manure with Miguel. This organization was based in South Central and, in one capacity or another, had been doing food justice work, among other things, since the 1970s. Food for All's mission was to offer fresh, quality, locally grown food to South Central, and to create and support grassroots, community-driven conversations to develop critical consciousness toward liberation. Lindsay was wholly committed to the long-term vision of liberation. While helping her set up for an event, I asked why Food for All was not at Food Day.

Lindsay turned from the piles of collard greens she was bundling and wiped her hands on the olive-green peasant dress she had owned since

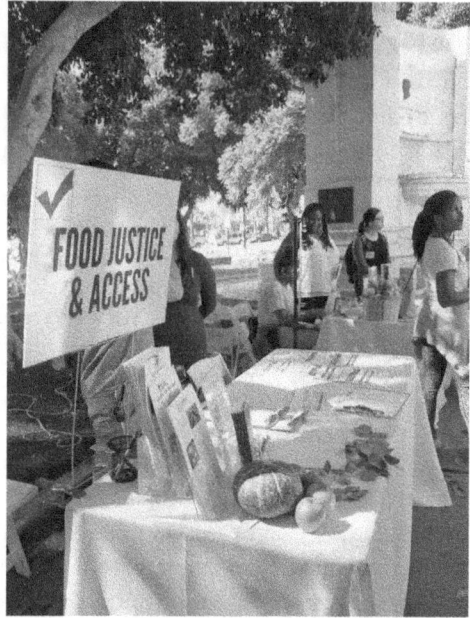

FIGURE 13. Food justice and access. Photo by the author.

the late 1990s. Tiny, ripped pieces of collard green fell onto her well-worn classic Swedish clogs. She brushed the wavy dark blond hair that had fallen out of her bun back from her face with the backside of her hand. She paused and gave me a confused look, pushed up her glasses with her right knuckle, and said, "What day?" I empathized with her state of confusion, remembering how much work she had on her plate. For a moment I felt bad about even asking her the question. I reminded her that Food Day was an annual event at City Hall. "Oh yeah, that," she said. "That's not really for *us*." Helping her with the collard bundles, I asked Lindsay what she meant. She continued:

> I mean, it is a day that is, like, for blowing smoke up City Hall's ass. It's, like, so they can pat themselves on the back about all of the quote-unquote good work they are doing. But it's not what we are about. Our mission is *to be of service*. To serve the needs of the community. What has City Hall ever done for this community? Plus, it's always, like, in the middle of the week, in the middle of the day, and we have actual work to do. That kind of stuff actually makes us angry; it is, like, part of all this new stuff that is sucking up all this attention and taking away money from the orgs that are down here doing the real work and have been for a long time. They like shiny things with good imaging for PR, but it's, like, fake, plastic, not real.

A white woman from a middle-class background, Lindsay was now working class, or what she called "lower-middle class."[3] She lived adjacent to South LA in the West Adams area. Like many of the food justice activists I met, Lindsay was not from South LA, but she lived much closer than many of the others who were not from the community. Her way of seeing these divides was not drawn along racial lines but along ideologies, ways of thinking, and ways of seeing the problem. Nevertheless, she understood that the issues surrounding food justice were still fundamentally tied to race and racism in the United States.

People like Lindsay and Sarah Cunningham, introduced in the book's introduction, helped me to see that the forms of racialization wrapped up in food justice work are not always linked to individual identity but can be enacted across racial lines. I started to view Lindsay, like Sarah, as a white woman who was committed to fighting for Black and Brown liberation, always trying to disentangle herself from white supremacy (even if imperfectly). Like many others who saw justice as part of working toward liberation, Lindsay was working on a much longer timeline, such that the organizations that had been at Food Day for several years already were new in her mind. The timeline toward liberation was much deeper and had many ebbs and flows. Lindsay told me that her inspiration for this work was freedom fighter Ida B. Wells, famous for her racial justice and anti-lynching activism after the lynching of the Black owner and staff of the People's Grocery in Memphis, Tennessee.[4] This kind of historical knowledge and the ability to make these connections was rare among the people I studied, so I appreciated Lindsay's ability to connect this history and long-standing struggle to her work.

Comparing and contrasting Garcetti's speech with Lindsay's reflections, I started to dig deeper into understanding what the activists I was working with meant by "justice" and what it had to do with race. I had to figure out how these organizations operated on a day-to-day basis and access the microlevel discourses and practices that shaped their work in particular ways. By focusing on the operational logics of the organizations, I was able to get beyond the rhetoric to see how their distinct visions of justice are operationalized in their projects, often in problematic ways. I slowly observed the patterns in how different people and organizations defined "us" and "them" and how those divisions ideologically shaped their work, positioning them differently with respect to the way they intervened in South LA. Their discourses significantly shaped their actions. For instance, many organizations presumed that they knew what "healthy" was and conflated small projects to increase access to healthy food, such as placing some bananas and apples for sale near the cash register at a liquor store, as "us" enacting justice for "them." Terms like "justice" and "healthy" were often deployed with the assumption of shared meaning, even though people frequently have different understandings of these concepts. Narratives like Garcetti's created the illusion that justice is something that certain "kinds" of people possess and can share or bestow upon others. These narratives positioned those others as "needy" and helpless, further entrenching the idea that "we" need to help "them." These narratives stigmatize the Other and reinforce the dominant group's privileged position.[5]

In addition to Garcetti, a critical mass of people I worked with coalesced around the concept of "justice" as part of what motivated their food work. At the outset of my research, I assumed that food justice was part of a broader "social justice" project, which I understood broadly as the duty of the state and the people to distribute basic and vital means to provide equal opportunity for all and to protect human dignity. After listening closely to people like Garcetti and Lindsay, I saw many ways that people within this movement understood and mobilized justice. Yet I observed that people working within and adjacent to the movement often used the term "justice" as if everyone had a shared understanding of its meaning. In writing about the "intractable problems of rectifying perceived injustice," anthropologist John Borneman notes several types of justice, including "retributive justice" (or the "conviction of wrongdoers and restoration of the dignity of the victims"), "distributive justice" (concerned with "giving each their proper share"), "corrective justice" (which "is intent on rectifying harms"), or Borneman's central concern, "retributive justice" (which deals with "moral injuries, wrongs that frequently do not result in material injury or harm").[6]

In my experience each of these different ways of understanding justice might be brought into any conversation about food justice. Sometimes the same person might define justice in multiple ways. Other times, each person might refer to a particular kind of justice that is distinct from how others understand justice. Nevertheless, for many working in this field "justice" seemed to connote a sense of ethics and values around the "right thing to do," as if there was a shared understanding of what was best for everyone. "Justice" connoted action and urgency to move toward this unspecified good. In general, however, there was a shared sense that working within a justice framework differs from (and is better than) charity work and that social justice is distinct from (and more helpful than) unfettered market capitalism. Garcetti and many of those working for food justice organizations imagined that they were serving a "public" that was different from them. The "public" included other members of the group, who would conceive of us as "us" and a broad, wide-ranging imaginary "them." These publics include populations that are understood as "in need" of services provided by the city and these organizations, and they are also stakeholders and political constituents. Among the organizations I worked with, many different terms were used to refer to those they imagined their work would serve. Terms included "users," "clients," "participants," "residents," "Angelenos," and "the public."

These labels did not, of course, represent the groups of people who showed up to events like Food Day. Lindsay had admonished those kinds of events as geared toward the wrong audience, specifically not residents of South Central that Food for All serves. This discrepancy was entangled in how food justice organizations defined their "stakeholders." I had assumed that "stakeholders" would be residents and community members that the organizations sought to intervene upon or serve. However, over time I saw that gatherings like Food Day and stakeholder meetings did not focus on the communities the organization was charged to serve. Instead, stakeholders were most often staff or leadership at other nonprofits or governmental organizations who were in powerful positions in the food world or other adjacent organizing spaces. These stakeholders were present at critical planning meetings, shaping interventions, missions, visions, and goals for food justice without the presence of the clients or residents the organizations sought to serve.

The positioning of the interests of these stakeholders rather than the needs and interests of clients was central in shaping the outcomes of the food justice organizations I worked with. Those outcomes often did not significantly affect the community but instead served to uphold stakeholders' visions and needs for their own work. The people within the movement who had the power to select stakeholders held and wielded the power to shift the food justice movement in particular directions.

BUS TOUR #5

In the fall of 2016 I drove to South LA, parked at a local community center, and boarded a yellow school bus to participate in my fifth bus tour of South Los Angeles.[7] Right away, I noted that most of the participants appeared to be white and looked like they were over fifty years old. Over the course of the day, as we got off and on the bus at ten different stops across South LA, I spoke with and sat next to many participants. Most of were lifelong residents of Los Angeles, from the Westside, and few had ever been to South LA—except for events they had attended at the University of Southern California (USC), the neighboring museums at the Expo Center, or a sporting event at the Coliseum. Many of them were excited and eager to see the "real" South LA.

Our first stop was at the community garden of another food justice organization working in the area. As we departed the bus, we were greeted by a dozen or so young people who all appeared to be Black and Latinx. The young people took turns making rehearsed presentations about the organization's work. I had been tracking and studying this organization for several years and knew that the commitment to being a site on the tour tied into the organization's goal to empower youth in the community and develop future leaders. I also knew that they had spent hours over many days preparing for this visit and that it would "count" as an "outcome" of the organization's work. The youth explained each of the programs that the organization ran and walked us through different parts of the garden, "explaining" steps in the growing process as a display of the knowledge they had acquired through their participation.

As we moved through the garden, a bus participant named Mary Louise commented to me that "these young people seem so articulate, the organization has really done a lot with them." The loaded word "articulate" piqued my interest, so I asked Mary Louise to tell me a bit about herself.[8] She was learning to become a master gardener and had seen this bus tour advertised on her garden organization's listserv. She had only been to the edges of South LA to go to the museums, and hoped that after she received her master gardener certificate, she would be able to put her skills to good use and help the people of South LA. The tour was to acquaint her with the area in which she already had hopes of intervening before arriving. As we boarded the bus again, Mary Louise and I sat together. I asked why she felt South LA was the best place to apply her soon-to-be-acquired skills. She told me that she just felt that she *should* give something back to the community. Life had been good to Mary Louise, she had inherited a bit of money, made good money, and owned a beautiful home in Pasadena—where she planned to use most of her master gardener skills. Offering her skills to communities in South LA was "just the right thing to do," she had decided. South LA needed her based on how she imagined South LA. Her reasoning was not unique. She was just the kind of person who might become a "stakeholder" in a food justice project.

BECOMING A STAKEHOLDER

After a year of working with several local food justice organizations, I was invited in 2009 to participate in a series of stakeholder meetings held by a large food justice organization. The first stakeholder meeting that I attended was held during the middle of the workday in a downtown LA office building. As a graduate student then, I had the flexibility to participate. I drove there and paid a flat fee of twenty dollars to park, which was steep while living on my graduate stipend. As I was paying for parking, a young white guy came behind me to pay for his parking. He asked if I was there for the meeting. I said yes, and he started to complain about the cost of parking. "Why did they hold it here? I mean, who can afford to pay twenty dollars to park and leave work for a half day?!"

His point was well taken, but he and I had endeavored to make these sacrifices to attend. The fact was that we *could* afford to pay for this and take the time to attend, while others, undoubtedly, could not. As we entered the building, I learned that he was the head chef at a wildly popular new local restaurant that had recently garnered a lot of media attention. Reporters and community members blamed the restaurant for single-handedly sparking gentrification in a small, previously ungentrified area adjacent to Silver Lake, LA's hipster hub at the time. I asked the Chef how he had heard about the stakeholder meeting we were attending. "Jonathan Gold told me about it," he said. "If Jonathan tells me about something, anything, I am there." Gold was LA's beloved food critic, reporting for the *LA Times*, where he created his annual coveted list of the top one hundred restaurants. An unconventional food critic, Gold defied the food-critic-as-snob image. His genuine love of all kinds of food took him to beyond the Michelin Star tier to various local mom-and-pop operations, often reflecting cuisine of immigrant communities as seriously as fine dining. He was *the* source for determining the best cuisine in the city.

As the meeting was being called to order, Chef and I found seats next to each other. We were introduced to what the organization had done thus far. The concept of food justice was introduced, and the word "race" came up during an explanation of the lack of supermarkets and the high number of liquor stores in South LA. During this portion of the meeting, Chef turned to me as I took notes and said, "What is this thing about? I thought it was going to be about food." I smiled at him and kept listening. Later, we were asked to break out into small groups for a continuation of the discussion that was more focused on the areas we were interested in. The Chef and I headed for different groups, and I didn't see him again that day.

Experiencing the introduction to the stakeholder meetings with the Chef offered me a glimpse into the kinds of people that were invited to participate and attracted to these kinds of vision and planning meetings. These meetings were for Angelenos who were passionate about food in some way, shape, or form, who wanted to talk about a vision for the future of food in LA, to network with others who cared about food, and to be a part of something bigger than themselves, or, like the Chef, who saw this as an opportunity to kowtow to an esteemed food critic. Most of the people who attended these meetings were interested in urban agriculture, farming, and gardening. The extent to which people thought about issues of justice, inequality, or equity was not entirely clear at the outset. Later, it became apparent to me that there was a great deal of internal tension among the participants. Some were passionate about understanding how histories of structural racism, such as redlining, had affected the problem, while others, like the Chef, were only interested in food. Given the focus on food justice, the Chef himself questioned why he was there.

The small breakout group I participated in offered an additional glimpse into the processes whereby the opinions produced by these kinds of "stakeholders" were incorporated into food justice visions for the city at large and in places like South LA. I observed that the group appeared to be majority women, mainly dressed in business attire, and most appeared to be white. We opened the breakout group by introducing ourselves. There were three other MA students in fields such as urban sustainability, urban planning, and public policy from various area colleges and universities. Three participants came from a progressive Jewish organization, one from the Department of Public Health, one from a councilman's office, and one from a local food-related nonprofit. Although we would be planning interventions in South LA, none of these stakeholders were residents of South LA, where most of the interventions were taking place, and very few of them had regular contact with any residents of South LA. This skewed representation was partly due to the meeting location and time circumstances, which the Chef had commented on earlier. The kinds of people who can spend half of their workday in meetings like this, drive across town, and pay twenty dollars to park would inevitably be skewed to people who were able to do this work as part of their paid employment or as tied to their educational projects—and not people working for small, South LA nonprofits, small business owners, or local residents who had other obligations during the times these meetings were held.

It was also telling that during this meeting we discussed the plan for an upcoming bus tour of the South LA food system so that stakeholders could get to know the landscape better. The fact that this was preplanned suggested that the organizers knew who their audience would be and that they would lack knowledge of the area. This implied that the people in the room did not have prior familiarity with the area, and what little exposure they would have would be through the windows of a school bus peppered with short visits to area nonprofits, markets, and schools. After the bus tour there would be a forum for small retailers coming from South LA and East LA. This group was trying to convert small local stores, including corner stores and liquor stores, into "healthy neighborhood markets." This forum would allow the stakeholders to meet with local small business owners to determine how the group could "support small community businesses" and "understand their fears of competing with big grocers."

After the announcement of these two events, the first question to come from the group was a concern about language: "Will there be translators? Because we won't understand what they are saying." Another question: "What is the purpose of these visits? And another: "How is this related to the focus on food?" Followed by an assertion: "We need to think about scale here." Before understanding the specific situation of each store and its clients, the group launched into a planning discussion of some of their interventions in South LA. One person chimed in to defend a proposed project, saying: "There is value in piloting any new program with small groups before trying to scale up at all." Someone else made a suggestion to "simplify the language for what the group does" so that the residents with "different competencies" would understand better. Another person who pushed for "healthy food" felt the focus on health was getting lost with the emphasis on businesses. Someone else chimed in that the "store owners should be trained on what is healthy so they feel solid on it." In an excited revelation, they added, "We can call it an orientation!"

From my vantage point, these stakeholders had drifted into a territory of condescending and patronizing characterizations of the residents that they hoped to intervene on. They assumed that residents would not be able to understand—both because residents may not speak English and because the concepts being deployed might be too difficult for them to understand, therefore requiring simplification. I could see that the stakeholders were not reflexive about their own knowledge gaps with respect to "understanding the area," speaking the language of the community, or fully grasping how much they really needed to learn before they could adequately understand what this community was facing. The stakeholders instead focused on what skills and connections they could bring to the table. The room roared with cross talk as participants started to bring up friends and people who were good event facilitators. The person beside me said, "I know someone who worked with Bristol Farms to redesign their stores." Another person blurted, "It would really be great to organize refrigeration vendors into our movement." They paused and added, "so they give us discounts." The conversation moved into sourcing and accounting, and moved away from food—until someone said, "Okay, let's get back to food!"

These conversations illuminated the ways in which expertise is produced and reproduced and how certain forms of knowledge and skill sets are routinely highlighted and prioritized over others. People who have done projects before and can draw on what has worked and what has not worked are seen as having valued experience. Those with connections across the nonprofit sector and to various related industries, such as the "refrigeration guy" or someone who offers "technical assistance," are important. Above all, the most valued contribution to these projects seemed to be connections to money through microlenders, pro-bono services, city-based grant funding, or private loans. The ability to access money to fund projects is a highly valued skill set.

In thinking about the "orientation to healthy food for storeowners," someone offered up a critique: "Other groups have come through this community offering free trainings/workshops that weren't very good so that the group might be skeptical of us." A response in agreement came up: "Yeah, we can't make too many promises, like [that other] organization that said they were doing all these things and lost funding before anything even got built." Someone else responded: "Yeah, we should focus on handing off skills." Another person added: "But we need a better understanding of the real conditions on the ground first." This last assertion piqued my interest because it offered a rare statement that more knowledge of life in South LA was necessary for the stakeholders. A much more common approach in stakeholder meetings was instead the comment on handing off skills and focusing on the long-term sustainability of the project. This session revealed the many competing discourses that come to a head in food movement work—few points in the conversation related to justice, and many points were part of business logics and economic discourse.

In these meetings there was minimal discussion of the themes I had assumed would relate to justice when I started doing this research. I imagined there would be discussions on the histories of redlining, police violence, loss of good jobs in the area, and many other issues that I saw as related to the problem of food access in South LA.[9] I was also surprised that there was minimal explicit discussion of race. These differences in my expectations for how the problem would be approached illuminated key characteristics of the food justice movement and other similar efforts to intervene on issues in places like South LA. These conversations revealed the complex relationships between social justice organizations and their relationships with stakeholders. Keeping in mind that the "stakeholder" here is not necessarily a member of the community but instead a person or group with some level of power who can facilitate or block programming, we should carefully define the term. The stakeholder is concerned with things like public relations, funding, sustainability, or scaling up. Stakeholders are crucial to the sustainability of projects because they can carry the mission forward, and their support will allow for expansion. They are thinking about issues related to fundraising, large donors, and sometimes upcoming political campaigns. They tend to be broadly constituent-facing, thinking about the kinds of programs and services that have tangible outcomes before the next election cycle. Their relationship to "the community" is in the form of representation or considering their best interests but not necessarily creating programs that directly address the community's needs.

Over time, I began to see that these stakeholder meetings and planning sessions, which rarely included residents of South LA or people food justice purported to help, were where the power lay in the food movement. These places had the potential to build radical change. However, because the people involved tended to be limited to a particular kind of stakeholder, these spaces usually involved one-sided discussion and an imagined Other being intervened upon. Ultimately little emphasis was placed on understanding "what is happening on the ground" or how to reach out and involve the community beyond concern over translators and trainings. In general, these meetings and the outcomes generated tended to be more about highlighting Los Angeles as a progressive, liberal city and less about the needs of the actual community members being intervened on. After attending these meetings, I realized that in order to study food justice, I would have to interrogate my own assumptions about the meaning of justice and dig deeper into how activists understood justice as a concept driving their work.

THE MEANING OF JUSTICE

Sarah Cunningham had recently finished a master's degree in public policy at a large research university in Los Angeles. At various points during our regular long walks around the Silver Lake Reservoir and over shared pots of herbal tea in Echo Park cafes, we discussed the meaning of justice in her work. She insisted that justice was the center of her work and that her goal was social justice for all. However, Sarah struggled to connect her ideological leanings with bigger liberation projects, and her training taught her to focus on formulaic approaches to targeted interventions with tangible outcomes and outputs for reports and future funding.

During one of our walks, Sarah mentioned the American political philosopher John Rawls as having a strong influence on her understanding of justice. Referring to things that continue to influence and inspire her work today, she explained simply: "You know, Rawls—'justice as fairness.'" She assumed I understood what she meant. Her reference to Rawls made me recall that Chase Bledsoe, who came out of the same graduate program as Sarah, once told me of similar influence. He said: "I think a lot about reading Rawls. . . . His work really resonates with my own orientation—justice is fairness. It's about everyone having equal rights to access basic needs like food, and we should have an egalitarian system. My work is to make that happen, to make justice as fairness happen for everyone." Drawing on Rawls in this way, Chase essentially equated justice as equality (not *equity*), specifically equal access to the same foods across race, neighborhood, and class in Los Angeles. Many leaders in the food justice movement derived their understanding of "justice" from their educational experiences—the majority were educated in the United States, attended elite colleges, and had graduate degrees in public policy, urban planning, public health, or adjacent fields. Graduate programs and undergraduate concentrations at local universities offer "justice"-based programs that attract students to their programs. In their curricula they often draw from classic Western philosophical ideas of "justice." However, these academic programs may lack a truly shared definition largely because Western philosophical ideas of "justice" have shifted over time.[10]

Chase, Sarah, and I understood that the approach to justice grounded in Western philosophy is fundamentally tied to Enlightenment ideals of individual pursuits of life, property, and liberty.[11] This body of philosophical and political scholarship is the foundation for and continues to influence "social justice movements" across the globe. However, many social justice movements have shifted the conversation toward human rights and equality. Many of these movements aim to ensure that all members of society have fundamental human rights and equal access to the benefits of their society. These philosophical tenets are central to how many participants in the food justice movement understand their work. Related to the definition of social justice as sharing the benefits and burdens of society, while those involved in the movement often want to envision and give Others access to the good life that they have imagined as best for all, they do not want to take on more burdens of society or lose their own freedoms in order to improve the lives of others. In other words they want to circulate the benefits without taking on the burdens.

I was initially surprised that Chase and Sarah felt that Rawls had shaped their visions of justice. From my perspective Chase and Sarah were much more radical because I also regularly heard them reference people like Angela Davis, Assata Shakur, and Franz Fanon as well as Paolo Freire, the Black Panther Party, the Nation of Islam, and Ida B. Wells as people and groups that they admired. Instead of deriving their definition of justice from these thinkers, they turned to the Rawlsian approach they were exposed to in graduate school. Were they influenced in this way simply because a professor had decided that Rawlsian justice was worth teaching over other forms of justice? I found it interesting how they both distilled their understanding of Rawlsian justice into the simple idea that "justice is fairness." It's not surprising to learn that John Rawls's work, particularly his 1971 book *A Theory of Justice*, was highly influential in social justice circles—I read it as a graduate student too. In *A Theory of Justice*, he proposed that "each person possesses an inviolability founded on justice that even the welfare of society as a whole cannot override. For this reason, justice denies that the loss of freedom for some is made right by a greater good shared by others."[12]

In other words, I understand these food justice activists as framing justice through Rawls in a particular way, specifically that justice is not a zero-sum game, and they see their work as sharing the benefits that society has bestowed upon them with others. They sometimes interpret this as "giving others justice" by teaching them how to behave.[13] However, this approach does not understand the historical and contemporary conditions of Black and Brown Americans as excluded from those state structures; it is part of what anthropologist Savannah Shange calls "a multicultural fantasy" that all people can live good lives within a postracial egalitarian state. Sarah and Chase, whom I had pegged to be on the more radical end of the food justice spectrum, used this logic, and so did people like Julian (mentioned in the introduction). I encountered others, like Randy Johnson (leader of the food justice nonprofit Build it Better), who thought of criminal justice and the need to punish or avenge, and still others who thought of justice as akin to reparations. I also encountered more radical-leaning food justice activists who drew on such thinkers as Davis, Fanon, and Marx to ground their work. These conversations made me realize that the people doing food justice work did not always fit neatly into typologies.

I came to understand "justice" as what political theorist Ernesto Laclau would call a "master signifier" where the meaning of the term is unclear, allowing individuals to assume the definition of their own positions and interests. In this context "justice" was an "empty signifier" that expressed a universal idea, without defining it.[14] The murky space of assuming shared understandings of "justice" and the oversimplification of justice as fairness allowed organizations to only attend to surface-level issues that appeared to offer problems that could be quickly and cheaply solved. This was the very thing that Sarah Cunningham was struggling with, as her intuition pulled her toward more complex understandings of justice derived from genuine grassroots community concerns. I witnessed how wielding the concept of justice in particular ways can also be a form of power whereby the easy solution to a surface-level problem is bolstered by the idea that it is "justice" and therefore necessary.

Although social justice is often associated with the demand for structural change, many of my research participants and their organizations remained focused on individual- or household-level behavioral change in their programming. Likely influenced by the popular media of the early 2000s, which idealized "real" foods and pushed the individual- and household-level change, the focus on individual-level behavior change as a form of justice continues to perpetuate the separation of space along racial lines in the city, rather than understanding the problem of food access through broader structural lenses.

RECONCILING JUSTICE AND NEOLIBERALISM

In addition to struggling with how to understand social justice broadly, Sarah and I often grappled on our walks with the tension between social justice and neoliberalism in our work and our lives. My partner and I had recently bought a small house in a highly coveted Silver Lake neighborhood, within walking distance to grocery stores, coffee shops, queer bars, and our reservoir walking path. Sarah wrestled with feeling happy for me, jealous, and wanting to completely turn away from private property and all the neoliberal capitalist ideals that are wrapped up in the process of buying a house. She was living in a small house on the other side of the reservoir with four roommates, and though she was "pretty happy" on a day-to-day level, she had this nagging critique that she should be living more like a "grown-up" with her own place by now. But working her way up in food justice organizations meant Sarah was living on a salary that was way too low to live on her own in the city's high-priced areas. Without a partner's income to lean on, she felt that she was stuck. Sarah relentlessly worked on overcoming these feelings and reasserting her commitment to justice. Our conversations made us each reflect on the entanglements of social justice and neoliberalism.

While people like Sarah and Chase grounded themselves in Western philosophical orientations to social justice, they understood that the food system itself is embedded within a neoliberal market economy and that neoliberalism has particular ramifications for how things like food and housing are distributed in Los Angeles. They sometimes had trouble seeing how neoliberal logics were also central to the food justice work that they were undertaking. Scholar David Harvey defines neoliberalism as "a theory of political economic practices that proposes that human well-being can best be advanced by liberating individual entrepreneurial freedoms and skills within an institutional framework characterized by strong private property rights, free markets, and free trade."[15] In contrast to the Keynesian political economic approach, which is characterized by market regulation, neoliberalist approaches prefer less regulation in the name of efficiency.[16] The ideals of "entrepreneurial freedoms" and liberating an individual's ability to tap into those freedoms are central to much of the food justice work that goes on in Los Angeles. Many projects undertaken are efforts to improve local business practices and are part of the neoliberal promotion and expansion of business.[17]

Although the organizations want to initially help businesses and communities, once they begin talking about the success of a project, they shift their focus to "sustainability," "scaling up," and whether the project is self-sustaining. This usually includes a focus on the ability of a business or program to reinvest in itself and generate consistent profit year after year. For both Sarah and me, these concerns that propelled work "up" and into the future invoked a different kind of temporal relationship to justice work than those who looked to the past for inspiration from people like Ida B. Wells. The trend toward expertise and entrepreneurship tended to center on individual action rather than collective struggle. As Sarah was on her journey to figure out what kind of food justice activist she would be, and I was trying to get the lay of the land for my research, we both found ourselves looking for folks who were thinking on these longer time scales and of collective struggle. We struggled to find those folks.

Sarah also struggled when her visions of justice were not aligned with what residents of South LA told her that they wanted. Years into our relationship, as we shared a pot of tea at an outdoor table at a bohemian café in Echo Park, Sarah reflected on problems of neoliberalism and food justice, referring to it as "the Walmart problem." In 2016 the Baldwin Hills Crenshaw Walmart in the vicinity of South LA closed. Folks from the community felt that Walmart was an important place for them to access affordable foods; they wanted Walmart to come back. Sarah reflected on "the Walmart effect":

> So Walmart comes in and displaces all these community businesses, and then Walmart goes away, and it's very difficult to get back all those community businesses. All of the individuals and families that were business owners within the community were displaced. And it's very difficult to recoup that capital, that social capital, that cultural capital, that actual ownership of business and space, which we've seen. I mean, that is the Walmart effect. So people are just really starting to be willing to think about those things as we're thinking about the issue of access. It's not just about access. I mean access to just whatever, just produce or organic produce or sustainable whatever, you know what I mean? Access to GMO produce, really? Is that what we're talking about? Is that justice? You know what I mean? In terms of health, wellness, longevity, thriving communities.

For Sarah, there is a fundamental tension between her ideals of "justice" as a more radical-leaning activist and members of the community she works with who are calling for Walmart to return. She was supposed to be doing work that served their needs. For some residents a more equitable food system would give them access to the affordable foods sold at Walmart. She lamented that the food justice movement as a whole was more about "capitalist development" than the radical visions of a different food system she hoped to see. "I am interested in decolonization and the end of capitalism," she told me. "I mean, I feel like that's just a process that will unfold anyway. But a lot of the strategies that are put forward in food justice are in the context of capitalist development."

Sarah paused, looking up from her tea. She caught my gaze and held it momentarily. I assumed she was trying to discern if I shared her views. She continued with this train of thought. "The whole premise implicit in that is this need to perpetually develop in this capitalist context. That's where I have the same concern and question that comes up in the food work, and it relates to this question of like, well, Walmart. And it's about power." Sarah's use of the term "power" piqued my attention, and I wrote it down in all capital letters on my notepad: POWER. As Sarah looked at the word, she asked:

> Who holds power in those situations still? Someone said to me the other day—we were talking about freedom—and they said we cannot be given what is already ours. Like how do we create food justice initiatives that affirm the innate power and self-sufficiency of every person in every community? And that doesn't reproduce this dynamic of dependency and reliance on the same food system we are trying to get away from? There's some leveraging there, but it's pretty limited. And it's also naive to think that the public sector is a site of sustainable power. Food justice should really be about sustainably affirming the power of communities.

To me, Sarah was expressing her frustration and uncertainty about different approaches to food justice. When she referred to her conversation about freedom, she was indexing to me that she was tapping into other kinds of food justice that were part of the longer struggle toward liberation. She saw those approaches as linked to self-sufficiency and the power of the people. But that was different than those that she imagined when asking "who holds the power still," which implied that she was critiquing the ways in which food justice work often maintained status quo hierarchies.

Sarah related her critique to similar problems I had observed with stakeholders. She continued:

> I mean, I really believe in *collective* stakeholdership. I don't do this work *for* other people in a charity sense. I do it because I really believe that liberation is a collective process. We all need to be free, get free from the system. But I do take seriously the practice of following the leadership of folks from the community who are in it in terms of the stakes being really high for their day-to-day lived reality. So, there may be things that I just don't find myself on a soul level aligned with, but I appreciate the tactic or the strategy, and I get it. And I also honor that it's coming from the community that is most in need at that moment. Honoring that, just honoring and being like, okay, well, there's questions that come up for me around that, but I hear that it's really important to this organization or this leader or this community to move forward that piece right now. And I honor that. It's tricky.

Here, Sarah reflects on the complexity of her own more radical politics when she does not live in South LA or face the day-to-day struggles of affordable food access there. She is deeply aware of the power dynamics at play and the need to respect the position of those in the community. She had what communication scholar Rebecca De Souza would call "a social justice sensibility" in that she tried to identify with others from a position of solidarity. Sarah's sense of solidarity is grounded in the realization that we share a world with others and are ethically obligated to listen and respond meaningfully to their stories. A social justice sensibility requires engagement and action to redress structural inequalities, not simply doling out the leftovers.[18] At the same time, Sarah felt that she was actually much more radical than the residents she was talking to. Although she wanted to participate in collective stakeholdership and move toward justice through collaboration, she could not reconcile how a huge chain tied to a large international corporation could be part of a food justice vision.

Beyond Sarah's specific concerns about Walmart, although many people working in the food justice movement thought that the work that they were doing somehow operated outside of neoliberal capitalism, the logics of market capitalism were central to the plans and projects that these groups enacted. Although food justice advocates touted moving away from corporate food regimes, the logics and frameworks underlying their practices still supported the market capitalist system at the base of the global industrial food system.[19] Because food justice was focused on food access inequities, which inevitably must address grocery stores and the global industrial food system, these tensions between status quo capitalism and more radical visions of food futures were almost always at play. Sarah touched on the complexities of power in the food justice movement and the tensions between outsiders with visions of food justice that differ from those who live in the community. From her vantage point, within a lot of food justice work, she felt that the power was in the hands of the outsiders intervening in South LA rather than her ideal vision of collective community power. To me, Sarah was questioning how outsiders can create justice by fostering collective community power, breaking down the barriers between those she might think of as "us" and the people of South LA, referred to as "them."

THE "US" AND "THEM" OF STAKEHOLDER MEETINGS

In addition to grappling with questions of justice, neoliberalism, and the breakdown of "us" and "them," I watched Sarah struggle to articulate her more radical visions of food justice as she navigated how to manage "stakeholders" and their many-sided concerns. I saw some of these difficulties when I joined an invited group of food justice stakeholders in July 2015 for a working lunch discussion to reflect on the state of the food justice movement. We gathered near downtown Los Angeles in a trendy art loft space. The group included Sarah, then working for Produce Power, Federico Jimenez and Javier from Barrio Bite, and Matt Smith, who had just wrapped up a project with Bettering Life and was working with Growing Health.

Several people attended whom the organizers considered important stakeholders; they were staff members working on food-related projects linked to their various organizations. Some came from a program within large for-profit health-care systems, others came from county-based organizations, and still others came from a large food bank, a large research university, and a local philanthropic organization. One of the conveners of the event, who came from a community-based organization that I was not studying, opened the conversation with the following reflections: "There is a food distribution crisis in our country. Low-income and communities of color are disproportionately disadvantaged when it comes to accessing fresh fruits and vegetables, *and* they have a disproportionately high numbers of fast-food and junk food retailers in the areas where they live. Here in LA, we are in the midst of a burgeoning food justice movement that is working to change things. All over the city, groups are partnering to try to change food consumption behaviors by increasing access to healthy foods."

Following this opening reflection, everyone at the table introduced themselves and said what organization they were from as well as what motivates their work in the community. Answers included: "I am interested in bringing healthy markets to the community"; "We are trying to figure out how to best support the food economy"; "We are creating a healthy zone"; "We want to deploy micro-lending and offer technical assistance to build sustainable healthy food businesses"; "We are trying to give access to capital for increasing healthy eating and healthy food in food deserts"; "We work with area farms that go to farmers markets to help them scale up their business and brands"; and "We are trying to lower the cost of healthy foods."

As the stakeholders communicated their goals, they framed their approaches as individualistic "I" or as a group of "we" from an organization. Like Mayor Garcetti's framing, the "I" and "we" have a desire or interest in "offering," "lending," "giving," or "helping" the Other, articulated as a "they," "them," or a subject-less "healthy zone" or

"food desert." This type of framing was common among the food justice activists coming from outside of the communities being served,
while those who live in the area and those who identify as people of
color tend to use different language to describe the work they do in the
community. From my perspective most of these ideas were focused on
economic and business-based solutions and less oriented to social, race,
or "justice"-based interventions. Sarah spoke up about this. She tried to
remind the group of the inequities that places like South LA face by
offering a different take on the situation:

> It really starts in the foundation of this country in systemic inequality and
> there's been an effort to achieve social and racial equity in this country. There's
> been a lot of incredible work done to remedy the reality of food deserts such
> has been named here already which is that we know some communities do not
> have adequate access to healthy [food]. Access to food and a healthy diet is a
> foundation of our well-being. This has resulted in all kinds of health dispari-
> ties along class and race and so if we move through twenty years of food jus-
> tice community organizing, that is the foundation of what we are doing.

No one in the room responded verbally to Sarah's reminder of the history of racial violence and inequality in the city and the broader US
context. However, I saw Federico and Javier nod their heads in agreement. The silence and body language in the room did not indicate that
there was much uptake of these ideas. This was despite the softer, seemingly more approachable language they used to keep the focus on inequality, access, and disparities rather than racism, racialized violence,
and discrimination.

Shifting from the topic of inequality, Sarah continued, pivoting
toward language that the group could latch onto: "The idea was we
have resources as a city that we can invest. I think [this is] an important
moment in the story because there was a time where obviously public
health and a public health community and health advocates had been
looking at this issue for a very long time. There was a real marriage I
think between public health and economic development community to
figure this one out and to take these investments to the next level." Here
again "we" is cast as those who work for the organizations and the city.
Investment was part of the neoliberal logic that Sarah had critiqued. But
after the energy was sucked out of the room at the mention of inequality, the power of the stakeholders pulled her toward those logics despite
her own values. In response, Matt chimed in:

> One of the things I want to talk about is how we looked at the problem and,
> what is the problem and what are the multiple problems and different layers,

dimensions of the problem that we can confront. I started to look at that and said, "Wow, we have so many skills and so much know-how in this sector that we could probably help out in such a project." Whenever we take a role in any project, we are just giving support. We're trying to help the goals of people, it's really about *them*.

While he emphasized "them," Matt framed the "we" as a group of outsiders with skills and "know-how" to "help out" Others. But he back-peddled the "savior-ness" of his remarks by underscoring that the work was really about the Other. Matt was focused on intervention and working on a rapid timeline that did not tie to historical struggles or collective action but instead focused on individual fixes.

Matt was part of a broader type of food justice activism that revolved around "skilled" outsiders helping the "less fortunate" Others of South LA. In meetings like this and others that I observed, when a participant wanted to dig deeper into the causes of inequality in Los Angeles, as Sarah did, those in the room did not quickly take it up. It may have been that everyone in the room implicitly understood that the mention of racial inequality is something that must be said in these kinds of spaces, but that it is not normative or necessary to go beyond just mentioning the issue. Or it may have been that only the person mentioning race really had the capacity to discuss it, and the others simply did not. In any case, the conversation shifted back to providing skills and resources for those in South LA.

The dominant approach of "us" providing resources and "skills" for "them" remains in place. This understanding of social justice is in line with the ways in which members of this community conceptualize justice as fairness. They understand their work as an effort to create more egalitarian distribution systems in society without reducing their own access or privilege. In this framing, social justice has colonial and assimilationist undertones, and the stakeholders in the room jockey for the power to keep those undertones in place or move toward conversations to dismantle those associations. Not knowing how to navigate the silence in the room, Sarah pulled back from her initial attempt to shift the conversation. Matt pulled things back toward familiar territory to most people in the room—the good intentions, technical expertise, and benevolence of the group and their interventions.

After sharing lunch together, the group departed. As I walked to my car, I reflected on the long history of stigmatizing food charity and the myth that those who use it are lazy, irresponsible people who do not take responsibility.[20] By contrast, the activists in the room that day did not seem to frame the residents of South LA and East LA in this way. Instead, they used forms of soft Otherizing to mark these community members as Other, framing them as in need of help. I reflected on their comfort with neoliberal language such as "output," "entrepreneur," and "choice" and the fact that they would often shy away from conversations dealing with terms such as "racism" and "equity." In the case of the Angelenos at work here, the concept of "justice" (and occasionally "equity") was central to their work, but they struggled with the ways neoliberal economic concepts were applied to justice work in seemingly contradictory ways. Like Matt, rather than dealing with these contradictions, many activists fall back on the idea that overall they were doing the good work to "help Others" through "justice."

NOT ABOUT JUSTICE AT ALL

While searching for the more radical food justice organizations, I stumbled on Build It Better, a food justice nonprofit run by Randy Johnson. Based on their website, social media posts, and what others in the food justice movement were saying, I thought this organization was interested in interrogating the structures that caused food access inequality and working with community members to break down existing power structures by building from the knowledge and needs of the community to push for fundamental changes to the food system. However, once I sat down with Randy, I saw his approach did not embody my understanding of the kind of work toward radical change to the structure of food access inequality generated by the communities most impacted. Instead, the approach was about Randy himself taking on power and enacting his vision for how to "get things done."

Randy was deeply involved in local community organizing and neighborhood-level politics where he lived, about ten miles or a twenty-five-minute drive from South LA. He regularly shared his opinion about how things "ought to be." Randy was a white, middle-aged, left-leaning parent who was deeply invested in his local community and schools. He told people that he was driven to this work simply by his "desire to improve access to healthy food." His general philosophy was "Take care of everybody, and everybody will take care of you." When I asked Randy whether he felt that there was a "food justice" movement in LA, he first told me about some of the failures and struggles of his organization, alluding to the notion that he too had faced adversity. He said:

So I don't like the term ["justice"] because it just makes it a little patronizing. . . . To be honest, I don't think there is. I think it is being approached in
all of the wrong ways. It is not a justice issue. It is a, a, . . . this whole patronizing approach to it is a problem. You can't be patronizing to a Spanish
mom, you can't go in there with an English accent and say "Well, I know
better than you. You should be eating this, this, and this." If someone came
up to me with another accent, I'd say, "Who the hell do you think you are
telling me how to eat?" It tends to be white middle- and upper-class activists
who are in the movement, and that's kind of stupid. So my wife and I recognize that we are so freakin' white, so we see that the very people who are
going into these South LA [places] need to be from there. So, we are changing that [part of the program] this year, so we hire or figure out who is down
there and have them do it rather than us. I think it would be a lot better way
to do it.

Randy's use of the terms "us" and "them" was quite telling for me. It
was not that he disagreed with the condescending view that middle-
class white folks should tell lower-income communities of color how to
eat; it was that he felt it was not effective. But he wanted to "figure out
who is down there" and hire someone who looks like a community
member to spread *his* message. Randy's approach in this respect is very
common among these types of organizations in Los Angeles. This pattern of hiring has the effect of perpetuating and redrawing the divisions
between Black and white/"us" and "them." This maneuver keeps
Randy safely ensconced in his white, upper-middle-class world of "us,"
far enough away from "them." He asserts that he has outsmarted the
more patronizing attempts of food justice where outsiders ("we") tell
"them" (the Other) what to eat. Instead, he saw himself as cleverly con-
scripting minoritized people to work for him so that the messages about
the proper ways to eat appear to be coming from within the community
rather than from outside.

In our interview Randy discussed details related to hiring difficulties
but summarized his view on justice by saying, "To frame it as 'justice'
makes it sound like you're punishing us, the white people, when we
really didn't do anything wrong." Randy thus frames "justice" as a
"conspiracy":

It's not so much that . . . there's not a conspiracy out there, obviously.
There's nobody writing this conspiracy, but there are people who are now
exposed to stuff that is clearly not good for them and they're being almost
funneled into this where this is all you can buy. There's nothing else available to you based on the price we're offering it to you. That's unfair. With
better education, with better appreciation, people can make a choice. Others, I see them having almost zero education when it comes to that. They

don't know that what they're eating is destroying them slowly, *blah blah blah* [*sic*]. But it's not a conspiracy, it's not a justice issue.

Here Randy takes issue with the set of meanings associated with "justice," particularly the idea that differences in access to healthy food are structural issues and that those structural issues have anything to do with race. In essence, he conflates "justice" with "racial justice" in a way that very few food justice organizations do, and he is opposed to the idea of using a racial justice framework in his food-related work. His initial framing about punishing white people reflects an understanding of justice as "retributive." To Randy, the concept of "food apartheid"—the notion that folks in places like South LA have access to different kinds of foods than people in West LA because of institutional, structural racism—is a conspiracy theory. Instead, he positions the Other from places like South LA as lacking knowledge and education and in need of outside intervention.

Despite the fact that Randy's work is regularly categorized as "food justice" and the literature produced by his organization uses the term, he shared critiques of the food justice movement in LA, making an explicit link between the social and cultural cache of "justice" (and specifically "racial justice") and the thirst for fame that is so prevalent in LA:

> The problem is Los Angeles, it seems to be a city of dreams or a city of speeches or a city of . . . This is not just rhetoric. I've seen it firsthand now in my few years. People like the photo ops. People don't like the work. People don't want to work. I'm sorry. LA is kind of a lazy city. People are kind of lazy. That's one of the things that's been stopping the food justice movement because it requires work. People are simply not used to work, you know? Is [the food justice movement] just talk? In LA, again, the talk seems to be far ahead of the reality. That's the truth.

Randy seemed to be characterizing a whole host of Angelenos—from food justice activists to residents of places like South LA—as lazy and unwilling to put in the work. When he cited LA as a place where this kind of thirst for fame and the spotlight is particularly problematic, I remembered that Lindsay Adams had also made that connection, even though she was really differently positioned than Randy in terms of her approach to justice as more of a liberatory project. I could see how this problem impacted their work in different ways. While I imagine Lindsay would have worried about the thirst for the spotlight attracting people who weren't genuinely dedicated to liberation, Randy focused on work ethic.

"You've heard more about the justice movement," he said. "There has been some actual stuff. There have been people saved, but not nearly as much as people would say, you know? You go to some of these gardens, and they don't look anything like the pictures that we might have sent out to our donors. That's frankly just lying, and you're really not helping your customers. It's exaggerated. It's too much based on photo-op things, and there are too few people actually there, down and dirty, doing the work."

Although Randy admits that even his organization has created images that depict their work as more put together than it actually is, something he considers to be lying for some people, in the case of his own organization he only lightly critiques that kind of embellishment. Instead, he offers a searing critique of those who are only involved in the food justice movement, or any social movement, for the time in the spotlight and virtue signaling that comes along with that. To Randy, the problem with superficial people in search of the limelight was that potential stakeholders or donors who were more conservative would see through them. "There's a whole segment of this city who believe this is just total crap," he said. "There are conservatives in the city who are like, 'You're fucking kidding me. Really? Really? You're planting vegetable gardens? Really? What kind of hippie are you? Really? Is this going to really make a difference?' You know? You have to bring them along with you if you're going to make this widespread. Any time you behave in a superficial way, they catch you out. They're always on the lookout. They've challenged me many times." To Randy, the trendy, fleeting involvement in food justice that is too lefty-feeling excludes more conservative folks who might also care deeply about food access for all. "Because a lot of people out there who believe that young kids should be exposed to farming," he explained, "because they believe it's good for their work ethic and obviously good for eating healthy. They are often conservative people. You've got to bring them along with you."

For Randy and his organization eschewing the "justice" narrative, distancing from "hippie" politics and lifestyles, and focusing on values like "working hard" and "eating well," which he associates with conservative politics, has yielded results in the form of donations and political support. He was not the only executive director who told me that catering to conservative politics was essential for managing donors and nonprofit boards. Still, of all the people I studied, Randy was the most explicit and most inclined to agree with conservative values. He talked about people who do food justice work just for the photo ops and social media posts. He made an explicit link between the ways people manipulate the meaning of justice in the service of their own images and as a broader process of virtue signaling. He casts his work in contrast to this and instead focuses on getting work done, creating an opposition between "justice" and real work.

Randy's point about how people use food justice for virtue signaling or advancing their careers was something that I saw often in food justice work. Indeed, even the comments of Mayor Garcetti at the outset of this chapter echo these sentiments. He refers to his work "serving" on boards, "connecting people with ideas," and the "movement" that is the "justice" "they" need, positioning himself as part of an "us" that needs to help "them." Zooming out to think about all of the things that Randy has said, he offers a clear example of how activists within the food movement leverage their power to pull the movement in a particular direction. Like Randy, these activists often do so without the voices of those they have deemed to be "in need" of help.

CONCLUSION

As I burrowed deeper into this ethnographic project, I saw how the work of Food for All, the organization that I started with and thus built a lot of my assumptions about what food justice would look like, was quite different from the work of Build It Better or Produce Power. I understood these organizations as generally operating on an ideological continuum, moving from organizations narrowly focused on interventions to those who want to improve South LA through empowerment and placemaking to those who move toward a broader goal of liberation. Over time, however, I saw that organizations and the people within them were not fixed on this continuum. They could move from being interveners to empowerers to liberators and back again, and at times there were elements of each type in their approaches. Framing these activists within specific typologies would be too confining. Indeed, doing so might do the very thing that I critique many of them for doing to South Central residents. Rather, I focus on the practices these activists undertake and the processes they go through in this work.

Like me, Sarah Cunningham was unsure where to land in the vast food justice movement. Our regular walks were peppered with her reflections on how different organizations understood the goal of their work and whom it should serve. I served as a sounding board as she questioned the words people used, and the things organizations prioritized. Sarah saw that while folks were inviting "stakeholders" to food justice gatherings, they were not creating inclusive spaces with the potential to build toward her vision of collective stakeholdership. Instead, whether intentional or not, Sarah and I could both see how some organizations created exclusive spaces for developing the vision of food justice by excluding residents and other kinds of activists from South LA. This exclusion systematically limited the potential of food justice stakeholder meetings as spaces for multiracial or radical organizing. By drawing the boundaries of food justice gatherings in this way, some activists bolstered their own power to produce a movement in their vision and had the power to limit the vision of others. This had a way of undoing or limiting the possibilities for justice.

Possibly counterintuitively, the way that the term "justice" was used could have an effect of undoing or diminishing the power of justice. The concept of "justice," which operated as an empty signifier with shifting meaning that could be molded to fit what is needed from moment to moment, situation to situation, was leveraged to support particular kinds of power structures. The concepts of "health" and "good food" were operationalized as empty signifiers with presumed beneficence that everyone should agree to be good things for "us" and "them." In the meetings I attended, participants leaned on the concept of "justice" to do the work of rhetorical virtue signaling for them. If they and others describe their work as "justice," it must be inherently good. They wielded the concept as something neutral, capacious, and able to serve everyone. I saw a subset of activists narrating their work as "spreading justice," "opening things for justice," and "allowing for justice to come forth." They positioned themselves as the bearers of justice, spreading it through their programs and projects.

At the same time, the people involved in the movement lead complex lives that sometimes involve contradictions, such as the Chef who complained about the cost of parking in downtown LA but has been at the forefront of gentrifying another part of the city, or Sarah's personal debates about homeownership versus a radical liberated future where profit is not derived from homes and people are giving the land back. I observed other food justice leaders say they are anticapitalist and talk about the problems of the capitalist food system while at the same time using entrepreneurship and business savvy to enact their food justice work. Each organization had slightly differing ideas about social justice and how it was imagined. Some thought that financial inclusion and business capacity building were the best ways to empower residents of South LA. Others focused on building leadership capacity and empowering community members with confidence and agency.

Nevertheless, these orientations to justice are couched within a multilayered scaffolding of virtue signaling and moral relativism wielded on multiple scales to further ensconce people in their positions of political and social power. Justice becomes about making the Other less Otherly, essentially folding the Other into "us." By "giving" them access to the same things as "us," they would have no reason to engage in "unhealthy" behaviors. I consider these moves as assimilationist civilizing projects attempting to fold "them" into the idealized healthy and morally sound lifestyle that people in the food movement share so that they may become the "good citizens" who make "good choices" with respect to food.

Ms. Veronica

Ms. Veronica had been a teacher at three different high schools in South Central over the course of her career. At each school she was linked to various food justice projects that were part of K–12 interventions. One afternoon, I chatted with her after a gathering that brought together food justice leaders and local political leaders. She had attended but did not say anything during the meeting. I asked Ms. Veronica what she thought of all the different food justice interventions she had seen in her wide-ranging experience. She thought about it for a while and told me that the families in her school area had a lot of food insecurity issues in general. She said:

> Kids would always ask me for snacks. Of course, we had breakfast in the classroom—99 percent were eligible for free breakfast so it was just for the whole class. I always just had snacks in the room that I bought, but I would also keep any extra breakfast food, and kids could come and get it throughout the day. All the teachers did that. But I had one kid I remember specifically ask me, in addition to the regular snacks, to buy them peanut butter. They knew that it was a high-calorie food that could fill you up, so they knew if you have bread and you have peanut butter, you have a meal. So I started to always keep those in my classrooms.

Ms. Veronica was pointing out a form of food insecurity that often went unrecognized among the food justice activists I worked with. In telling me about the student's desire for peanut butter, she both conveyed their deep knowledge of nutrition and also the fact that students might be looking for different things from many food justice programs like calorie-dense foods, the opposite of what most food justice activists wanted. Ms. Veronica explained the kind of needs she saw in her student populations:

> I had another kid tell me about living in a warehouse where his dad was a security guard at night, the kids were sleeping on these hard tables. They didn't really have a place to shower, and the only food they had was at school. That was the case with some kids, they only had food at school. I also did this thing where I got donations, like on GoFundMe, and I had this thing where kids could apply for things they needed. Like, you know, school supplies or if they wanted to do puzzles with their little siblings or games. And a surprising number of students asked for food. Or money to buy food. We have eight hundred kids at our school. I ended up only having about $5,000, so there was no way every kid was going to get something. But yeah, kids would basically want things like cereal or chips. Snacks. I have a whole spreadsheet of what they requested. That money went straight to the corner store. Kids are spending like five bucks a day there.

None of the food justice organizations that I had worked with were seriously considering what food justice might mean in the context of homeless families. I wondered if the fact that Ms. Veronica's kids were asking for snacks above all else meant that they were not eating this kind of "junk food" at home. "Wow, if they are really doing that," I said, "it's $4,000 a day just from that school alone." I asked Ms. Veronica where they got the money to buy this food, and she explained:

> I know some kids were getting money from their parents, but also a lot of kids would buy food for each other—like I would hear them ask each other, "Hey, will you buy me this?" and it was like consistently some kids buying for others. Some of the older kids, more juniors and seniors, you know they worked. It was a social thing, it's like you go with your friends to hang out and buy snacks after school. They will do a lot to be able to do that because that is like their friends. It's their life in high school.

I thought this was really sweet and viewed this as part of how students were building community through food and taking care of one another. Ms. Veronica continued: "I think about how kids think about food a lot. I have worked with the [Healthy Families] food justice nonprofit, and this other one too [that was involved in the corner store conversion]. Trying to teach kids of to eat healthy and, you know, 'Let's do gardening, farm-to-table type stuff.'" Her voice heightened into an almost whiney pitch, and she swayed her body and waved her hands back and forth as she described what food justice organizations do in the school:

> We were trying to do these things, but I am realizing it was not really system-atic or actually connected to the kids and how they think about food. You know? It was almost like a different thing. Kids come away from that saying, "Just eat vegetables." My perspective was like, "Yeah, we all know that maybe fast food isn't that great, and maybe vegetables are good for you." But not just that, I was always like, it's not just about knowing what to do, it's about the behavior and the systems that make it difficult to do what is quote unquote healthy.

Ms. Veronica related this to her own life. She told me that she mainly shopped at a Food for Less near her house because the prices were rea-sonable, and it was a place where she could usually do all her shopping at once rather than having to go to multiple stores as many other resi-dents did. With her job and family life, she did not feel she had the time to shop around for the best bargains or go from store to store looking for the best quality produce or meat products. Ms. Veronica had a son who was just a few years younger than my oldest. We both experienced our kids starting to eat "a lot" and wanting to ensure they had healthy food at home while balancing our food costs. We knew that given what they ate at school and with friends, we could not control what our kids ate. All we could do was offer them healthy choices. Ms. Veronica always had apples, oranges, and bananas at home because her son would eat those things. Though he loved berries, she would rarely buy them because of cost. She tried not to buy packaged snacks but kept simple things on hand for him to snack on, like carrots and hummus or the ingredients to make a quick quesadilla or peanut butter sandwich. These things were within her budget, and she knew they would get eaten rather than thrown out.

I wondered how many other South Central families were doing this at home. I asked Ms. Veronica to explain more about her understand-ing of her students' knowledge of the connections between food and health. She said:

> Kids just think, "Well, it's junk food, and junk food is bad. Junk food and fast food are bad." Why? "Because they make you fat." Kids would say things like, "It's just sugar. Bread is just sugar. Rice is just sugar." So we would talk about that, like, is that really true? Is that bad? What does it do in your body? But I also think about this in terms of fatphobia. To me, it's like quickly the kids go from learning about gardening and vegetables to this

really intense fatphobia. Like the other day, I overheard some kids pointing at another kid and laughing at him for eating a cheeseburger after school. They pointed at him and called him "Diabesity." And I was just kind of horrified. I was like, *What are we doing to these kids?* So, I just, it's just something to think about.

Ms. Veronica's story made me reflect on the complex social factors surrounding eating behaviors and the ways in which oversimplifications can have unexpected negative repercussions.

3

Whiteness

On a beautiful late May afternoon, I drove to South LA from Silver Lake. By that point in the day, traffic had already slowed to a crawl. I took Vermont Avenue southbound, driving through Little Armenia, Koreatown, and West Adams before arriving in South LA. The route took me down neighborhood streets lined with jacaranda trees in full bloom, their purple flowers illuminated by the Southern California sunshine. I pulled up near a middle school where an event I was attending was hosted, and I begrudgingly parked my silver Prius under one of the jacaranda trees, lamenting that it would likely become covered in sticky flowers. As I walked down the residential street, I smiled at children playing in front yards being watched by grandmothers. I tightened up as I passed barking dogs.

Reaching the school, I walked through an open wrought iron gate leading to an inner parking lot. In the lot a group of kids was trying to teach some of their white teachers how to Dougie while playing the previous year's hit "Teach Me How to Dougie" by Cali Swag District. I thought it was kind of cute that the kids were showing their teachers how to do the dance, but I also felt weird about the kids and their teachers singing the song's explicit lyrics together. I did not linger and soon found an open school door with a handwritten sign: "HEALTHY FOOD WORKSHOP HERE/TALLER DE COMIDA SALUDABLE AQUÍ." The workshop was led by Melissa, a new employee of a small nonprofit that had been funded as a community partner through a large, national-level research organization's community-based research grant program that a team at a local university had received. The overarching goal of the grant was to implement programming to reduce obesity. The university project leaders had proposed to do food justice work as part of their grant. The team had specifically enlisted this nonprofit because they already had established connections in the community. However, the nonprofit team had no prior experience working on issues of health or nutrition. Nevertheless, they enlisted Melissa, fresh out of a master's program, to conduct a series of healthy eating workshops for South LA residents. The workshop focused on a cooking demonstration to create a simple, healthy dinner. The attendees would later receive a bag of groceries that included the ingredients used in the cooking demo.

I sat in the back of the classroom, in the last row of metal desks. My body felt large as I squeezed into the desk with my knees up against the bottom of the cubby. The desktop was sticky and its cubby, like others, was filled with crumpled papers and broken pencils. I observed the workshop participants: all South LA residents, mainly Latinx, with some Black participants. As they entered the room, most chatted with one another, which gave me the impression they already knew each other. People with smaller bodies sat at the desks, and those with longer legs and larger bodies sat on top of the desks in the back row or stood at the back of the classroom. Most people congregated toward the back, making it feel like the participants were very far from the workshop leader.

Once it was time for the demo to start, it took a while for Melissa to get the room to quiet down. Melissa welcomed everyone in English and explained that the meal she would demonstrate was baked chicken breasts with a vegan "cheezy" kale salad. She informed the participants that, due to a lack of refrigeration, the bag of groceries they would receive at the end of the workshop would only contain the ingredients for the salad. They would not receive any chicken. There was an audible groan and palpable eye rolls. Although the recipe they would take home was for baked chicken, since there was no oven in the demo space, she sautéed a chicken breast in a small pan on a hot plate. She used a drizzle of olive oil but no seasoning. The participants looked on with blank faces. I could not help but wonder: *Does Melissa think the adults in this room do not know how to cook a chicken breast? And, if they were leading the demonstration, wouldn't they season it?* The demonstration struck me as insulting to the people in the room.

Melissa next focused on the kale salad, showing participants how to rip the leafy part of the kale from the stem. Imploring them to massage the kale to help make it more tender—she noted that she sometimes added oil at home when massaging kale, but it was healthier to do it without oil. She cut two avocados and mashed them in a bowl. She cut a lemon in half, squeezed the juice from both halves into the bowl, and added about a quarter cup of nutritional yeast before mixing it with a fork. As she took out the nutritional yeast, the volume in the room went up as participants asked one another what nutritional yeast was and if anyone had ever heard of it.

After the workshop ended, participants lined up to receive a bag that contained two bunches of kale, two avocados, a lemon, and a small container of nutritional yeast. I walked out with a small group, and as we were leaving, they laughed and asked, "You sat through that and didn't even bother picking up the bag. That bad, huh? The free food bag is the only reason we come to these things." They had assumed I was a participant who had come to get the free produce bag—their central motivation for participation. They seemed dubious that they would actually use the contents of the bag, but they took it home nonetheless. Though brief, these comments indicated that the participants did not take up the programming as the organizers intended. The participants could see through the performance that the organization had put on in their "educational outreach" and only sat through the workshops to receive the free food at the end. While the workshop successfully got some healthy foods into the hands of residents, the efforts to change behavior undermined the organization's work to build rapport and trust in the neighborhood.

I wondered how such interventions, which could be insulting, severed the potential for the community to trust the organizations trying to help. I also wondered how this kind of work undermined the possibility of coalition building and limited the possibilities for food justice. I was interested in the implicit forms of power that allowed people like Melissa to lead such a workshop, and the ways the organization wielded power over the participants by promising them a bag of groceries if they sat through the demonstration. As I reflected on what I had just seen, I realized that I needed to understand how whiteness was being deployed in food justice work and how it operated within the specific contexts of race relations in South LA, where Black kids teach white teachers how to Dougie and white recent graduates teach Latina moms how to sauté a chicken breast.

Melissa later explained to me that the vision of baked chicken and kale salad grew out of the assumption that families were eating fried chicken and collard greens cooked with pork. The idea was to be respectful of cultural foodways but to teach people how to "healthify" what food justice activists assumed to be their audience's favorite foods. The demo was planned mainly over phone calls and emails between the university research team and the nonprofit team. To my knowledge, no residents had been involved in the planning. From my vantage point, the food justice organization viewed itself as intervening on stereotypes of Black food traditions even though they know that the area is predominantly Latinx (and indeed most participants of this workshop were Latinx). I thought about all of the scholars, leaders, granting agencies, and administrators who had agreed to back this work, giving the organization implicit and explicit forms of power to intervene in South LA.

What became clear was that the organizations were guided by racial imaginaries of South LA as a "Black place." This racial imaginary of food consumption implicitly links unhealthy food with Blackness, which was extended to Latinidad as well. Without any background in nutrition, the organizers swapped "unhealthy" Black foods (i.e., fried chicken and collard greens) for the "healthified" versions of the same thing. These new versions of Black foods were racially coded as white foods (i.e., unseasoned baked chicken and massaged kale). In this intervention specific foods and ways of preparing foods were tied to racialized understandings of virtuous behavior and the production of the "healthy" subject.

I observed many other workshops, classroom presentations, and conversations about "healthy eating" between food justice activists and the residents they target for interventions. Another involved an organization called Bettering Life that conducted a class in an East LA high school centered around both healthy eating for the students and mobilizing the students to encourage their families and community members to change their dietary habits.[1] Although "healthy" was not explicitly defined by this organization, the implication was that fresh fruits and vegetables were the kind of healthy foods that people *should* be eating. When the executive directors and I first got to know one of the classes they were working with, they had everyone introduce themselves and tell the group what their favorite food was. I jotted down the student's answers—tamales, BBQ ribs, pozole, pizza, carne asada, and tortillas with butter. When it came around to me, I stated my name and that my favorite food was macaroni and cheese. Later, one of the executive directors chastised me for this response, implying that I was a bad influence on the students. They were "here to get the kids to change the way that they eat," she explained. "To get them to stop eating things like tortillas or macaroni and cheese and eat things like Brussels sprouts, kale, broccoli, you know healthy food."[2]

The narrative of Bettering Life implied that the culturally significant foods that the students and their families had been eating all of their lives were unhealthy and glossed as "bad." In contrast, the foods that were more commonly associated with white communities, such as kale and broccoli, were healthy and therefore "good." The Bettering Life leaders were either unaware of or uninterested in the many texts, films, and TV shows that amplify the food traditions of Black, Brown, and all kinds of other people as linked to commensality, care, family, and love.[3] Teaching people to eat in this way was a form of discipline deeply linked to power within the food justice movement. "Health," "healthy food," and "healthy eating" were rarely defined by the food justice activists that I worked with. Instead, like the concept of "justice," the language around health operated as an empty signifier, where it was assumed that everyone knows and agrees upon a shared understanding of what is healthy.[4]

In specific settings, like the cooking demonstration, I could see how concepts like "good food" and "healthy eating" could take on raced and classed coded meanings.[5] To me, these ways of framing the problem and "healthy food" as the answer are part of a broader racial lexicon that is deployed in ways that "sustain racial thought, index particular racial meanings, and prescribe social practices."[6] In these interventions whiteness becomes the foundational background underlying the assumptions about what is "good" and "healthy," even as whiteness remains unacknowledged or "unmarked," instead "taking its meaning from those surrounding categories to which it is structurally opposed, such as blackness, indigenousness, and foreignness."[7] Here, whiteness only becomes visible or noticeable in contrast to something Other.[8] This is not only in terms of the ways in which Others are subtly encouraged to assimilate into whiteness, as the above examples show, but also in the assumptions regarding why this work is important and should be done in the first place.[9]

I observed the ways people doing food justice work tacitly operated under the assumption that the best way to improve the lives of people living in South LA was to make them behave (or, more specifically, to make them eat) more like people who live in other parts of the city—like West LA, commonly invoked as the counterpoint. These places are seen as healthier by both food justice activists and most South LA residents I have spoken with along various metrics, including regular consumption of fruits and vegetables, but they are also more demographically white and middle or upper class. In my observation most South LA residents *do* regularly consume fruits and vegetables, but perhaps not as often as food justice activists would like. In addition, the types of fresh fruits and vegetables and how they are incorporated into meals by food justice activists often differ from practices residents are used to. For instance, residents who were used to eating simmered collard greens might be encouraged to eat a raw kale salad instead. There was an underlying assumption that part of the work that was being done was to try to assimilate people in South LA into white, middle-class American norms or whiteness. In other words, in this imaginary, West LA was the developed, first world while South LA was the developing/underdeveloped world.

I started to see how the multifaceted role of whiteness was shaping the food justice movement. In addition to assumptions about health, the multiplicity of whiteness seeped into nearly every nook and corner of the food movement in varying ways. Once I could see the various ways that it operated, I tried to pull whiteness from behind the shadows to view its trickster character and slipperiness as whiteness moved through conversations on food justice in varying registers, marked and unmarked. Anthropologists and other scholars have analyzed various dimensions of whiteness as a process, system, or analytic.[10] Black studies scholar George Lipsitz proposes whiteness as "an organizing principle" of social relations, which, drawing on philosopher Walter Benjamin, requires a "presence of mind" to understand and deconstruct.[11] As I fine-tuned my ethnographic sensibilities over the course of the research, I began to see the ways in which whiteness facilitated forms of power. Whiteness was a powerful barrier to the inclusion of racial justice frameworks in food movement work.

ON WHITENESS AND WHITE RACIAL PROJECTS

While terms like "health" and "healthy eating" could be used to index whiteness, whiteness itself was rarely spoken of. Within much of the food justice work that I observed, race and racism were often ignored or assumed to be no longer relevant. Nevertheless, racial codes were consistently embedded within the language, logics, and practices of food justice practitioners in Los Angeles. Of course, the language of race has shifted over time, and my research primarily took place during the Obama presidency (2009–17), when many people in the United

States wondered if we had entered a "postracial moment."[12] Even if the United States never became postracial, this research took place before the racial reckonings that followed George Floyd's murder in 2020, when it was less common to speak openly about racism and white supremacy, and forms of "color-blind" racism prevailed.[13] Rather than using biological and moral racialization, color-blind racism moves away from the language of race entirely, instead turning to "market dynamics, naturally occurring phenomena, and imputed cultural limitations."[14] These implicit forms of racialization use "soft otherizing " to imply that people of color are lazy and lack knowledge and skills.[15] Importantly, white racial projects and related forms of racism operate to maintain white privilege without doing so explicitly.[16] While race and racism were often left unmentioned, the specter of whiteness also remained unmarked, as those working in food justice organizations rarely attended to the ways whiteness and white racial frameworks influenced food justice and how they are enacted.[17]

Although white supremacy has shaped Western political thought and the formation of societies across the globe for hundreds of years, it has never been made explicit.[18] Like what Michel Foucault has called "discourse," whiteness also operates as an opaque ideology built upon an assemblage of taken for granted, mainstream knowledge and power. Of course, W. E. B. DuBois has been writing about whiteness since at least 1899, while Black feminist scholars from Angela Davis to Barbara Smith and the Combahee River Collective have been writing about the violence of whiteness since at least the 1970s, and scholars like Brittney Cooper, Ibram X. Kendi, Robin DiAngelo, Ta-Nehisi Coates, and Ijeoma Oluo wrote extremely popular books during the course of this research that clearly defined white supremacy for the broader public.[19] Nevertheless, for many of the food justice activists that were part of this research, white supremacy and whiteness more broadly remained an unnamed, invisible political and social system that has unacknowledged power in social and political relations today.[20] For many, the invisibility of whiteness made it challenging to analyze and understand. That said, over the course of this research, I noted and attuned my focus to various apertures in the multiple forms and logics of whiteness in the food justice movement.[21] I found that whiteness is "continually restructured, revised, and disfigured" and operationalized by white people and non-white people alike.[22]

The people who make up the organizations in this research primarily identified politically as liberal, progressive, or radical. The forms of racialization that they engaged in operate within liberal-democratic political frameworks that frame state-affiliated and nonprofit organizations as helpful while avoiding or ignoring race and racism as a cause of current inequities.[23] Unlike the common understanding that people in the United States are critical of those who need food assistance and negatively associate welfare programs with Black and other people of color, my research participants tended to frame those they intervened on as "in need" of help from a benevolent outsider.[24] This imaginary serves to create and reinforce social distance between "us" and "them" as "givers and receivers" and works in tandem with the more extensive system of racial capitalism.[25]

I started to see that many of the programs and interventions I was observing were, in effect, "white racial projects."[26] A racial project is an interpretation, representation, or explanation of racial dynamics and an effort to reorganize and redistribute resources along racial lines.[27] Clearly, many food justice projects are attempts to reallocate resources to Black and Latinx communities even though discussion of race is often avoided. However, these projects are also specifically *white* racial projects in that they are based on the tacit assumption that the ways in which middle-class white people live and eat are the norm. In contrast, those who live otherwise are deviations from that norm and are encouraged to shift their behaviors toward the white norm. This tacit work is part of liberal racial projects that are often done without explicit commitments to racial redistribution. It falls within broader efforts to "get beyond race" and to "strenuously resist any concept of whiteness that equates it with the preservation of 'a sense of group position,' much less with the maintenance of racial privilege."[28] I found that much of the work done and the programming created under the guise of the food justice movement actually served to reinforce racial structures and ultimately benefit outsiders intervening in Black and Latinx communities. This is one among many social justice projects that are entangled in racial capitalism and long-standing settler-colonial projects.[29]

The underlying logics of food justice interventions were often inextricably bound with the particular histories of white–settler colonialism that gave rise to moralizations of manifest destiny and the need to civilize or help the Other. Western continental philosophers, specifically John Locke and the anthropologists who built from these lines of thinking, have had a significant role in tying the ideas for self-governance and property ownership to Eurocentric ideas of white racial superiority.[30] From European colonial land seizures across Latin America, Africa, and

Asia to Indigenous dispossession in North America, racializing logics about the capabilities of local people to govern themselves were used to justify violent actions and render these processes benevolent. Woven into racialized justifications for dispossession and eliding the massive campaigns of murderous violence against Indigenous and Black populations across the globe, the settler-colonial project of "civilizing the Other" came into view as a service offered by settler-colonizers.

"Civilizing the Other" reinforces the superiority and power of those in control. Building from hundreds of years of "civilizing" projects as forms of benevolent service for those "in need," at home and abroad (sometimes glossed as "social justice"), these are part of a historical, national project that relates to colonial and imperial projects of the United States. In other words, as anthropologists Aisha M. Beliso-De Jesús, Jemima Pierre, and Junaid Rana have theorized the relationship between whiteness and power has been foundational to the "construction of the racialized modern world."[31] Sociologist Ruha Benjamin has argued that these systems and ideologies, derived from the enslaver "caring" for his property, help to maintain the idealized contemporary figure who "benevolently feeds, shelters, and trains" his childlike dependents.[32] These ideologies persist in contemporary service and social justice work that is motivated by the idea of a duty to help the Other. What some might construe as benevolent service can be seen as what philosopher Lewis Gordon calls "white license," an authoritative stance that assumes the right to intervene and change the Other, regardless of the needs or desires of those communities.[33] The historical and political ideologies that support global development, settler-colonialism, and white supremacy are all part of overlapping systems that underlie the reasoning and assumptions around contemporary interventions that value particular ways of eating and build off assumptions that eating in other ways is a sign of ignorance or lack of self-restraint.

Within this broader context I found that *whiteness* was a central foundational tenant that both motivated and grounded food justice interventions. In the book's introduction, Andrés probed the idea of food justice itself as a concept that some "white liberal came up with." He indexed whiteness in the materiality of "vegan, organic food." He noted the power food justice activists had in erasing what does exist in South Central by "making sure that there were none of our foods present." Like Andrés, I see whiteness as both grounding and grounded in the forms of power that allow unprepared outsiders to intervene in their own ways. But whiteness was almost always unspoken, barely visible, and only lingering below the surface, referenced in veiled concepts like "vegan, organic food" or "kale salads." In turn, kale, unseasoned boneless skinless chicken breasts, and nutritional yeast index whiteness in particular ways in these contexts. This was part of how the mutability of whiteness helped to facilitate its role in veiled power relations within existing racial hierarchies. Following DuBois, I see whiteness as a set of complex, situational factors that are constantly shifting and mutating. This multiplicity of whiteness is not universally shared and can be experienced simultaneously in different ways by white people and nonwhite people alike.

Legal scholar Cheryl Harris's groundbreaking concept of "whiteness as property" illuminates some specific ways food justice can operate as a white racial project.[34] Although in popular understandings people think of property as material possessions or "things," Harris shows that the concept of property extends to intangible things, like whiteness. Whiteness fundamentally defined the legal status of "free," conferring "tangible and economically valuable benefits and was jealously guarded as a valued possession, allowed only to those who met a strict standard of proof."[35] Harris argues that the law as we know it in the United States was established to protect property interests in *whiteness itself* and that whiteness is a central characteristic of freedom. Whiteness is not just about racial identity but also the "assumptions, privileges, and benefits that accompany the status of being white."[36] She notes that whiteness is rarely apparent and instead implied in the ways white status and all the benefits conferred by that status are protected by law and the great lengths people have gone through to confine the status of whiteness to only certain kinds of people. I understand whiteness as a bundle of social, political, and legal benefits that were tethered to certain types of people and, critically, that whiteness could also be tethered to associated physical, material, affective, and other elements. This has allowed me to see how whiteness could be foundational for certain kinds of interventions and be represented in certain forms, like kale or baked chicken.

While whiteness has clear associations and is represented symbolically and discursively in relatively straightforward material ways, whiteness can also be elusive, tricky, and slippery. It can morph and latch onto different icons and symbols in unexpected ways. As I worked on this project, I saw the ways in which whiteness was articulated through various kinds of material representations and discursive practices that served to position whiteness in different ways vis-à-vis the Other and their practices. I became interested in how whiteness was produced and reproduced on the ground and in turn the power of whiteness in shaping the food justice movement.

WHITENESS AS MOTIVATING: FROM HELPING ABROAD TO HELPING AT HOME

Sarah Cunningham and I carpooled together from Silver Lake up Sunset Boulevard to a meeting held in the board room of a fancy building in Hollywood. Josh Anderson, a social entrepreneur who had been offering his skills for free to several different food justice organizations around town, was hosting the meeting at the headquarters of the company he worked for. Along with Matt Smith and Chase Bledsoe, two other people eager to "help out" the food justice movement, we were invited to convene that day to "a brainstorm" about how various food justice organizations could leverage the skills of experts in various areas working around the city.

Josh Anderson, a newcomer to Los Angeles, became involved in the food justice movement after being frustrated with the work he was doing in Africa as a volunteer with an international aid organization. Originally from the Midwest, Josh rented an apartment with roommates in Culver City. Born in the late 1970s, the tail end of Generation X, he identified as male and white. With a bachelor's degree in social justice from a Midwestern university, Josh moved to LA to work at a for-profit social enterprise that provided consulting services for high-paying clients and offered those same consulting services free of charge to low-income clients and nonprofits. After getting to know Josh, I came to see him as a social entrepreneur who believed in the power of innovation, design thinking, and technical solutions to address critical social problems and solve problems for "minorities."[37] He felt that "systems thinking" and "design thinking" were necessary for social movements to succeed and "scale up." He wanted to do more with his life than what his paid work allowed, and he "had always thought about how the work that we do could be applied to other meaningful projects in the community and we had a discussion one day about food deserts and their existence in urban areas." He wanted to "make a difference."

Josh had been living in Los Angeles for two years when I first met him in 2014. He situated his food justice work in his upbringing. "I was brought up in a very activist, volunteerist home," he said, "and I kind of grew up with the expectation that I would contribute, I guess. Right after college [I] actually joined the [aid organization] and did that for a couple of years and then from there transitioned into teaching elementary school [abroad]. So, I taught for several years and came back to America to pursue a different career path." Josh credited his family for instilling in him the virtue of helping others. However, after spending time abroad, he developed a less idealistic picture of international service. He explained: "With the [aid organization]—I don't know if it was because it was international and it was definitely like 'we're here as the American,' I mean here we were—the white people—but like with the [aid organization]. Some of these people have never seen Americans—white people—before."

Josh contextualized this work by the histories of geopolitical relations and the development dollars the United States brought to places in Africa. "And so, [. . .] they had a very clear idea of what they wanted," he said, "and it wasn't usually driven by what they actually needed, it was driven by prestige or ways that they could skim off the top." I interjected to clarify, asking *who* exactly he was referring to. "Sorry, the locals, so be it—the principal of the school, the community, and like, NGO partnerships they had with the government, neighbors . . .," he said, trailing off. "I felt like everyone had their agendas. It was pretty obvious. You had to be blind to not see what they wanted, and it was because there was very often a very clear ulterior motive. And again it was either driven by corruption or prestige projects." For Josh, aiding others meant doing so on his terms, not theirs. Instead, he characterized local demands based on needs that were agreed upon by locals and the NGO as exploitation of the NGO because it did not align with Josh's idea of what was appropriate.[38] In reflecting on Josh's framing of his family ethos around helping others and his assertion that he knew better than locals in Africa that he suspected were all corrupt, I saw the ways in which white saviorism and fundamentally racist ideas also motivated his work in South LA.[39]

Ultimately it was not the outsider dynamic that turned Josh away from international aid work. Instead, his experience led him to believe that international organizations were too constrained by international policy, local agreements and laws, and the rules and regulations created by the organizations themselves. To me Josh was saying that there were too many checks and balances stopping him from doing whatever he wanted abroad, but that there was no one stopping him from doing similar things in South LA. In our meeting that day, we sat around the conference room table with coffee drinks, snacking on muffins while Josh stood at the whiteboard. He started out by reflecting on the process of planning a recent food justice intervention to help convert a corner store into a healthy market. "We identified that the actual particulars of this project weren't your typical food desert scenario," he said. "There were actually a lot of food options in the area, but we also saw still that that didn't deter it from being a very positively potentialed [*sic*] kind of laboratory to, I guess, execute some of the work and processes." He explained: "We were looking for ways to experiment." Instead of thinking of their work as an intervention in an area of high need, Josh and his team thought of it as a laboratory experiment or a way to test out some of their ideas in a real-life situation. This way of thinking of low-income communities in the United States or the Global South as a place to test something out has a long history.[40] I found it telling that they did not want to let their client know that what they were doing was an experiment.

Attempting to move away from the white savior nature of international aid work, Josh crafted another narrative for the domestic work and tried to create a space that felt authentic to the area. "The client is an immigrant," he explained, "and he had come to this area that, this neighborhood that had been traditionally Black and is transitioning into more Latino, and we thought that was a positive story to be told around the bilingual nature, the international kind of mashing dynamic interaction of cultures in South LA and LA in general." I was pleased that Josh was aware of the demographic transition in South LA. He continued: "So we really wanted to create something that was fun and engaging, educational in a playful, familiar, comfortable manner that still spoke to some of the key, I guess, the key tenants of food desertism, or whatever that you would call it." I assumed that Josh was referring to the fact that some people, like Andrés, preferred to call the situation food apartheid. Josh explained their vision for the project:

> Like, you know, offering fresh food options and dealing with obesity epidemics, understanding the fact that there are schools nearby and providing healthy food options to people from lower-income neighborhoods and stuff like that, but understanding at the same time that we couldn't, we had these parameters of, the realities of the socioeconomic situation, what people actually want, what school kids actually want, and then also starting very early on to get a clear idea of our own budget constraints. I guess also just the kind of general market environmental constraints, understanding just because we necessarily offer bananas and fruits and vegetables and stuff like that doesn't mean that people will actually get it or want it.

Josh understood that some aspects of this work could be problematic: "From my, more, kind of, personal anecdotal experience of just understanding that there are a lot of issues with nonprofits and development, international development, or any kind of local community development. It's the road to hell paved with good intentions, and that you know—you can lead a fish to water or a horse to water, but you can't make them drink kale." I understood Josh as framing the problems with these approaches not as the fault of those intervening but as a failure or refusal of those being intervened upon. I laughed at his play on a pun about getting people to eat kale. Or, rather, *trying* (unsuccessfully) to get people to eat kale.

I asked Josh if the fact that this client was not a paying client but that the work was done pro-bono changed or shifted this project. "He was definitely more easygoing in a way because he was very appreciative, I think, of our efforts," Josh said, "and so I felt like he, once we gave him options, we provided different concepts and different approaches, so it wasn't like we were providing directives to him, but I think he was always incredibly appreciative." I wondered if his client was enacting a form of racialized deference, especially considering that the work was being done at no cost to him. I remembered that Ms. Veronica had told me she saw this kind of deference among Latino parents that she knew from working in area schools. She felt that it was linked to why these parents were willing to subject themselves to the insulting cooking workshops that they sat through. "So he was, he was very receptive, I guess, I'd say very open," Josh said. "There wasn't, the back and forth wasn't built as much on personal taste, or internal politics of a company."

On some level Josh was aware that the power dynamics of an outside company offering free services and goods to low-income clients results in those low-income clients yielding power and decision-making to the outsider. Yet in framing the process as part of his own personal fulfillment, Josh seemed to think of this as a benefit of this type of work and did not dwell on the negative repercussions of this dynamic for low-income communities. I asked him to explicitly reflect on how this work was personally fulfilling. "The best way somebody can contribute is through their skills, through their expertise. It's not necessarily just standing in the soup kitchen line and just giving somebody soup, it's not just necessarily giving twenty-five bucks to [organizations], it's actually contributing the very same thing they do during the day, that's their skill set, and that's what they're good at, and they should be employing some of those things for this. This is their part and that's the best way to really maximize your contribution and the organization's return simultaneously."

Moving from this more general characterization of why people should be involved in helping others, Josh shifted to a more personal reflection:

> I don't personally get much fulfillment out of seeing [a company's] revenues increase. It just doesn't do it for me. I know it's essential to what I do, and I know that it gets more business, so I don't condemn it by any measure, but I just don't get any—I don't derive any fulfillment out of it. It doesn't make me feel like a better person, like I'm contributing to the world. So this was a way I thought, you know, on a very small scale that I could actually contribute to helping this guy out. But more than that, I still did hold onto the idea that maybe [we were] creating a model that could be used in other parts of Los Angeles or wherever else or other urban areas. Yeah, so, more than anything else, it's a personal thing.

Josh paused and reflected on how this kind of work benefited him:

> I think it's necessary for me, it's a selfish thing in a way because I just feel like I need to do certain things in order to have that equilibrium. It doesn't help me sleep at night, it's not like that kind of thing, but it's just something I don't know you gotta do, and it's good to also deal with different clients, different kinds, I mean to treat them as nonpaying customers or different environments, different contexts. I think it does make you—it can make you—better, whatever you, to learn the necessary adaptability to be able to work within these different circumstances, I guess. But in the end, it was just more of a kind of a personal chipping in.

Josh crafts himself as an expert whose intellectual skills are more valuable than just his physical volunteering or monetary donations. Implicit in how he understands his contributions to South LA is his belief that he knows the best way to implement an intervention, and through his food justice work, he has found a way to enact his vision of what is best without the rules or checks and balances of the work he found so frustrating with the international NGO work. Josh spoke with such confidence that I could see how people like Sarah Cunningham would just take him at his word that he *knew* what was best in terms of the intervention. This could slip into assuming he knew what people in South LA needed as well. Whiteness travels between global and local scales here. Yet in Josh's critique of food justice interventions that offer fresh fruits and vegetables that no one wants, he also seemed to understand that these approaches to improving access to healthy food may not be effective. The inefficacy of such programs has been supported by research.[41]

Josh's own understanding of what he is doing is a perfect example of the power of white license and the assumption that it is helpful to intervene on others. He describes the process of intervening in South LA mainly as something that has benefitted him and allowed him to "have equilibrium" to balance his life in more affluent parts of the city and the busy pace of that life and his job. Intervening in South LA expanded his social network, introducing him not only to clients but also to other people like him who felt passionate about "helping others" by testing their ideas and experimenting in places where it was feasible to do so, and no one would stop them. Thus, as Josh and the people involved in this project act upon particular forms of power and white license to intervene, they build their own social capital and bolster their positions of privilege, all while drawing on the unspoken benevolence of whiteness and narrating themselves as virtuous, selfless people. Although not totally explicit, Josh appears to be motivated by deep-seated ideas of manifest destiny and broader settler projects tied to whiteness. His story illuminates the ways various aspects of white license are entangled with volunteerism. More broadly, in the food justice work that I studied, I found that there was a heavy focus on the ways this kind of work mainly benefits the volunteer. The impact on those being intervened upon was secondary or completely cast aside.

After Josh spoke in the meeting that afternoon, Matt chimed in. He agreed with Josh: "We should do more projects. Allow more junior people to take on projects that they wouldn't be allowed to do for a real project. For people who want to play a role, they could play a different kind of role. It gives them something to practice on." Like Josh, Matt thought of these interventions in South and East LA as experiments or projects where relative novices can practice their skills without any pushback from the community if they make mistakes. Matt referred to the places they were working on as "dumps" and reflected that "it just strikes me as —you could do better—you could do something more interesting here." But given how he saw these places, even having a novice come in and experiment on "making this better" was an improvement in his eyes. To me, Matt's idea that he can "do better" is a clear manifestation of white license.

Like Josh, Matt was a recent transplant to Los Angeles who became involved in the food justice movement. He was initially approached by an organization and asked to contribute a particular skill that he had. However, he told me he was not interested in helping out in the way that they wanted and instead offered to help in the way that *he* preferred, telling the organization: "There's other things I can do, I would like to help." He got his "feet wet" in the movement by teaching a high school class on behalf of an organization that had been funded through a large federal grant to create programming that encouraged students to shift to healthier eating habits. Admittedly, Matt knew nothing about teaching or healthy eating, but he offered up his time for free, and the organization needed help. From that experience, Matt shifted into a position that helped the organization and others to save money by getting more highly skilled volunteers to work on projects. When I asked him why he made the change, he said, "I just thought it would be fun for us to work on this."

I asked Matt what motivated him to get involved. It was a variety of factors but mainly, he told me, "I have this job, and it's a good job. I mostly like [it], but it's a very corporate job. So, there's all these things I know and couldn't I, shouldn't I apply that knowledge? I lived in [a somewhat low-income area of Los Angeles] for a long time, and we could see it there. We were like, 'People eat terribly around here,' and we wanted to help these people. And I was like, well, I kinda know a few things, I should do something." Matt viewed South LA as a place with fewer barriers to experimentation, where the City of Los Angeles is less likely to check if work is permitted and where rules and laws can be broken or circumvented. He feels that he has a lot of knowledge and skills that he cannot or should not apply in his corporate job. It is too risky for high-stakes projects, too risky for job security. But South LA offers a place to play around and have fun without taking on risk; instead, the risk is shouldered by those who live and work in South LA. The risk is offset onto the lives of the Black and Brown people that they experiment on or with. But Matt is confident that even his unexperienced junior colleagues knew enough to make things better in South LA.

Continuing about why he was driven to "help these people," Matt grounded his motivations in broader issues, saying, "Obviously, everyone should be horrified by the obesity epidemic in America." He shared personal connections to health issues exacerbated by obesity that have been a part of his life: "Everybody has got this issue in America. I know what it means to eat poorly and to do these things to your body that you shouldn't be doing." He returned to more personal motivations: "I want to be more human, more well-rounded, about . . . . how do you connect with people." While explaining why he volunteers his time, Matt made the assumption that I would agree that the obesity epidemic in the United States is "horrifying." I thought about Ms. Veronica's critique of the ways in which food justice interventions can easily turn into fatphobia and bullying among her students. While these logics are grounded in the problems that Others face, Matt underscores how the work helps him more directly to be a better person who is more closely connected to his broader community.

In a follow-up interview, Matt reflected on why so many other people from outside of South LA were getting involved, telling me that there was "a lot of ego" in the movement: "It is interesting to see how interested regular people are in these issues, to the point where I sometimes wonder if it tends to cloud these other food justice—justice issues. But also, probably I can imagine if you're working on social justice issues, you're like, Are you kidding me, like you're interested in selling apples and oranges, what impact does that even make?" The category of "regular people" deployed in this way is another form of normalizing whiteness. Matt finds it surprising how many "regular people" are interested in food issues. Still, he understands that the flood of these outsider volunteers and activists into the food movement makes it difficult for those who care about justice issues to get them onto the table and across to those who have difficulty understanding them or feel uncomfortable engaging issues of justice. He sees how the narrow focus on "healthy eating" overshadows the more "justice"-oriented social issues others are trying to incorporate into the food movement.

Drawing on what they assume to be transferrable skills with little to no knowledge of the area and its residents, organizations create programming that helps to "build capacity." The locus and direction of capacity building are almost always assumed to go from the organizations to the community. The one-directional nature of this kind of food justice activism in LA is in line with approaches to global development outside the United States as well. There is an assumption that the need is "out there," that these communities are spaces of lack that need to be filled, but what the accounts Josh and Matt, and others like them, show are that *they* are the ones that are in need. Their egos need to be fulfilled. The accounts detailed here show that the concept of "need" is not as straightforward as these organizations assume.[42] These workers may be unfulfilled at work or home. They may "need" to practice their skills but find themselves without opportunities at work to do so. They feel the need to utilize, share, and spread their knowledge and skills that they otherwise have no outlet for in their everyday lives.

While their areas and levels of expertise varied, there appeared to be a relatively common inclination toward design, entrepreneurship, or technical solutions to food systems problems. Most of the interventions that I observed were derived from the logic and experiences of outside interventionists and did not draw from local knowledge or experience. For instance, both Josh and Matt pointed to their expertise in design as something they felt compelled to offer to help Others—their logics were akin to the humanitarian design movement, a broader global movement that tries to address "need" and social precarity through technical solutions.[43] Building from neoliberal values, this framing of the work ties it to particular American values around democracy and freedom, which in turn bolsters the power and apparent urgency of such work. This resonates with anthropologist Tania Li's critique of the use of technical solutions to problems that are social and political in nature as part of a process of depoliticizing problems, which I argue undermines the need for collective, grassroots approaches to solutions.[44]

In my experience LA-area nonprofit executive directors and other staff often felt they did not have the time to do the research and gather the information necessary to implement the programs they had come up with. In turning to these "experts," like Matt and Josh, the organizational leaders implicitly assumed that the "experts" would either already know sufficient information about the context or do that research as a part of the project. However, rather than spending time on the ground in South LA and working toward figuring out the complex problems of food access issues in the area, the "experts" I observed seemed to feel that they had the ability to warp their expertise to solve any kind of problem. They generalized their previous experiences or assumptions about ongoing social issues and assumed the problems of South LA would fit their abilities. These assumptions speak to the forms of power that they enact through their interventions based on technical fixes.

Sarah and I reflected on the meeting during our drive back to Silver Lake. She was "super excited" about the conversation. She thought about how she could "leverage" the free labor of people like Josh and Matt. She saw them as offering skills to create "leveled-up quality" in the food justice interventions she was working on with Chase Bledsoe at Produce Power. Sarah was eager to report back to Chase so that they could brainstorm how to bring Matt and Josh into their future work. Although I did not say anything, given that I felt very hesitant about the approaches Matt and Josh were using, I was surprised by Sarah's enthusiasm, given her desire to build coalitions with the community and her decolonial and liberatory motives for her work. I was unsure how the types of entrepreneurial thinking that Matt and Josh were using aligned with Sarah's values. I wondered if her values might be shifting. Nevertheless, I was intrigued by how much she had bought into the conversation that day and how quickly she wanted to incorporate these approaches into her work. I wondered what Chase would think.

DEFLECTING WHITENESS: THE SILENT POWER OF WHITENESS

Initially racial justice was at the center of Chase's food justice work. I followed his work from his first position as an intern through his rise to the level of executive director of Produce Power and then after leaving the nonprofit world to start a social enterprise. In our first interview in 2009, Chase characterized himself as "radical from a young age," telling me that his mom was a "white feminist" who had instilled in him an ethics of responsibility to "do something" about injustice. Chase told me he spent his college journey "thinking a lot about the history of white supremacy and racism in the United States and what it means to be a white person in that context and what it means to be an ally in that context." For Chase, that was the "foundation of the kind of activism I was involved with in college and beyond, it was all with an eye toward, you know, really focusing on my piece of the puzzle in terms of the work of dismantling racism, white supremacy, and systems of oppression." When we first met, Chase and I shared an understanding that race and whiteness were at the center of the problem that he was dedicated to working on, which he termed the "question of access, equitable access to food for low-income communities and communities of color across the country and here in [Los Angeles]." Back then, Chase viewed white supremacy as the deep underlying cause of the rise of the suburban supermarket and related divestment from urban center food retail. He understood that part of the failures of previous attempts to improve the conditions of South LA (like the Rebuild LA debacle discussed in chapter 1) were deeply entangled with race and whiteness.

In 2014, when Chase had risen to the level of executive director in his organization, I sat down with him again to talk about how food justice had changed over the years, and the topic of racial justice came up again. "With respect to the racial element," he explained, "we are really trying to work and develop an equity or justice framework that's really centered in everybody's work. To do that, we need to help build capacity to do that well, and to orient it around racial justice is, uh, complicated." Chase offered an example of a new intern who was finishing up her master's research in Oakland and had gotten him interested in the idea of "capacity building."[45] He said, "So, we were like 'yes,' capacity! We all care so much about it, but we're kind of like, 'So, how is this gonna get done,' you know? And she volunteered to really do leg work and research. It's looking and feeling more like it will be a document, but also a tool kit, and maybe a set of training or something that's really for participants and leaders." Chase talked about how great that intern was, and how the organization was now focused more on "skill building": "You know, to really build our skills and our language and build our analysis around what equity means in her work. You know, what that means in terms of race and class and gender and all these things. You know, so that's really exciting, and that's great."

Chase told me that he had been "doing this work" on racial equity "above and beyond my position, like as a volunteer for basically the last year. I'm really *really* invested in that, um, and then I mean, not a per se, something I'm moving in a very, like, manifested way, but something that is very dear to my heart and something I pay a lot of attention to and talk a lot about." He understood this work as something more profound and also part of how he approached building *his* community:

> So, like, there's folks who I'm in community with who do cleanses together who do, like, a week-long raw food cleanse together, but it's all together held in the context of building community and doing it consciously knowing it's subverting the food system as we have inherited it so it's not just quote-unquote "just for health" or "just for vanity" or whatever. It's about, healing ourselves, and being with each other in that process, and that's something that I got a lot of joy and, um, connection around. Folks who were on that tip to exchanging ideas and you know exploring plant-based diets is something that is culturally and politically meaningful for our lives. Does that make sense?

I admitted to Chase that I had kind of lost the thread of racial justice in his explanation. He paused, took a very deep breath, and said, "Hanna, you have seen what I am up against. I am just not sure what I can do here."

While Chase and others had originally come to the work of food justice as part of a deeper fight against white supremacy, his drive to do "the work of dismantling racism, white supremacy, and systems of oppression" through his food work diminished over time in part because so many people working in the food movement were not interested or lacked the capacity to discuss race and whiteness in meaningful ways. Over the course of five years Chase had shifted from a radical, antiracist approach to food justice to much more mainstream, status quo framings. This made me realize that I needed to check in with folks over time to see if and how they had shifted their thinking with more time in the movement. The positions and logics people used were fluid and not fixed.

In a different conversation with Sarah, she told me that she had tried to have conversations about the role of race and racism in food access inequality. Although she was very attuned to the connections between race, racism, and social justice, as a white woman she found it extremely difficult to get others to connect with, understand, and incorporate these issues into their mutual work. She told me a story of one interaction that characterized things for her:

> We had that conversation [about how to think about race and food justice], and it's true that there are just gaps in capacity. Gaps just come forward, in terms of everyone's ability to hold that in the work we're doing, um. Which highlights the "whiteness" of the space and how whiteness and privilege shapes what we're doing, and that's not necessarily white people engaging in that, but it is a very white space. The woman who is actually from [A Food Production related nonprofit], um, didn't like . . . when she . . . when she finally waded into the conversation, like she took it somewhere else, like I spent a good six minutes trying to see where she was headed, and at the end I felt it was her reaction, in not knowing how to directly engage with race.

Sarah paused and looked off in the distance. She seemed to be reflecting on what had happened in the room that day. She continued:

> Because she was acting defensive, but she started talking about local food about how grocers should source locally, while we were in the midst of talking about what does racial equity look like, and then she responded and she was very frustrated and went somewhere else and the best that I could understand that there was a gap in capacity, maybe she didn't get what we were talking about or know how it related to her, so she took the conversation somewhere else, so it wasn't like she was that stupid, but she was like that, she was frustrated and then she was looking at her watch. And then people were responding to her, and I was like, "We're talking about something different that's important," but I don't think, I don't know if she purposefully derailed the conversation. She didn't have the capacity within herself to, I don't know, to integrate with what we were talking about to have that conversation, but she felt like she needed to be there but couldn't talk about these topics.

Even in a space where Sarah was aware of the relevance of issues of race and histories of discrimination, these efforts are often thwarted by other stakeholders who do not have the capacity or interest to think through, deal with, or even discuss the role of race and discrimination in the food system. Within the food justice world these practitioners felt entitled to "take up space," both in terms of how much they spoke in meetings and the extent to which they wholly redesigned spaces in these communities. The colonization of space and time in this way is central to how whiteness is enacted in food justice work. This taking of space is at the expense of the possibility of others taking up the same space.

Similarly, during a side conversation at a citywide food justice convening, the executive director of Rooting Change, Jamarcus Green, told me that it was hard to balance their clear racial justice mission with the "feelings" of their nonprofit board members. At the time his board comprised mainly white men who worked in business or at very large nonprofits. Even though racial justice is part of their mandate and written into all their documents, Jamarcus felt he had to avoid talking about race and racism with the board. He could sense that some of them got "squeamish" when the topics of race and racism came up. So, to keep his board happy, he tried to avoid talking about race, racism, and racial justice in their presence but felt assured that it was still central to their work even if they bracketed it out of those meetings. Here, even though they did not explicitly engage with race, the board members tacitly communicated with Jamarcus that talking about whiteness and race is off limits. Jamarcus accepted this silencing of whiteness as the "culture" of the nonprofit world. However, he had his own sets of tactics and strategies for maneuvering around whiteness when necessary while also leveraging and manipulating whiteness to achieve certain ends (I elaborate on these strategies in chapters 4 and 5).

Cases like these show the difficulty of addressing issues of race and whiteness in the food justice movement. These were multiracial spaces where people had opportunities to think through ideologies of whiteness, to potentially disrupt it, and to increase their capacity to process issues of race and racism in the food system. However, instead of addressing the ideology of whiteness, the discomfort or inability to discuss whiteness led to thwarted or shut-down conversations. This is in part because of underlying beliefs that any acknowledgment or discussion of race is racist, and the unmarked category of whiteness makes it seem like a neutral and unbiased position. Some food justice activists want to acknowledge and unpack whiteness, to pull back the curtain, or to speak about the elephant in the room. However, as Chase and Jamarcus would attest, there are many barriers to talking about the role of whiteness in food access inequality and in the food justice work being planned in these meetings.

While whiteness is usually a given norm or baseline from which people in the room are operating, it is intangible and difficult for people to understand. People do not have experience discussing whiteness as a concept and have been explicitly taught that being "color-blind" is virtuous. Therefore, when whiteness is intentionally brought into conversations by people like Chase, others in the room often do not know what is being said nor how to respond. They might feel uncomfortable or squeamish or just genuinely lack the knowledge to speak on the issue. These people have the power to shut conversations down, to shift the focus away from whiteness and back to the issues they feel comfortable dealing with. In some cases, given the multiplicity of whiteness, whiteness itself can hold various forms of power to shape discourses and in turn shape practices.

WHITENESS AND THE POWER TO SHAPE MOVEMENT DISCOURSE

Reflecting on the many different kinds of food justice activists I had worked with, I thought of Randy Johnson as someone who was precisely the kind of person that Chase or Sarah might be "up against." I recalled how Randy responded when I asked why he chose to spend his time working to improve food access and nutrition education in South LA. He reflected on his own position: "I have been incredibly fortunate. I mean, ridiculously fortunate. I am the cheesiest version of the American dream. . . . Super lucky, super in the right place at the right time. Obviously, I worked really hard, not a question, but basically I feel like I have been given this privilege." He had made his fortune when he was young, in his thirties, and never had to worry about money again. That was when Randy turned to serving the community. "It's not something that—I wasn't born as the Dalai Lama, but it's just simple. At some point, you invest in your financial affairs. You take care of those things. You invest in your education, and at some point, you have to invest in your karma account. There's got to be something more, or what's the point?"

Randy explained that though there was a bit of guilt in the fact that he had made so much money at such a young age, he mainly did not want to "waste away." "We're comfortable," he said. "We live in a nice house in a nice neighborhood. What else is there? So, I had the privilege of nobody really standing in my way as I tried to achieve my dreams, and then returning that favor. . . . It's as simple as that. I owe it. Yeah." Delving deeper into his motivations, he talked about his own children and their future. He told me:

> Only a fool thinks that if he takes care of his only family, he will be fine. It's gonna come back to you. It happened in LA in the early 1990s. They [Black people] didn't riot because they're bad people; they did it because they were desperate. We [white people] have it all. They don't. Obviously, I see that other kids don't have the same thing all across the city, and I suppose it is mostly about the young kids. I see everyone's kids as technically being my own child,

and I'm not just saying that because you can't just take care of your own because if you don't take care of everybody, *eventually they are going to come and steal from you and resort to crime or whatever.* Just because they are desperate. If you don't take care of them, you don't give them a good shot at a future. Whether it be health or education, or opportunity, or whatever. It's really simple. You take care of everyone, [and] you have a harmonious neighborhood, *[if] you don't, it's eventually going to come back and bite you.*

In connection with organizing in his own neighborhood, Randy reflects on the work that his organization does in South LA as firmly grounding his motivations to "help" in protecting himself, his property, and his family. He may be doing useful work, but his logics of improving the lives of others to protect *his* family from the purported future criminal activities of those imagined Others are rife with racist logics and the same forms of paternalism and patronizing that he goes on to critique. Although in many ways Randy is exceptional with respect to the amount of power he had and the positions he was able to access, I observed that many of the people involved in the food justice movement covertly draw upon several dimensions of whiteness, as connected to broader liberal projects, as a superior and favored position—as coveted and fragile and fundamentally as a property to be defended and maintained.[46]

CONCLUSION

Our regular conversations helped Sarah and me both see how many food justice projects are deeply entrenched in ideologies of Western individualism, whereby their actions to "help" Others are motivated by their desire to craft themselves as good, moral individuals worthy of their social and economic positions. Some of them specifically speak of the ways in which helping others and serving those in need is central to making them whole, well-rounded, or "good" people. We started to see how whiteness plays several different roles in the Los Angeles food justice movement, sometimes serving multiple purposes at the same time. Some of the food justice projects we saw in South LA were actually starting to look much like attempts to "civilize" unruly, out-of-control, and barbaric Others.

For some involved in the food justice movement, whiteness and white privilege evoke a particular kind of expertise that allows them to enact that expertise in interventions on Others. People like Melissa, Josh, and Matt had no knowledge of nutrition, food distribution systems, social justice, or race and racism, yet they and others around them felt that they had essential skills that should be used to improve the lives of others.

Since it *appeared* to them that no one else was doing this work and that those who were being intervened upon would take whatever was given to them, some people who did this work thought of it as an "experiment" to see what they could do, or as a free and easy way to "practice" their skills on a community. Assumptions by people like Josh and Matt that they have skills and knowledge that *should* be deployed to "help" Black and Brown communities is one way that the food justice movement operates as a white racial project that links "significations or representations of race, on the one hand, with social structural manifestations of racial hierarchy or dominance on the other."[47] This work is also about the power to draw on assumptions without any real expertise to shape interventions and the movement.

Whiteness, in its various forms, becomes the backbone of power that pushes the food justice movement in particular directions over others. Whiteness supports the power to assume everyone shares a vision of what "healthy eating" is. If some people do not share that understanding, it is therefore easy to assume they are helpless, lack knowledge or skills, and need to be educated by outsiders. These kinds of projects are about the power to shape the narrative around health and what is "good" as well as the power to distribute material resources. These forms of whiteness are not unique to food justice but part of a much broader "structuring logic that serves as a baseline for modernity and its cognates of liberalism, democracy, progress, and rationality" and are integrally connected to global power structures.[48] In other words, white supremacy—the assumed superiority of people perceived as white, and by extension, the assumed virtuousness of practices and objects associated with whiteness—is an overarching global system that underlies the possibility of power within this particular organizing space.[49] Whiteness serves as a crucial foundation for the forms of power that pull the food justice movement in specific directions over others.

Nevertheless, there are completing forms of power here. On the one hand, people like Chase want to have the power to shift narratives around white supremacy, and others within the movement refuse and will take Chase's power by thwarting conversations or preventing Chase from rising up in power. Their own forms of power tamp whiteness, keeping it in the shadows and just below the surface. On the other hand, people like Jamarcus can also be deeply aware of how whiteness operates and deploy different tactics and strategies to make whiteness and its various inflections work in their favor.

Kween

I arrived at Produce Power's Fall Fest with my oldest son just as things were starting to kick off. The nonprofit Produce Power, based in South Los Angeles, had been holding regular Growing Good Food Gatherings, and this one was called Fall Fest. The event was held at their community garden, and it had the feel of a fall harvest festival or apple picking and cider-making event, although the fall Los Angeles climate meant it was nearly 100 degrees that day. Unlike some other food justice events around town, this one was put together on a shoestring budget. There was no swag, no fancy marketing, no web presence associated with the event. Perpetually understaffed, everyone on Produce Power's payroll and their crew of regular volunteers had arrived at the garden early to wipe down dusty folding tables, bring out old rusty folding chairs, shake out rugs and mats to be laid on the ground under the garden's largest shade tree, and set up half a dozen shade canopies precariously held together by duct tape. Born and raised in South Central, Produce Power staff member Candace, who was also an amateur DJ and photographer, would be spinning and documenting the gathering.

Spread throughout the garden between raised beds, white vertical hydroponic planters, and the established fruit trees, there were different stations set up for Fall Fest—some open for use all day and others involving scheduled activities. There was a blender bike set up for people to make their own smoothies, powering the blender by peddling the bike. There was an information table where people could sign up for raised bed gardening classes, composting classes, and classes on keeping backyard chickens. People could sign up for Produce Power's weekly CSA deliveries or pickup. Another area showcased partner organizations offering information and assistance including Los Angeles Department of Water and Power (LADWP) with a free rain barrel program, folks assisting with EBT applications, an organization giving away fruit and shade trees, and a sister nonprofit offering information on backyard aquaponics. There were tables set up for drawing and mandala-making for kids as well as a station for making jewelry with seeds and flowers for participants of any age. Throughout the day there would be opportunities to weed garden beds, harvest certain fruits and vegetables, as well as a free yoga class, a free mediation class, a poetry reading, a book reading and signing, and a jam cooking demonstration.

Kween, a young mother of two who lived nearby, sat next to me as I got my son set up at the mandala-making station. She commented that she did not usually bring her kids to these events. She loved attending these events, it was like her "me time," a chance to recharge and enjoy the day without worrying about money or anything. In a later conversation Kween told me she went through different phases where she would heavily participate in Produce Powers events and then seem to disappear for months at a time. I wondered why, assuming her answer would be related to the busyness of life and raising young kids. But that was not it. Kween took a while to respond, thinking about why she had fallen into this pattern. Looking off into the distance, she said, "Sometimes the vibes is just off. You know?" She continued:

> I don't know, I sometimes go to their stuff and I just feel like dark, like I need to get out of there. Sometimes it's like who is there from the staff, there have been some folks from the neighborhood working there like Candace who just give off these good chill ass vibes and you want to be around them. Then when the boss walks in, you can feel the air get sucked out the room, like you see Candace tighten up and you just want to get out of there. Sometimes it can start to feel like too many white people telling us how we should be acting and eating and all that. When I start to feel that, I just lay low, I might go to one of their events and just get the free food and leave, but I am checking out the vibe so if it seems cool, I will stay. You know what I'm saying?

Kween's words made me reflect on how different people sense whether food justice organizations and their work are aligned with their values and have their best interests in mind.

4

Placemaking

Ms. Mary gently called out instructions to a group of young Black boys as they cleaned and sorted the black plastic crates that held the food items for Mission Marathon's weekly food distribution. Ms. Mary never slows down. She sees herself as picking up the baton in the marathon started by Nipsey Hussle, whom she knew personally before he died. She viewed Hussle as a philosopher and was inspired by his view on life: "You got where you're at and where you are trying to be." Palms facing one another, she held her hands about a foot apart in front of her face. Like Hussle, she felt a pressure to strive for something more for her community. She started Mission Marathon out of her home off Crenshaw Avenue in the heart of South Central, where she has lived all her life, over sixty years. She inherited her home from her father, who came to South Central during the Great Migration.

After years of working as a caregiver and seeing the daily struggles of her community, Ms. Mary wanted to pull together resources and services to offer her friends, family, and neighbors. "I needed a place for my community to come and heal. I wanted to empower the community. I wanted to enrich lives." She conceived of the idea for Mission Marathon in 2016, when the Crenshaw Walmart closed. She and her neighbors were angry. "Where are all these people going to get food that they can afford?," she worried. Around the same time, she heard an interview on NPR with the executive director of one of LA's largest food rescue operations. He spoke about how their program started with residents and public parks donating fruit and other edible plants growing on their property. Specifically there was an abundance of citrus growing all over LA, but in wealthy areas in particular, the bounty was often considered only ornamental and not consumed by the property owners. His organization collected gleaned fruit and other foods no longer deemed sellable by grocery stores and wholesalers. They then redistributed the food to people and organizations who needed it.

After Ms. Mary heard that NPR interview, she knew that redistributing that food would be central to Mission Marathon's work. Recounting the story to me, she peered over her reading glasses, smiled, and said, "I thought about calling the food distribution program For Us, By Us, FUBU, you know, like the clothes from the nineties. It's not exactly true, like we did not *make* the food. But I wanted folks to feel dignified about what they were getting. I wanted to encourage people to better their lives, to feel like we have a place in this world, in this city. You know?" In addition to the food pantry, Mission Marathon had a community garden, an annual backpack and school supply giveaway, a holiday gift giveaway, a holiday meal support program, and a program where local vendors and caterers could teach others how to start similar businesses. They also worked with LA County social workers to offer team-based "wraparound services" using a comprehensive, strengths-based approach to address the complex needs of individuals and families in the area with coordinated services for various needs—from food access to mental health.

Ms. Mary only had one paid employee. Everyone else was a student from the community who worked as an intern or community volunteer. She understood Mission Marathon as offering a job-training service and hoped to expand to multiple centers and add coffee shops to each site to create a comfortable, aesthetically pleasing space where community members can gather to grab a bite and a hot coffee. Though places like South LA Café had opened in South Central in recent years, I knew from personal experience that there were not many spots in the area where you could sit down and enjoy a cup of coffee or a meal. Many residents complained about this to me, questioning why the Starbucks near them was drive-thru only, or the fact that they had to drive to the edges of South Central to go somewhere like Sizzler or TGI Fridays for a sit-down dinner. A few residents told me that one of the reasons they went to McDonald's was that it was one of the few places in the area that would still let you sit inside. These places are what scholars have called "third spaces"—churches, bars, cafés, libraries, and other spaces where people come together that are not their homes or places of work.[1]

These spaces offer a different setting for socializing across different kinds of life experiences. I wondered if other food justice activists had heard these complaints, and if they would consider Ms. Mary's coffee shop as food justice or not. I also wondered what Ms. Mary thought about distributing food sourced through rescue programs. She did not dwell on the fact that the food she distributed to her South Central community was gleaned from places like Beverly Hills or came from castoffs from Westside grocery stores and restaurants. Instead, she focused on nourishing the community with affordable food while offering networking and cultural events, block parties, and access to other free goods and services, from clothing to health checkups. Beyond Mission Marathon's food access work, I saw the organization as engaging in placemaking, a framework I noticed several other food justice organizations latching onto. Ms. Mary never actually used the term "placemaking" to refer to her own work, instead focusing on ideas of "healing," "enriching," and "empowering." Although I heard other food justice activists use these terms, after nearly a decade of doing this research, I sensed that Ms. Mary was doing something different from the other organizations I studied. A genuine grassroots food justice organizer, Ms. Mary was drawing on a lifetime of experience in South Central, the critical input of her neighbors' responses to Walmart's closure, and the LA County social workers who had reached out to her about the need for more services. She had built her organization from the ground up with her own savings in her inherited home in the heart of South Central.

The language that Ms. Mary used to talk about what she was doing is similar to the way that David, the former executive director of Bettering Life, spoke about his awakening and realization of the importance of "placemaking" and "empowerment" in food justice work. Over the course of my research David's understanding of his food justice work shifted to center placemaking. He shared his path to this new approach with me in a lengthy interview at a small, local Cuban café in Silver Lake. Although his degree was in politics, David had always wanted to work at the intersection of art and organizing. With espresso machines whirring in the background and amid the bustle of a lively café, David explained:

> Back when I was running Bettering Life, we were doing all of this work, but we had no real connection to the community. I was doing what is now known as "social practice," which is basically working with people from the worst areas of the city on projects that involve a lot of education. And I was just getting tired of that kind of myopic way of approaching all of these

things and I wanted to branch out. So, the work I have been doing is a kind of place-based. It's about exploring an area through a process that's creative. That involves people in it through dialogue, through exploration, through use of media through use of art, through creativity. With the idea that one starts to look at areas and get familiar, and also understand what your role is. But [you] also to start to see, well, *Who actually makes the decisions about where people live and how can I play a part in that?* Along with that generally comes a heightened sense of not just awareness but sense of like, oh you know, passion and responsibility. And it's more about this idea of sense of place.

Although David is not originally from the area, after running a local nonprofit for a while, he recognized that the work he was doing was relatively superficial and the impact was short-lived and thin. When he focused on the question "Who actually makes the decisions about where people live and how can I play a part in that?]" I sensed that he was picking up on the forms of power that are negotiated within food justice movement spaces. He was interested in what kind of role he might play in shaping that power.

David began making connections between his own interest and love of aesthetics through his art practice and the work that he was already doing related to food access. He said:

I started working in things that were related to food access that had to do with being in a part of the creative world where there's a lot of discussion about the built environment and how that impacts the world. You know? That's certainly justified, but I always felt like that was also a really limited understanding of place, and this happens a lot too—people always talk about this concept of "placemaking," which, you know, basically means like "Well if we put a really nice-looking cafe on the corner, all of a sudden that will create community" and it's like, really? Is that creating community, or is that just creating a business that has people that consume the business and somehow utilize the business, right. Community and sense of community and sense of place, there's something better, a generative thing that they take—they take direct action.

I agreed with David's criticisms of many other food justice organizations, such as those profiled in earlier chapters of this book, including his former organization. David was critical of the oversimplified or naïve assumption that improvements to one food-related business will solve the wide-ranging problems of communities like South LA. For him, food justice solutions must involve "creating community" rather than just creating more businesses where people spend money. In David's analysis, placemaking and community building will lead people to become involved in their own communities through "direct action." However, unlike Ms. Mary, David had no ties to South LA. From my point of view, David was essentially operating from a position similar to the philosopher Paulo Freire, that people have to go through a process of awakening or critical consciousness about their own oppression before they can begin working toward justice or decolonization.[2]

Although David genuinely wanted to generate a spark that would encourage others to work in food justice, I remained skeptical about the ways he wanted to shape that work around his values and vision of what food access in South LA should look like. Nevertheless, David's approach piqued my interest. I had observed other activists using what they describe as "place-based" approaches to improve and reform local food systems. Some of those organizations were not actually engaging in placemaking or community empowerment. Instead, just as others had used the term "justice," some organizations were capitalizing on the popularity of the term "placemaking" to garner community support and access funds. "Placemaking" was the new, emergent buzzword in food justice organizing. Some organizations were leveraging that to advance their work and their careers without actually believing in the value of placemaking or community empowerment. Instead of latching onto the terms people used, I had to ask myself: *Who benefits from the work, and who is extracting resources and social capital for their own benefit?* Through understanding such dynamics, I could see the ways in which food justice was also about the possibility of coalition building and how the co-optation of concepts like placemaking had the unintended consequences of undermining the potential for radical change.

"Placemaking" is a way to understand the possibilities people have for shaping and reshaping the physical environment and the social spaces around their collective desires and needs. It assumes people living within communities have the agency to know what is best for their communities. Beyond understanding urban life as merely deprivation, a placemaking framework offers the possibility of mutual aid, social support, and community building. For instance, in the contexts where Ms. Mary works, where many households cannot rely on the state to adequately supply their basic needs. Many people do not trust that the government has their best interests in mind, people often come together, build community, and create forms of placemaking that facilitate access to basic needs and enable survival. Rather than understanding this through a lens of individual struggle, in theory placemaking has the powerful potential to foster community growth and empowerment when generated from within the community.

For example, working in the Echo Park area of Los Angeles, historian Natalia Molina has focused on restaurants as urban placemaking institutions that foster a "politics of the possible."[3] Molina analyzes establishments that have become hubs for placemaking and part of the process to make cities like Los Angeles more hospitable to everyone who lives there. Analyzing her family's Echo Park restaurant, The Nayarit, Molina shows how offering a place for enjoying comfort food "from home" created a space for social connection and community building.[4] Placemaking thus provides the possibility to "make a way out of no way," to create a "politics of habitability," and to build "the conditions in which new forms of life emerge."[5] Anthropologist Rebecca Louise Carter writes of placemaking as a way that members of a community shape human geography. Carter sees placemaking as drawing upon the strength of Black histories and experiences to reconfigure power structures and lay claim to Black urban space.[6] In this way, placemaking is about decentering outsider perspectives that might render places like South LA as vacant deserts in need of outside help, and instead centering the ways in which residents make places like South Central home.

Critically, scholars like Molina interrogate *who* gets to define place and *how* it is defined, implying a question of whether outsiders can "help" residents of South LA or East LA make a place, or whether placemaking must always be grassroots-generated by (often) disenfranchised people trying to carve out hard-to-find spaces to build community and flourish despite the hostility of public space for these communities. While Ms. Mary focused on community need and her lifelong experience to create a meaningful community organization, I witnessed other people and organizations with different understandings of placemaking and its role within the food justice movement. In contrasting cases I saw outsiders attempt to foster or create placemaking among community members rather than allowing placemaking to grow organically from the community. As I observed how the term "placemaking" was used to frame different food justice projects, I became less interested in theorizing placemaking and more focused on the ways in which food justice organizations use the concept as an ideological tool to shape food justice work in particular ways. I perceived the power struggles within these organizations, revealing how easily "the politics of the possible" can be thwarted by the need to tackle immediate needs and tangible goals, sometimes rendering food justice projects as part of a politics of the practical. I observed how the idea of placemaking was used alongside different forms of power that pulled projects and ideologies in specific directions over others, often forcing food justice solutions that were commensurate with existing systems and status quo ideologies.

While placemaking and community empowerment provide one framework for the kind of work these organizations are doing, when this work is not generated by the community or coalitions across groups, it could be understood as attempts by outsiders or a few dominant people to shape things as they would like. The question as to whether it is possible for those outside of the community to generate placemaking within the community remains open. Still, the attempts at generating placemaking from the outside that I saw within the food justice movement could not develop the kinds of vibrant spaces that anthropologists have theorized as placemaking. Beyond questions of the feasibility of placemaking, this chapter explores the ways organizations can ultimately use placemaking as a foil for the same kinds of assimilationist interventions that had been done under other guises.

STREET FOOD AND THE COMPLEXITIES OF PLACEMAKING

In mid-January 2019, I joined hundreds of thousands of Angelenos who took to the streets in solidarity with thirty thousand Los Angeles Unified School District (LAUSD) teachers who were striking for better pay, smaller class sizes, more adequate support staff, and better benefits. The strike and solidarity protests lasted six days and fell at a rare time when the city was inundated with heavy rainstorms. Because of the cold and rain, groups of supporters collaborated to offer hot food to striking teachers and protesters. I was part of a crew of parents who brought hot coffee, hot chocolate, water, and massive amounts of packaged snacks to our local schools in the Los Feliz area. One morning, while picketing in front of our school, Randy Johnson and his wife, Clara, pulled up with a trunk filled with hot meals for the teachers. I chatted with Randy about what he had been up to lately at Build It Better. He said he had dropped everything he was doing to support the teachers' strike. I asked him where he got the food, and he said that he had purchased these meals out of pocket. However, he told me about a campaign called "Tacos for Teachers," a solidarity effort organized by local street food vendors. "Yeah, now that they've legalized street vending," Randy said, "it can all be above board." His way of framing the tacos as "above board" stood out to me.

The Tacos for Teachers effort was supported by the Los Angeles Street Food Vendor Campaign, the same organization that had been fighting to legalize street food vending in the city. Tacos for Teachers can be understood as another form of food justice, an expression of solidarity with organized labor and LAUSD teachers as a critical foundation for public education and supporting local communities. I thought about the micro-community that emerged each night around different street food vending spots, like those outside of the clubs in Hollywood or the ones that set up each afternoon outside of the Numero Uno Market at Ninety-first and Fig waiting for folks like me or those getting off the Number 81 bus to grab a bite to eat, lingering in each other's company before heading home. To me, street food vendors—from taco trucks to *fruteros*—were already essential to placemaking across various Los Angeles neighborhoods, including South Central.

After Randy left, Alejandra, a young mom who was picketing alongside me that day, said under her breath "Such Bullshit." I asked her what she meant. She explained that her mother was a street food vendor. Ever since Alejandra was a kid, her mother had been selling bacon-wrapped hot dogs to exiting concertgoers after a show at the Hollywood Bowl. "Because of that bullshit legalization campaign," Alejandra explained, "she had to quit." Back in 2018, when Governor Jerry Brown signed the Safe Sidewalk Vending Act (SB 94d), Alejandra's mother and her usual crew of vendors in Hollywood started getting harassed by the LAPD. Alejandra felt that the campaign drew attention to the fact that street food vending was illegal in the first place. "Before that," she said, "no one even cared, my moms would see a cop coming up and know he just wanted a hot dog. Now they see them, and it's all pack this shit up, let's go."[7] She and her mom were undocumented, and there was no way they were going to file paperwork with the city to get a permit because they feared the city would turn them in to US Immigration and Customs Enforcement (ICE). She also pointed out that the permit was supposed to be $500, and her mom felt like that was just the City trying to take away her hard-earned money. Alejandra viewed the legalization of street food vending as another kind of settler-colonial imposition from the state.[8]

While Randy was celebrating the legitimization of street food vendors into a formal labor market through official permitting and licensure with the city, Alejandra understood the entire project of legalizing street food vending as increasing state surveillance and extracting money from people who had been working within a well-established informal market for decades or longer. From the vantage point of those organizing to legalize street food vending, it was a form of placemaking that legitimized street food vendors as a long-standing fixture in LA communities. From Alejandra's point of view, the street food vendors she had known all of her life were already a part of placemaking. For her, the formalization of street food vending was actually undermining the community-driven placemaking that her mother and many others had fostered. However, the ability of street food vendors to legally provide food in all kinds of settings across the city can facilitate just the type of placemaking that Natalia Molina writes about.

CORNER STORE PLACEMAKING

In 2013, I started tracking a group of food justice activists involved in converting a South LA convenience store into a "healthy corner store." I was first looped in by a designer who was sketching a complete rebrand of the store. Because I spoke Spanish, he asked me to help him brainstorm the new name. "We've been exploring alliteration phrases," he said, suggesting the first thing that came to mind was Piggly Wiggly, America's first self-service grocery store. He underscored that the name had to be in Spanish but also accessible for English-only speakers. I thought for a minute and then suggested "Si o Si" or "Pin Pan" or "Timba Tamba." Ultimately the name chosen was totally different, but I was intrigued by the multiple scales of work happening behind the scenes on this store conversion project. Part of what made this project different from other store conversions was that it involved designers. Another key difference was the store owner, who explicitly wanted to do something that looked good and was not just "throwing some vegetables in a box on the floor by the cash register," as he had observed in other corner and liquor store conversions. In meetings without the store owner or any residents, the intervention team wanted to create a warm and welcoming store experience that was unique from generic chains. They wanted to give the store a community feel, to have design touches that would make customers feel "at home." I understood this as a form of placemaking.

In late March 2014 we all gathered at the store for the grand reopening. The conversion team made a huge event of the grand opening, inviting various leaders from other food justice organizations, area students and teachers, council members, and other local business owners. When I arrived, Sarah Cunningham greeted me with a big hug. She did a little dance and sang along to the song the DJ had just put on, Drake's "Started from the Bottom." She laughed, and sang the lyrics "Now we're here!!" She pulled me into the store. "Look how different it looks!" The store was dramatically different. Where there had previously been displays of chips and candy, new, sleek-looking shelves held "healthy" snacks— healthier chips, nuts, and dried fruit. There was a new refrigerated case with yogurt, bags of baby carrots, bags of sliced apples, and containers of locally grown fresh berries. Everyone that I spoke with that day said the store looked beautiful. They seemed proud and happy about the transition. The store was, in many ways, different from any other corner store in South LA. However, most of the people at the grand opening were not residents of South LA. This made me see that the intervention team had designed the store around their *imagined* sense of place within South LA. In other words, with the exception of the store owner, this form of placemaking had been imagined and designed almost entirely by outsiders. I wondered how outsider placemaking would intersect with organic placemaking that came from residents.

In 2018, I visited the store with my summer research assistant, Jorge, who had been helping me catalog the existing food retail in the area. That day, the store looked very different from how it had been transformed back in 2014. The cases that once held nuts and healthy snack bars were overtaken by Honeybuns, Zingers, and packaged sugary donuts. The refrigerated case with yogurt, string cheese, baby carrots, and small containers of fresh berries was gone. In its place there was an M&Ms rack that displayed a wide variety of Skittles and gummy candies. Another refrigeration case was unplugged and held boxes of Great Value bottled water and Shasta brand soda that the owner bought at Sam's Club. I recalled talking to the owner before the process of converting the store about the fact that low-cost Great Value brand bottled water and the Shasta brand sodas were his top-selling items, and he understood providing these lower-cost drinks was a service to his customers.

As we walked into the store that day, Jorge looked around and seemed confused. He turned to me and asked, "I thought you said this was a healthy corner store." I sighed and said, "Well, it *was* . . . but I guess it's not anymore." I spoke with the owner about what had happened after the healthy corner store conversion. He explained:

> At first, they [the team who did the intervention] were bringing me the fresh fruits and vegetables and delivering the healthy snacks. You see all the items I sell here are delivered to me by companies, Frito Lay, Pepsi, Coca-Cola, they [representatives from the companies] bring these things here. Well, I have some items I sell myself as well, but it's very few. So, after all of the

people stopped coming to bring the healthy snacks, I was going to pick things up downtown myself for a while. But you can't just buy a small amount downtown, you have to get at least a box. And I just wasn't selling enough of that stuff, it was going bad. I was getting too tired to drive downtown and be back here in time for my morning customers. I realized I was burning myself out for like fifty cents, and it wasn't worth it. So, I had to stop doing it. But the store looked bad with those empty cases, so I put other things where the healthy items used to be.

The store owner described the fallout of a food justice project focused on short-term solutions and had not planned for long-term sustainability. I thought about his initial vision that the store would become an important place in the neighborhood where his customers could feel at home. I recalled how my conversation with the designer tried to take the owner's desires to heart. Beyond the logistics problems, I wondered if centering outsiders' ideas had also thwarted the attempt to create a genuine community space. I wondered if placemaking actually had very little to do with the aesthetics of the store but was centered around the little things the store owner did for his customers, like purchasing lower-cost sodas and bottled water. After all, those two items were his best-selling products.

Why didn't the team that created the corner store intervention have a workable plan for the store owner to source healthy food and snacks after they left the project? While I observed the process of the project, the problem of long-term sourcing was a frequent concern voiced by team members. Sometimes a short discussion would follow, but most of the time the question was ignored, and everyone just pushed forward with the project. This is partly due to the fact that creating a self-sustaining project was beyond the capacity of those intervening. It is also partly due to the fact that the scope of the work was only focused on the short-term and actionable completion of the intervention itself.[9] It was an experiment to see if a healthy corner store could be launched, not to see if it could be sustained. This is part of a broader process whereby experimentation and testing ideas in places like South LA is understood as acceptable and part of affirming the position of those intervening rather than upholding the real needs of residents. After observing the fallout of this store, I questioned whether these kinds of corner store conversions could really be placemaking. But I also knew that plenty of corner stores and bodegas are vital gathering places in different communities. What then is the key to making these kinds of projects effective forms of placemaking and community building?

BARRIO BITE

While I observed many food justice interventions that similarly failed to create long-term plans for self-sustainability, I also tracked the work of the nonprofit Barrio Bite, another Los Angeles food justice organization looking to develop a solution to distribution challenges. After being involved in a series of corner store conversions, a common type of project within LA's food justice movement, the staff of Barrio Bite knew that they faced an uphill battle to make these healthy corner stores self-sustainable. Their team saw the potential for corner stores to be critical sites of placemaking in South LA. Barrio Bite spent years figuring out the barriers to selling fresh fruits and vegetables for store owners, and realized that one of the critical problems that repeatedly came up was sourcing: How and where could store owners source fresh produce?

Big food distributors sold food in large quantities; a pallet of bananas usually contained sixteen boxes of bananas with about six bunches per box. There was no way a small corner store in South Central could sell a whole pallet of bananas before they were too ripe to appeal to customers. Bananas have a relatively limited shelf life, and clients at these stores will likely buy only one banana at a time as a snack. During and immediately after corner store conversions, corner store owners or staff from Barrio Bite would go to produce wholesalers to buy just the small amount of fresh produce the store could cycle through before the food spoiled. They delivered the items daily during the conversion process but knew it would be impossible to do this forever.

Federico Jimenez, the executive director of Barrio Bite, brought on Javier and Magdely to develop a long-term, sustainable solution to this problem. Magdely had grown up in nearby South Gate and was influenced by environmental justice activists there. Anthropologist Karen Brodkin's book *Power Politics: Environmental Activism in South Los Angeles* was particularly influential for Magdely because it documented the community coming together to fight for environmental justice. Magdely pursued a bachelor's degree in environmental studies at a local college. There, she took a class called "Place-based Environmental Analysis," which she credits with giving her the skills to develop a healthy food–purchasing program for corner stores using "place-based conservation planning and management."

Barrio Bite's purchasing program was a small shoestring operation. In 2016, Javier and Magdely joined me for lunch in downtown LA to discuss how Barrio Bite functioned. They explained that the program involved Magdely calling a dozen corner stores across South LA and East LA once a week to ask what fresh produce they wanted to be delivered. After placing the orders, Javier used Barrio Bite's pickup truck to purchase produce from a wholesaler in the City of Commerce. Barrio Bite chose to use a local wholesaler rather than other kinds of producers like farmers markets or community growers because this would be a one-stop location for all of the types of produce that corner stores wanted, including foods that do not grow year-round in Los Angeles, like cavendish bananas and apples. After purchasing for all the stores, Javier would drive to the Barrio Bite offices in East LA, redistribute the items for each store's order, and personally deliver the orders to each store across South LA and East LA, often sitting in the city's infamous traffic jams for hours. This was a grueling weekly process for Javier. Still, in his eyes it was one crucial step in creating a sustainable way of distributing healthy food to area corner stores using locally based solutions that Magdely would call "place-based."

Although the operation would eventually grow to have more employees, when I interviewed Magdely and Javier, they did all the work for this small operation. While they were creating a nuanced technical solution that seemed to serve an immediate need, in the end their program did not address the deeper structural issues underlying the distribution problem. Based on what she was taught in college, Magdely envisioned her work as "placemaking," but I did not view Barrio Bite's efforts in the same way. Although Magdely and Javier were members of the community and they were looking for locally based solutions to the distribution problem, Barrio Bite was not directly engaging with community members to build on local understandings of space and place. By contrast, Ms. Mary was able to foster a form of placemaking even though she was sourcing the food for her program from wealthy Westside residents, stores, and restaurants. By comparing Mission Marathon and Barrio Bite, I could see that placemaking was not about where the food was coming from. It was about how the food was incorporated into broader dynamic aspects of the community and its desires.

FEDERICO JIMENEZ: FOOD JUSTICE THROUGH BETTER BUSINESS PRACTICES

In 2009, years before I would interview Magdely and Javier about their corner store food-purchasing program, I met Federico Jimenez, executive director of Barrio Bite, for a midafternoon coffee in the Highland

Park area. Ironically the café where we met is often cited as one of the first establishments to inspire gentrification in the Highland Park area, but I am not sure if Federico knew this. We were introduced at a food justice event the year prior, and I have followed his work since then. He reflected on how he ended up doing food justice work: "My bachelor's was in business administration. . . . When I went to school, I decided to study business not because I had guidance or because I had some businessperson to give me mentorship, but essentially because I knew I needed to go to school, and business sounded like you would make money." He laughed and paused in reflection before he continued:

> When I went to school, I learned that I didn't really like business, and I got politicized, and I started to learn about a lot of the inequities in our communities, then I decided to sort of leave business quote-unquote, and I ended up studying urban planning. Only because I was really interested in "How do you build community?" That was what urban planning is. It's the study of cities and the study of community and all the different elements in it. Little did I know that I was actually going to circle back to business because, as I was realizing, all the issues that were happening in our communities, uh, a center of that was the access to capital. And a lot of neighborhoods looked the way they did because they were denied capital. They were denied rights that other people had, and so I became very interested in capital. Um, in "How do you control the circulation of capital?"

Federico cites higher education as the place that politicized him and gave him the language and tools to understand structural inequality, something he had taken for granted growing up in low-income areas. I found it interesting that it was through higher education rather than his everyday life growing up in the area that he came to start asking questions about how to build community.

Federico understands the political and economic structures that have created current inequities in accessing funds. Redlining, both retail and residential, was just that—barring access to capital and long-term potential to build wealth. He connected to business because of his understanding of the importance of financial capital, or access to money for low-income people. As Federico explained it:

> I was working in a nonprofit organization in a low-income neighborhood. And that really began to fit all my interests together of, uh, justice and of inequality, but then also of capital. And I began to see more clearly that not only was I an entrepreneur at heart, but then one of the key actors in making our neighborhoods a better place are the entrepreneurs that already exist. . . . Because to me, they are all entrepreneurs, and they are trying to make money and or in order to pay their bills. Some of them are, unfortunately,

more successful than others in an exploitative way [laughs], but I do see them as folks trying to make this happen, and some of them have skills, and some of them do not. And for the ones that do not, I am interested in giving them the skills.

I followed Federico and his organization's work over twelve years, and (as I expand in chapter 5) he has been steadfast in his dedication to creating structures that allow low-income, disenfranchised, immigrant, and racialized Others to participate in the food system as producers, entrepreneurs, vendors, and people who have a say in how it functions.

Federico's advocacy is based on a deep-seated belief that another food system is possible—a politics of the possible. However, like the other food justice activists profiled in this chapter, he operates with a sense of urgency that drives him to try to work within and reform existing systems to improve the food system *now*. Federico was interested in supporting and pushing low-income entrepreneurs and small businesses run by people of color into higher-stakes businesses. He wants members of his community to have successful high-earning companies, and he hopes that the capital they earn will be reinvested in the community. His vision is to support these businesses and train them in more formalized business practices and necessary legal structures, such as permitting, licensing, and taxation.

EMBRACING POLICY: FOOD SYSTEMS AS POLITICAL

During the quarantine of 2020, Federico's organization pivoted to fulfill their mission around the confines of the COVID-19 pandemic. I reconnected with Federico on Zoom and asked him to reflect on his work since graduate school. "So, I guess I really embrace policy in that way," he said. "But for folks that think, 'Oh, I don't see it as a space for other things,' . . . what I would invite people to think about is to embrace the idea that food is political, it's a foundation of things because we're worried about the political framework that governs how we eat, how we consume, how we grow things. And if we are not involved and not even mindful of those things, we're just being oblivious to things that are really impacting us."

In thinking through the kind of work he is dedicated to, Federico pans out from the day-to-day needs of his client. Considering the structures and systems that have gotten us to this point, he concludes that the only way to change our food system is to be politically involved. Over the course of the food justice movement, he said, "many groups that were created and then kind of dissolved over time, . . . they didn't create really any political movement out of their work. It was just kind of a space to connect. They did events. There was [a short-lived food justice group]. And I don't think they created any political work out of that, but it was a space for them to connect. And that's valuable." Reflecting on projects that have been short-lived, Federico felt that their downfall was a lack of political, legal, or policy change tied to the project to create a more systematic change. He wanted to avoid this kind of short-lived work for his own organization but also saw that there was room for organizations that did not want to be involved in local or higher-level politics. Instead, these projects became a node for creating dialogue and connections, potential spaces for placemaking, which are also invaluable to food justice work and essential for a politics of the possible.

Federico and the various food justice organizations he has led throughout this research embrace a multipronged approach to food justice that incorporates the economic realities of capitalism, the political nature of food systems, and the everyday needs of low-income communities. While Federico had radical long-term visions, the work that his organizations did was grounded in the immediate need for practical, incremental solutions for the people they support. Even if the longer-term goals are not achieved, for Federico the process of building connections and community was a win in and of itself. He emphasized building community and placemaking as central to racial and economic justice. He saw policy, political action, and economic growth within capitalist systems as the most direct way to build community and create a sense of belonging in places like South LA. Keeping in mind that Federico was born and raised in low-income communities similar to those he intervenes in now, my interpretation of this approach is that he understands the need for longer-term systematic change to the structures creating food inequalities, but he also knows that the people he serves need immediate, practical solutions.

DAVID: PLACEMAKING THROUGH CREATIVE COMMUNITY-BASED PRAXIS

While David was trying to transition his organization toward a placemaking approach, he received an invitation to collaborate with a large food justice organization that did not share his vision for place-based food justice. I talked to David about how he reconciled his decision to work with the organization. I asked if he was worried that being linked to their approach to food justice would negatively impact his work. He explained:

> So [a big food justice organization] called me up one day, and they were like, "Well, would you be interested in working with us?" and, you know, my response was like, "If you're interested in a process that involves education that is really looking to expand your goals in terms of community engagement, and it expands your broader goals in terms of ultimately improving health outcomes in the community and wrapping those things together, then absolutely we're in." So fortunately, that was something they were open to and so that kind of the whole—the work that we do in terms of working with young people, working with community members, working with institutions, schools are around issues of healthy food access all kind of grew out of that and grew out of the kind of ideology.

When partnering with funders or other organizations, David was upfront about the fact that his organization was interested in more profound engagement with participants and not necessarily the shorter-term goals those partners might have. He continued:

> What I'm saying is I was already kind of thinking about, "Well, what is this relationship between a sense of place and the built environment and things around public health." So that all was easily, well not *easily*, but that all kind of led to having kind of an approach in terms of work and how to go about these things and thinking that you know people will always talk about community engagement, but what does that truly mean and how does one effectively involve people from a given neighborhood and community in the process of generating change but also generating, ideally, a structure that's sustainable and, you know, that's always a goal but way easier said than done.

David partnered with this large organization that was connected to a series of grants from large federal granting agencies, which involved creating "natural experiments" to improve childhood obesity in Los Angeles. I attended meetings with David and the principal investigator (PI), Cristianos, at a large research university in the area. During the team meetings, Cristianos and his team of researchers expressed that they entrusted the "natural experiments" to David and his organization. They made David's organization into a subcontractor and provided money from the grant, which served as a large portion of the organization's operating budget. Although David's organization did carry out the "natural experiments" that Cristianos and the research team cared about, for David the critical part of the work was this broader goal of fostering a sense of place and pride in the community among the youth that they worked with. David knew that the grant's goals did not align with his vision. However, he was okay with taking the money from a granting agency that had a different worldview. He understood that compromises must be made for his organization to finance its programs, and he was okay with those compromises as long as he could still work toward his more radical vision in some ways.

David clarified that although his organization stayed afloat on federal funding for the purposes of reducing obesity rates in LA, he was really after something else: "I always say that like the things that are most important—that the people that we work with walk away with—is a sense of critical and creative thinking and an ability to be, you know kind of critical consumers of everything that's out there." Although he wanted his program's participants to be critical consumers and understand the systems that push them toward consuming unhealthy food, he also tried to help them develop a critique of the research team and federal programs to reduce obesity. To me, David was trying to help them identify projects and programs claiming to be placemaking or social justice, when in fact they were just reproducing existing social hierarchies. He tried to give the students a sense of the complexity of these systems: "Whether that's about like the history of, like, well, say they live in an area that's a food desert, well, how did it get to be that way? Why is it that way? How is that linked to income, race, class, freeways, or, you know, redlining? Whatever it is that they need so that they understand those factors." Beyond just knowing the history and understanding the structural factors, David felt he had to give young people tools to make change.

For David, this awakening was the first step toward empowerment, which, he hoped, would foster radical change in the future. He did not want these young people to feel helpless:

> We also want them to know there's things they can actually do, but more importantly that we provide an opportunity for them to do something. So it's not just like get someone all riled up about all the social injustices and then hope that that goes somewhere, but really like provide some direct outlets and avenues. So, to me, that's all tied back to the education component of our work, in the sense that we're taking a very irreverent stance on certain ways in terms of engaging people in public health projects. We're not coming from public health background; we're not coming from directly from like a *social justice* background. We're coming from a creative background, and that means that the projects that we do—that the community members do—they look and feel different. . . . So hopefully it has a sense of creativity but also a sense of levity and hope to it because I think a lot of these messages—particularly around public health—well, they really boil down to: "Do this and don't do that." Fine, but the question is, who's telling you those things and why?

Even while working under an organization that he thinks has gotten the message all wrong, David is able to plant seeds in students' minds about the structural problems that underlie the issues they see in their communities. To him, planting that seed is one of the most important things that he does. While this kind of approach to food justice is more thoughtful than many of the others analyzed in this book, for me, planting seeds that are going to grow and thrive requires particular kinds of knowledge of the place where they will grow and ongoing forms of care that I was not sure David would be able to provide.

After becoming a subcontractor, David and his new organization were able to create programs that really supported the youth they were working with. They carried out the "natural experiments" for the research team by doing things like corner store conversions, cooking demonstrations, healthy eating workshops, and other typical food justice events. He described the goals of the programs they had created:

> So it's the community seeing itself. What we do really is also, again, it's not, say, limited to work around food justice, or it's really at its heart, I think it's educational and community-based and so it's really about leadership development. The programs we're doing are about healthy food access, but really, it's a community leadership class. To just give you an example, you know this, we worked with a group of high school students for two years on this project around healthy food access, and, you know, these students were just remarkable on so many levels, and they did all this work in the community, they transformed the stores, they did all the work to promote it, they were on like all kinds of national, international media. They've become really comfortable spokespeople for what they're doing. The work really shifted to them, so they were the ones organizing these projects in the two markets they transformed. It's the first time they've ever done anything like this. And, um, so you know, it's like a radical shift for them.

David's reflections made me recall one of their events I had attended a few years prior, where the students who were working with his organization hosted their own healthy cooking demonstration. Unlike the school cooking demonstration described earlier in this book, David had the idea to have area youth show how they can make healthy meals using ingredients that could be purchased at local corner stores on a budget. They creatively did this in the style of a cooking show challenge. The goal was to empower young people to cook for themselves and their friends, with the hopes that they would also show their parents that it was possible to eat healthy, locally sourced, affordable meals.

Living in close proximity to a store that could be described as somewhere between a corner store and a small independent grocer, the students were able to source fresh fruit to make a fruit salad and canned corn, canned tomato, and fresh chilis and lime to make a healthy salsa salad. Working within the limitations of a typical family in South LA or East LA, the youth participants decided what to make and created palatable, nutritious dishes. Although these are unlikely to be considered a meal and much more likely to be a snack, David and his organization cite these kinds of projects as forms of youth empowerment. While I appreciated the ways that teaching the kids how to cook with what was available to them was a great skill, I was not sure that this organization was exactly *empowering* them. That said, the approach was not based on assumptions about what people ate at home; it was designed around what was possible in the area, and the recipes were created by the youth participants.

David reflected on his organization's longer-term goals and hopes for the youth they work with:

> But, um, really, in terms of our goals, it's like, how can we create sustainable change? So, um, if they want to get to college, great, how can we help them, right? Can there be direct scholarships linked to what we're doing? Can there be some revenue stream that we can funnel to them. Can there be enough career connections so that if they don't go to college, there's a job waiting for them after our paid internship? So college is like $50,000 a year. It's really out of reach for the kids that we work with. Even if you get a really good aid package, it doesn't cover all the funds, and where your parents don't generate enough income to do anything other than sustain the family, there's just not the extra funds. It is just pure kind of economics. There are other factors too in terms of like certainly . . ., but I think the main driving one is really the money.

To address this issue head-on, David's organization established various programs, from paid internships to leadership academies to programs where his program's alums return to train new high school students, all of which pay area youth for their time. They were paid at rates that ended up being higher than minimum wage to do work that helped them to build a résumé that was legible to both universities and area employers. These paid internships not only provided the essential funding that area youth needed to be able to pursue education instead of working full-time, but they also developed a sense of placemaking and ownership over their communities and the work that was possible there. This was their way of enacting two different approaches to social justice work. They directly gave people resources ("give a man a fish") and instilled particular ideologies in them while teaching them specific kinds of life skills ("teach a man to fish").[10] Unlike programs that argue for "capacity building," which anthropologist Paige West has called "colonially anchored yet fully contemporary fantasies about nature, culture, savagery, discovery, temporality, and gender," David grounded his programs in placemaking and a practice of funneling money to community youth that was akin to a form of reparations or a cash transfer.[11]

David fundamentally understood that the "problems" in the area were the direct result of official policies, laws, and development practices, not some systematic flaw in the people who live there. Yet I also saw times when David's work felt similar to the forms of "capacity building" that West critiques, which positions the Other as lacking capacity, backward, and unable to function in modern capitalist society. He seemed to be aware that he fell into this way of thinking, but he saw this as a necessary step to "transform the whole ecology" of South LA. David viewed his work as enacting placemaking and as doing better work than other food justice organizations that were doing more superficial work in his eyes. Although his organization built from an understanding of the structural roots of food apartheid, their programs still tended to focus on individual behavior change. He added a layer of trying to train local youth to be "changemakers" and inspire their parents and others in the community to change their individual food consumption behaviors.

I was not sure that these paid internships were the kind of reparations that David envisioned, or if they were simply paying people for their labor or training them to labor in particular ways. However, the focus on healthy eating did not come from a community-based desire for change. Instead, it came from the mandate of the large university grant. The young people David worked with often reminded me of Journee (mentioned in Interlude 1). Recalling her reflections on jobs and food justice, I was not confident about the value of training area youth to be future leaders without addressing the root problems of the area's structural inequity.

JAMARCUS: EDUCATION AND SOCIAL EMPOWERMENT THROUGH FOOD JUSTICE

Through David's connection to higher education as a subcontractor on the grant, he adopted the tools of academic research, specifically Community Based Participatory Action Research (CBPR), in his attempt to "transform the whole ecology" of South LA. Another organization, Rooting Change, led by Jamarcus Green, similarly used the tools of

CBPR to do what he called "empowerment work." Jamarcus grew up in South Central. Reflecting on his childhood, he danced in his chair and sang, "I remember syrup sandwiches"—lyrics in a popular Kendrick Lamar song. He laughed and said, "But you know that was real, though?!" We laughed, and I shared my own childhood memories of syrup sandwiches during times when there was little food in my childhood home. Jamarcus, the leader of a very well-respected social justice nonprofit in the area, responded to my question about how he got into food justice work:

> I grew up fairly economically vulnerable, meaning we moved around a lot. I just had a lot of challenges growing up. We used to have powdered milk under the kitchen sink. And having been a poor kid who had holes in his shoes, and I would often go to bed hungry. I remember when Jack-in-the-Box first began to expand in the late eighties, early nineties here in [the area], and fast food has really taken off. Sometimes all we could afford—all my mom could afford—was like the two tacos for a dollar from Jack-in-the-Box. So that would be our dinner, or if we couldn't afford to, she couldn't afford electricity or gas, the gas get cut off. We'd have to use an electric stove, electricity would get off, you'd have to use the gas to try and cook, or sometimes we wouldn't have food to cook at all. And so, I think just growing up hungry, and growing up accessing the food that I did. I knew it was a challenge, but I didn't quite understand the systemic challenges that existed.

Jamarcus was the product of several diversity pipeline programs that tried to channel promising kids from low-income areas into higher education. He earned a BA and an advanced degree. In college he learned to navigate white-majority environments, he drew on the kind of respectability politics that his mother and grandmother had instilled in him to make it in those places. He wore khaki pants and a button-down with dress shoes to class. He sat in the front row and went to office hours. He did all the things he was taught he should do. After college he had a successful career in business and learned a lot. As he put it:

> And so, I came back and the kids at the [local] school [and I], we were already talking about like the material conditions of the community. We were already talking about food; they would have bags of sugar, Kool-Aid, gummy worms, and gummy bears they would sell on campus. We were already talking about how this stuff was not healthy. And then we started talking about like the built environment, and it's important to know that in the work that I did with my young folk, we utilize youth participatory action research to evaluate conditions. So we began to evaluate the physical conditions of our environment. And through that evaluation students began to explore and ask questions about why they didn't have access to healthy food.

Building from his own life experiences and the realizations of area youth about the poor-quality foods they were exposed to regularly, Jamarcus drew on the skill set he had learned in college and his advanced degree. He employed a form of action research that followed up each realization with more and more questions, allowing him to dig deeper into the structural realities of the problems faced by the community. He recounted:

> And so, we started exploring different options like, okay, well, if we don't have access to healthy food, then how can we make it happen? And so, by the end of that sort of term, we landed on this idea of launching a community garden. . . . You got to do research, and you need to do something. I mean, it's sort of action research, so it's really about understanding and how what you're doing works or doesn't work. . . . And then we started talking to people in the city about using land, went down to the city's planning department, and then we ran into all of these barriers, and we're like, why is it so hard to find land to put a garden here? . . . And so . . . we went to the city council member's office, we went to planning, we went to building and safety, we went to all these code [offices], we went to all these places, and then we finally sat down with [them], "Well, yeah, we're not using that parcel. Go ahead. You want to build a community garden?" Let's do it.

Jamarcus was driven to show the youth in his program that with hard work problems can be solved. His drive was rewarded when he was able to get the city to let him use the land for a community garden. He drew upon his experience in college and higher education, building on that networking and the forms of communication he had developed there. He used his own forms of soft power to negotiate within the (surprising) space of city bureaucracy and vacant lots to leverage his skill set to access land from the city. Rather than first deciding to enact place making based on assumptions, through collective, collaborative problem-solving with the community Rooting Change organically became involved in placemaking.

Jamarcus reflected on that experience as the moment when he realized that he couldn't do social justice work without engaging local politics and area businesses. He told me:

> It's all tied together. There is no way to do justice work without local politics. . . . And it was in the context of that we said, okay, well, let's take what the kids are trying to do, what this resident's trying to do, what other people in the community are asking for, what we're bringing partners together to do, and let's just institutionalize that work and make it a part of what we're doing. And so, you draw the dots, so we had to draw the connection to draw the dots between the conversation we were having in the classroom and the various systems that created the material conditions we're dealing with in communities. So, it's all intersections. It's all linked. It started with their

research. It started with the need that they identified. Which is why I fell in love with action research because I saw the power of potential it had to transform the material conditions that exist in the communities and not just theorize about it, right? But instead to say, hey, this is what the theory says, and let's ground this theory, right? Let's have a real, grounded theory, but let's also ground it in the lived experience of people and in their need and then help that become what it needs to become, which was, then, this is what led to all these other things that have now become in many ways a part of our identity, a core part of the work that we do.

Jamarcus draws upon his skills as a researcher in an interesting way here. He eschews theorizing for the sake of theorizing, implicitly critiquing the work of many academics, and he points explicitly to action research as an approach that is grounded in the real-world experiences of those who would be research subjects. What he takes from his academic training is the communication and networking skills he developed. He learned enough about working within bureaucracies to not only navigate those spaces but also pull some of the more conservative or status quo people within those formal institutions toward his vision. He tried to bring everyone together toward a unified goal of improving everyday life in South LA.

Through Jamarcus's own experience with education as a vehicle for social awakening and social mobility "we realize this can be a tool for civic and social empowerment, and then it wasn't and has never really been about the food. It's still not about the food, and the food is important. And trust me, we very much believe in food, and we eat healthy, and we do all that because we know it's connected to health. But what we were always trying to address was the multiple social determinants of health but utilizing education as a tool to help individuals within our communities move toward their own levels of self-determination and individual empowerment." Between the lines Jamarcus underscores that the real goal of Rooting Change is to empower young people in South LA to create individual and community futures around their own needs and desires. His goals are not necessarily tied to the shorter-term work Rooting Change does related to food and health, both areas that were of great concern for federal and state-wide campaigns, and thus themes that Jamarcus could latch on to for funding opportunities. He knew how to draw on the language that would excite people and leverage different funding opportunities. He could turn on the charm and convince people who were not on board, or not even interested, that his vision for change was worth their time and investment.

Jamarcus leveraged the work of Rooting Change by making broad connections to programming that would matter to funders or people on his board. Issues like empowerment, food, and health. As he put it:

> We have sort of a social empowerment framework, and I think it's that framework that connects the dots between these pieces. So, if the folks in our communities are trying to address social issues or so on multiple conditions, food might be an entryway into doing that, housing is another, the environment is another. And it's for us as an organization. It's about helping to provide the tools and the skills, and the resources people need to create a thriving community. And then to go on to change the systems that you know reify the material conditions they've done. So a lot of people ask me what it is that we do. I tell them we're in the people-building business, all right? We're in the business of building people and people who want to address these conditions as it relates to food.

Like Federico and David, Jamarcus's overarching goal was to foster a sense of belonging that inspired community belonging and civic responsibility in the young people that he worked with. He wanted to build community leaders, and he firmly believed that formal education, degrees, and other accolades that are recognizable to people outside of South Central are fundamental to leadership development. For Jamarcus, teaching youth how to undertake action research is part of cultivating a skill for understanding not only the structural issues underlying problems but also how to engage with the community and build understanding through the eyes of community members rather than outsiders.

"THE PEOPLE WHO WORK IN THESE ORGANIZATIONS JUST DON'T KNOW WHAT IT'S LIKE."

I met Ronica in early 2022. A twenty-three-year-old who identified as a multiethnic Black woman, Ronica was born and raised in South Central. During and after the COVID-19 pandemic, her economic situation became untenable and she began to rely on emergency food programming. Ronica was a proud graduate of a local university, the first in her family to earn a degree. She described herself as "currently unemployed," but she had previously worked in "social justice and community organizing." Ronica had participated in programs in her high school that were similar to the K–12 social justice educational interventions conducted by David and Jamarcus's organizations. Through these programs she became passionate about healthy eating, developed a strong desire to eat fresh produce regularly, and avoided fast food and junk food.

In many ways Ronica is a successful product of a food justice intervention: She has a college degree and worked as a community organizer in South Central. However, she also faced ongoing difficulties. Throughout college she remained food-insecure and used the food pantry on campus as her primary food source, shopping at the 99-cent store when she could. Although she had been on food stamps before starting college, she became ineligible for that support when she accepted a college fellowship to help her pay for school. Her last year of college coincided with the 2020 quarantine and she had to move out of the dorms, which she described as her "safe haven as far as having secure housing, the campus food pantry, and access to a space for cooking." After leaving the dorms, Ronica became homeless and very food-insecure. She described that period as a "huge struggle," telling me that she "didn't have a place to go" because her mom was also unhoused at the time. Ultimately she was able to sleep on couches and access emergency food and "a lot of mutual aid" to stay afloat.

Ronica reflected on her work as an organizer and experience being food-insecure in an interview in 2022. "I had access to these spaces through relationships and volunteering," she said, "but I didn't—I don't have consistent access to food. I felt disenfranchised. I had been working as a community organizer, and I reached out to all of the organizations I had worked with, 'Hey, I don't have stable housing, I don't have stable access to food,' but are there any programs that can help *me* out?" She paused in reflection at her own rhetorical question, then continued:

> I have been a community organizer for eleven years now, and I was a full-time organizer. I felt like being in a community that did support my access to certain things like mutual aid and like hearing about gift card giveaways and things like that, and I think that one reason that impacted my employment was like burnout and really navigating, like, poverty, food insecurity, and poverty and a lot of things that other people in the community-organizing world didn't relate to. So I feel like largely I am experiencing it and organizing against it and also having to pretend that I am not being impacted by these systems and injustices. And it's really hard to navigate, especially when you are working with people who are not impacted, people who don't identify as food-insecure or people who don't live in South Central, people who don't take public transportation. So in many ways when I did experience burnout, it wasn't acknowledged. It was just like "Keep going, keep showing up as you are." And it was very difficult to do all of those things at once. To organize for your community, while organizing for yourself, while also trying to be like a strong person and not let these injustices hold you down. That was very difficult. I have always been an organizer, but I feel like maybe people didn't really see my struggles because within community organizing,

you're really expected to put others before yourself, so it was difficult for people to hear—Hey, I really need support, I don't have stable housing, I don't have transportation. . . .

The people who work in these organizations just don't know what it's like. I think that sometimes, within organizations, they are really glued to the idea of doing something, "At least we are giving food," "At least we are feeding four hundred families weekly," and I think that there's a lot of layers within that . . . it's kind of like a slap in the face. No one ever sees the realities we [people living in poverty] go through, but they are just like glorified for the food that they give out to people. So it's really inadequate, basically, when people are serving folks who identify as food-insecure but not really taking the time to do it with intention.

As a participant in social justice K–12 programming and related higher-education pipeline initiatives, Ronica was precisely the kind of person that food justice activists, both residents and outsiders, thought they were empowering and shaping into a community leader with the goal of placemaking. They hoped that their efforts to mold people like Ronica into community leaders would be the ticket to lasting, grassroots organizing and change that was driven "from the bottom up." Like them, Ronica operated under the assumption that earning a college degree would afford her access to decent-paying jobs, respect, and authority not only within her community but across demographics. Her credentials and experience with local nonprofits were supposed to be the golden ticket that would break the cycles of poverty that plagued her family, and, as she was trained, she was supposed to lead the charge and "lift as she climbed" while "giving back" to the community.

But it did not work out that way. Ronica was devastated. Heartbroken. When we spoke in 2022, she reflected on the culmination of housing, food, and transportation insecurity that she faced despite all of her work to fulfill the roles that social justice organizers sought for her as "burnout." She reached a point where she could not in good faith continue to work with these people. For a brief period she was still technically working, but she described herself as "going numb," unable to perform any labor or even leave her house. When Ronica quit her job, she realized that what she actually needed was medical leave. She was unable to work because the burden of expectation that she continue to help others when she did not have her own basic needs taken care of. This was essentially a hostile work environment and had led to a medical condition that rendered her unable to work. In our conversations she vacillated between calling it "burnout," "medical leave," a "break," a "sabbatical," and a "period of reflection."

Since Ronica could not take a paid medical leave during this period—explaining that it was not something she knew to ask for nor ever imagined possible at a small nonprofit—her situation worsened. As she became more food-insecure, she became more depressed. This situation was particularly hard for her because she had been so successful in college. She had earned a BA, had won awards, and was honored by community organizations—in her mind there should be no reason for her failure other than herself, and now she felt she was "a statistic" and "a stereotype." Ronica could not get out of the downward spiral of her thoughts, and she continued into depression and immobility.

As someone politically motivated who was eager to learn, Ronica was the ideal subject for food justice "experiments." Various Los Angeles organizations intervened in her education to teach her about structural inequalities. With her growing awareness of the structural nature of the problems her community faced, Ronica knew that her situation and her mother's situation were not individual failings. Armed with this knowledge and the encouragement of the nonprofit leaders who were also her mentors, she resolved to "be the change" she wanted to see in her community. She started eating a "plant-based" diet and educated herself about her own health and biometrics, fearing that she and her mother were on a path to diabetes and other diseases. She advocated for others to choose a vegetarian diet and take care of their own health.

Yet just a few years after she was outside of the protective structures that the status of "student" gave her, Ronica found that she could not do things on her own. She could not find a job that paid a livable wage, even if she lived with her mother in low-rent areas of South Central. She could not amass enough money or credit to acquire her own form of transportation. And she could not afford to buy food consistently at all, let alone maintain the plant-based diet that she and her mentors had revered as "healthy" and therefore best. Since she had been told time and time again that her knowledge, her credentials, and her experience as an organizer would lead her to a healthy future, she simply could not understand what had gone wrong or if the problem was her. She knew that the problems she faced were rooted in structural issues, but because of the ways that her education and social justice nonprofits that shaped her had framed the solutions to these problems as not only within her reach but as a process she could lead, even Ronica could not understand that structural problems require structural solutions.

While Ronica is just one example, and thousands of students from South and East LA benefited positively from K–12 food justice interventions, Ronica's case points to the glaring problem at the heart of the issues outlined throughout this book. In addition to the K–12 interventions, corner store conversions, cooking workshops, and gardening programs, all well-intentioned, still fundamentally do not address the structural issues that cause food access inequality. In general, the lack of understanding and attention to the structural and racial roots of food apartheid is the central problem that plagues food justice projects like the ones detailed here. Only a few organizations, like Rooting Change and Mission Marathon, who were really in touch with the needs of their target clients could see the need to connect food access to broader issues of poverty, like housing costs, transportation, access to jobs, health care, and mental health services. Most organizations viewed other problems as beyond the scope of their mission to increase access to healthy food. By ignoring the interconnected issues of food access and poverty, these organizations were left focusing on individual behavior change or educational programming and only superficially addressing the realities of unequal food access in South Central.

CONCLUSION

Reflecting on Ronica's situation, I could see that there was a lot of nuance and complexity in the ways in which different food justice organizations invoked ideas of placemaking and empowerment. It would not be easy to discern who was doing "good" food justice work aligned with what I valued. Just like with the term "justice" or "health," I had to be diligent about scrutinizing the work and entanglements of these organizations. Ronica's story reveals the ways in which placemaking and empowerment can not only fail without full consideration of structural issues but also cause additional issues that reverberate through individuals and their links to the community. In that way even projects that try to empower community members can have the effect of undoing the radical potential for social justice. While someone like Ronica had the passion and drive to become involved in social justice work within South Central, the ways in which these organizations functioned did not allow her to do that work or to live a decent life there. These organizations pushed her away and into her own process of finding out how to channel her passions for social justice in different ways.

Still, despite this failure and other potential problems, to me, people like Ms. Mary, David, Federico, and Jamarcus were all starting from a good place. They were each driven to inspire a sense of community and belonging for residents. For some, that would ideally manifest as a sense of civic responsibility and encourage participation in the community. For others, that was about helping to shape future leaders or empowering young people to take responsibility for their communities. Beyond their focus on food, whether they called it placemaking or empowerment, these organizations were interested in creating spaces for the community to come together. Some projects were about gathering for the sake of gathering, which is an excellent pursuit in and of itself. Other food justice activists were about healing and dignity. Some focused on educating people about their history, histories of oppression, and the structural conditions that continued to negatively impact the community as the first step toward developing a critical consciousness for liberation.

Ms. Bernetta

By the second time I went to Ms. Bernetta's church, congregants knew me as Dr. Hanna, greeting me with hugs and questions of how my kids were doing. Bernetta told everyone that I was her niece. She seemed to really see me as kin, like the many other "adopted" nieces and nephews she had. I met a handful of them. Folks like me who had come into her life and meant something to her.

Her congregation was small. Folks really got to know one another. Though the church was running on a shoestring budget, they tried to celebrate special occasions for congregants with a post-church lunch and cake. On one of my visits I shared in a birthday lunch for a member of the congregation who was turning eighty-two. She usually held a birthday party for everyone at her home in her backyard in the summer, but given how many members of the church were passing away, the church members felt they should celebrate right away. They pooled resources, and some people cooked. They served spaghetti with ground beef sauce, corn, salad, and garlic bread, with lemonade from a mix and bottled water as drinks. There was a beautiful cake decorated with butterflies and an upside-down cake with mixed fruit and Hennessey. As we ate our lunch, Bernetta recalled another church member's Ooey Gooey Cake, as "Ooo, it's so good."

Bernetta mentioned to me that the other day a friend had brought her a lunch plate from a different church. "Toward the end of the month the churches give away stuff," she said. "Food, plates of hot food, clothes, shoes, diapers, anything you might need. They know that folks need a little help to make it to the end of the month, till they get that check on the first."

I asked Bernetta how often friends brought her plates of food like that. "I don't really know but usually at least once a month," she said. "Might be that I get a few plates in the last week of the month. Or they will come by and tell me about a free lunch, or a food giveaway and we will go together if I am feeling okay."

After lunch Bernetta and a group of folks from the neighborhood went back to Judy's house to watch the Chiefs versus the Ravens in the AFC championship. Judy and her husband are big Kansas City Chiefs fans. I rode back from church to the house in Judy's minivan. While smooth jazz played softly in the background, I noticed how happy and calm everyone was. It felt like a moment of liberation, tucked in between the struggles of everyday life, where we were all full, satiated by good food, good company, and for some the word of God.

Before the game started, Judy and Bernetta sat at the dining room table and laid out the produce from a few different produce bag giveaways they had received on Friday and Saturday. They divvied up the produce based on what each one liked. They each set aside the kale that was always in all of the free produce bags. They made a big pile of it to give to Ms. Corrinne, their neighbor across the street and the only person they knew who loved kale enough to eat it in these quantities. When Corrinne arrived to watch the game, she smiled at the big pile of kale they had gathered for her. I too reveled in the joy of this moment, which offered a glimpse into what a liberated food future could feel like.

5

Liberation

In January 2018, I attended a friend of a friend's afternoon meditation *sangha* at their home in the West Adams, an area adjacent to parts of South Central.[1] I brought my partner and son with me. About fifteen people gathered, sitting on mats and rugs in rows of half-circles that began in a converted garage space and spilled out onto a driveway and garden. It was winter in LA, a balmy 60 degrees, cold for many Angelenos. Most attendees gravitated toward the garage's space heater or a sunny spot outside to stay warm.[2] Citrus trees flanked the yard. In the center a winter garden was filled with flourishing kale and chard plants, onions and garlic peeking through the dirt, tomato plants that would overwinter, and broccoli, cauliflower, and kohlrabi that appeared to be struggling. After a thirty-minute silent seated meditation, our host played a recording of Tibetan temple bells with a faint, low humming chant in the background.

As folks opened their eyes, the host said, "All that you touch, you change. All that you change, changes you." Many in the group joined to close the chant: "The only lasting truth is change; God is change."[3] As a group, we stretched and moved our bodies and transitioned to a circular walking meditation, after which we gathered for conversation and vegan snacks in the garden. While the crunchy-granola stereotype of this gathering was not lost on me, I was also a genuine participant who sought refuge, community, and repair in this space. While we were gathering in the yard, my son walked over to one of the apple trees in

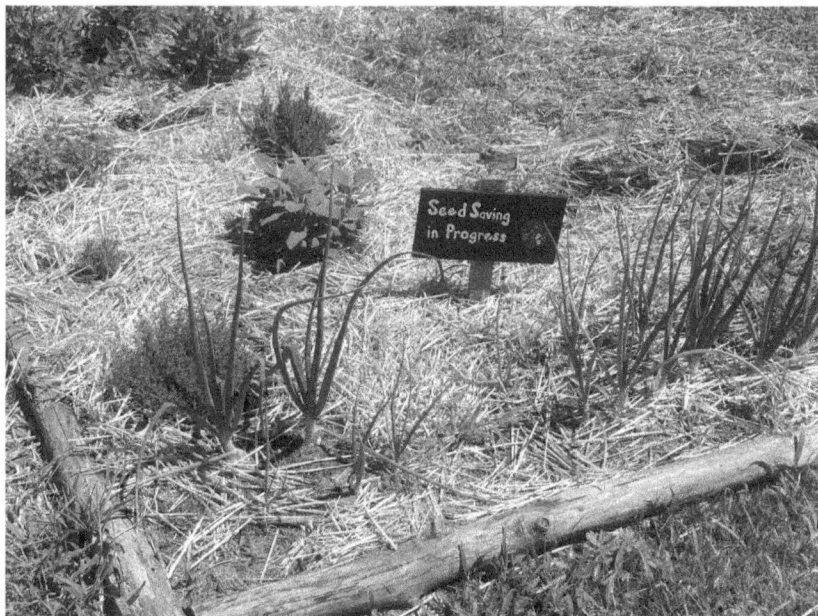

FIGURE 14. Seed saving in progress. Photo by the author.

the yard, picked a piece of fruit, and immediately took a bite. They were growing a particular kind of apple that does well in LA's climate. I felt the group grow silent; it seemed that everyone was watching my son bite into the apple. One woman turned to me and said, "What a beautiful thing. Your son just ate that apple." She nodded, looking musingly at my son. I smiled, grateful that my fear that someone might be angry about what he had just done, or that they would judge me for letting him eat an unwashed apple, was unfounded. I was happy to be there. From that day on, people remembered my son and this moment, often marveling about it when we would run into one another at other food justice events.

Although this particular event was not explicitly part of my food justice research, this was one space where the lines between my personal life and my research were not neatly drawn. Many people gathered there that day were involved in the food movement, and several were involved in abolition movements, including both police and prison abolition.[4] Perhaps these overlaps were coincidental, but this meditation *sangha* alerted me to the fact that parts of the social network of food justice organizing were linked with other kinds of movement organizing networks. As the participants and I chatted and crunched on fresh vegetables, I realized that the overlap of these communities with the influence of writer adrienne maree brown's 2017 *Emergent Strategy* pointed to new synergistic ways of thinking about food justice and abolition together.[5] For those in this overlapping community, whether thinking about food or prisons, "abolition invites a critical-historical awareness of *un*freedom and a creative prescription toward the possibilities of freedom."[6] A radical abolitionist approach to thinking through food apartheid is at once a refusal to accept the logics of racial capitalism that underlie food apartheid and a commitment to envisioning the radical possibilities of liberation and a liberated food system outside of those structures.[7]

When I returned home that day to write up notes on the event, I paged through a small handmade booklet titled *In the Liberated Future* that I had received at a previous food justice gathering. The hand-cut and folded seven-page booklet opened to a set of questions on each page:

Who do you consider your family/community? How do you communicate with one another?

What do you eat regularly? On special occasions, how is it grown and prepared?

What is your spiritual practice? Is there only one in your community, or many? What is sacred?

How do you spend your time?

What does accountability look like? How do you deal with conflict?

What does support look like? How do we ensure that everyone feels valued and has their needs met?

What does freedom look like? (Draw it!).

The booklet made connections between eating, family, community, the sacred, accountability, and how we spend our time. Without making it explicit, the booklet asks: What are you doing to get free? How do we get free? As time passed, the booklet sat on my desk and eventually became a benchmark: over the years, as my everyday life and fieldwork increasingly blurred together, I had forgotten where and when I acquired it.[8]

I do not recall working through these questions in a group setting. However, the handout and the questions within it exemplify an approach to movement work that applies abolitionist thinking toward a "liberated food system." As noted in the book's introduction, I understand "liberation" as an ongoing historical process, rooted in the struggles to abolish slavery, focused on freeing individuals and communities from oppression, inequality, and injustice. Liberation involves challenging and dismantling the systems and structures of power that have enabled conditions of oppression in the first place. It is about slow, long-term fundamental change to those systems and structures. Often the first step to liberation is simply creating awareness of how these systems operate and continue to produce oppression. Liberation often involves solidarity with adjacent social justice movements and an understanding of the interconnectedness of struggle. Ultimately liberation is about working toward self-determination for communities, and the ability to live a decent life as people define decency for themselves.

The booklet reminded me of some of Sarah Cunningham's provocations about what food justice *should* look like. To her, grounding the work in abolitionist logics and envisioning a liberated future were fundamental components of a good food justice approach. In the way the *sangha* brought people from these two movements together, such an approach would combine radical racial justice work and food justice work. Noting the underlying logics that would make these two movements align or misalign, I reflected on how the organizations I had studied aligned with these approaches. Many food justice activists who were trying to push toward more radical, liberatory approaches struggled through messy efforts to shift the conversation, to work outside of the dominant structures, and simultaneously to work behind the scenes that serve the community's immediate needs. That immediate work might be focused on pressing issues beyond food, or it might look like free food giveaways, community dinners, and other ways of getting food into people's hands when they need it. Though sometimes fraught, this messiness seemed inevitable in their attempts to move toward more radical, abolitionist approaches to food work.

Yet I could also see that developing a more profound understanding of the constraints of many contemporary approaches to organizing could open the possibility of working toward freedom and thinking through what a "liberated food system" might look like.[9] Nevertheless, radical approaches to food liberation can be problematic, complicated, and feel impossible in similar and different ways from other approaches to food justice. For some food justice activists and for the residents involved in food justice programming, this way of approaching the work was part of a broader set of practices of "refusal." Their refusal is not simply a matter of saying no but about selective participation in ways that can be "generative and strategic"; it can "illuminate limits and possibilities" and "stake claims to sociality" in specific and intentional ways.[10] This might look like sitting in a room and listening to a cooking demonstration, taking home the bag of produce associated with the event, and cooking those ingredients in different ways. Or it might look like observing and taking in conversations around food justice programs but refusing to participate. Or it might look like the situation I described in chapter 2, where Lindsay Adams was not interested in a food justice gathering that she did not think served the community. Refusal "marks the point of a limit having been reached: *we refuse to continue on this way*."[11]

These forms of refusal can be a set of practices that undermine dominant authorities and logics.[12] To me, this kind of refusal is centered on not conforming to logics and standards imposed from elsewhere that do not serve the well-being of the people or the community. This approach to food justice was part of ongoing practices of envisioning other ways of being in relationship to one another and place.[13] Like brown's "emergent strategy," liberatory approaches to food justice can attempt to "get outside of" or move away from dominant ideologies or systems, which include whiteness and some of the problematic elements of conventional forms of social justice. For people like Sarah Cunningham who questioned or became disillusioned with the way the food justice movement had been carrying on, brown offered them a framework to work toward the forms of justice they were not seeing, that had not yet been articulated. I came to see these types of frameworks as the platform from which radical approaches to social justice are launched.

To understand these approaches, following those in my research who envision radical liberated food futures, I chart brown's focus on "thinking parabolically" as influenced by novelist Octavia Butler and her fantastical fiction, brown's own work, and her collection with Walidah Imarisha, which illuminate the possibilities for abolitionist visions of a future not yet known. The ability to envision unknown futures where oppression and inequality do not exist, where communities have self-determination and live the dignified lives that they desire, is not easy; it requires concerted effort, one approach to which is laid out in brown's *Emergent Strategy*. A subset of activists in the food justice movement have tried to envision and set intentionality around what liberation looks like and how it is tied to food. However, as these activists attempt to "do things differently," they are constantly pulled into the dominant food justice paradigms, which prioritize neoliberal capitalistic nonprofit approaches.

Money, outputs, and immediate outcomes are the bottom line. They are also pulled into mainstream multiculturalist approaches that lean into color-blindness and superficially celebrate diversity. They contend with broader organizational cultures that place exceeding amounts of value on the priorities of the privileged—higher education, higher salaries, and more publicly legible accolades. As radical organizers continuously resist being pulled by mainstream elements of the nonprofit world, they face a constant ebb and flow as they balance their needs with their ideals and dreams for the future.

Radical, liberatory approaches to food justice align with Savannah Shange's abolitionist anthropology as a critical anthropology of the state. Following Shange, such a critical analysis of the state would mean including charity work, public service, and the nonprofit industrial complex as part of the state. Folks using these approaches acknowledge or *feel* these tensions but cannot consistently articulate the ways projects operating under the name of food justice can also be part of a "state romance" aspiring to "live happily ever after with the antiracist, distributive state."[14] As attempts to get outside of or beyond this "romance," these activists improvise strategies of refusal as they attempt to find ways to work toward a more liberated food system.

As I worked with groups of people organizing for liberation, I saw how they were also part of the system of jockeying for power within multiracial food justice organizing spaces. However, their orientations prioritize the project of pulling the food justice movement toward a more radical, liberated food system. This means that unlike efforts to build businesses, technical interventions, and incremental policy solutions, radical activists continuously push themselves to work toward a future disentangled from racial capitalism and the global food industrialized system, where fresh, healthy, culturally appropriate food is available in abundance in places like South Central. Whether that is possible or not, these activists continue to try.

NZINGA'S DREAM OF FOOD FREEDOM

Sitting in the outdoor patio of a cute neighborhood café near South Central, Nzinga described their journey to food justice as circuitous. Growing up in South Central, they ate mainly processed food, junk food, and whatever was cheap, easy, and tasted good. Nzinga prefaced their story by saying "It's going to sound weird, counterintuitive, but I really developed my vision for food liberation while I was in college [at a large public university]." Nzinga explained that it was not through coursework or formalized clubs; they made clear that the public university system was "still a hundred percent racist institution, but I still liked the little subculture of the place because I felt like that's the kind of energy that I wanted to take up while studying there." Their experience as a student in the public university system solidified their vision of food justice. "The thing is . . . I went out there, and it was the most hippie school, and I wanted for nothing," Nzinga said. "And I was there on a full ride. I left with no debt, and it was freaking awesome. The food pantry was like Erewhon level, 100 percent Erewhon level.[15] At first, I was like, 'Nope, no, it's not Whole Foods.' It was definitely Erewhon level. I mean, I was getting MALK for free."

"What? Wow!" I interjected with genuine surprise, given that MALK is a highly sought-after premium organic plant-based milk. "I was getting the highest grade of food for free," Nzinga continued. "And they had gardens of plenty. They had little communes. I love that place so much that I try to go back at least once a year just to soak that up again. Beautiful. It was super beautiful. I loved it there, and I would run the trails. So, when I was there, and I was reading theory, and that's when the first time I actually sat down and read Karl Marx, and I was like . . ." They paused as if to question whether they would make sense to me. "Oh, I don't know if you've ever had this in your studies?" I did not respond, uncertain as to what they would ask. Nzinga said:

> I had a physical feeling of being unlocked after I read *Capital* for the first time. And then when I felt like I got unlocked, I was just looking at my campus for the first time. And I am thinking about the demographic ratio and how I'm 2 percent of Black people that are on this campus. And there's at least 30 or 40 percent Asian people, but 60 percent white people. And I'm seeing it in real time. And I'm just thinking about where I come from—the level of comfort and access there. They literally built this whole place for people to succeed. And everybody, all they do is wake up, and they're able to just focus on the things that they're passionate about, and they're 100 percent supported.

I wondered if Nzinga saw things differently from other students or if most students understood college in these ways. I was doubtful and assumed Nzinga was exceptional in this regard. They continued:

> I didn't have to pay rent. I had therapy for free. I had a gym that was free. The campus was completely walkable, and I had a bike, and I was biking everywhere all the time. And I'm just thinking about how this structure needs to be replicated from where I'm from. And I was angry and delighted

at the same time. And so, when I left, I went right back to South Central 100 percent committed to—how can we replicate what I got at the college campus level, and what do I need to do? So that's pretty much, that's a long-winded way of, that's how I got into the food justice movement. A little bit of anger, a little bit of curiosity, but I think it came from more so from the fact that I was the process of developing wellness for myself. And once I learned the game, I was just like, all right, I want to spread this and help other people who are in my position.

The university offered Nzinga a glimpse of a system that fully supported its community, offering necessities and services considered luxuries free of cost to students like them. In some ways Nzinga's experience reminded me of the Great Society programs from the "war on poverty," in the 1960s under President Lyndon B. Johnson. The Great Society vision established many entitlement programs that folks still rely on (Food Stamps, Social Security, Medicaid) as well as broad programs to eradicate racial injustice like the Civil Rights Act of 1964 and the Voting Rights Act of 1965. Once Nzinga lived within this utterly beautiful and supportive space, where all their basic needs were taken care of, they could envision a world in which residents of South Central also shared in this kind of utopian space—a space "that was built for people to succeed."

Nzinga explained to me that after they started having health problems, they got a gym membership, "and then it began this whole trajectory of wanting to exercise better, wanting to learn more about food. And then the more I learned about food, the more it became evident of where the access was for good food." Nzinga grew up in the heart of South Central in a house within walking distance of an intersection with a big full-service grocery store, Food for Less. Reading about food justice and food sovereignty made Nzinga want more than what that grocery store—or any grocery store—offered. "I'm like, oh man, I want to learn how to grow produce," they recalled. "I was like, man, I want to grow my own food, and where are the spaces specifically in the hood where I could grow food, and why aren't there any green spaces in the hood? I want to be around hood people. And then I googled 'green spaces.' I felt like the first thing that popped up was this one organization that was known for growing food in South Central. And I was like, what is this?"

Nzinga checked out the organization with the hope of learning more about how to grow food in South Central. They described themselves as feeling immediately "locked in" with the executive director: "[She] was talking about the importance of growing your own food. She was talking about the necessity of self-efficacy and self-determination and how we're disconnected from the land. It was just like the gospel." A huge smile beamed from Nzinga's face as they thought about that vision. They were pulled into the organization. "I was like, bet. I was like, I need to go and just be in this energy and in this space. And at this time, it's like I'm not even thinking about working with them. I just want to volunteer; I just want to pick up training on growing my own food."

In 2024, when I talked to Nzinga about their experience with the food justice movement, they had left the food justice world a few years prior to start their own thing. I wanted to know more about what happened and why Nzinga left. Over the course of more than two hours, they told me of dozens of moments, practices, and ideologies through which the leaders of the food justice organization that they worked for enacted what Nzinga called "white supremacy." One key element of the work dynamic was that the executive director and leadership, who were not from South Central and not Black or Latinx, expected Nzinga and other staff from South Central to be subservient, subordinate, and deferential to them. This was hard to bear for Nzinga and many different staff members, but they were used to these kinds of dynamics. It was disappointing but not surprising. However, the fact that the leadership did not respect and spoke disparagingly about long-term residents—the people the organization were supposedly serving—was the final straw for Nzinga. The leadership was "just talking down, lack of regard, and just utter disrespect to the historical community members. . . . This is making me mad all over again." They continued:

> Externally, as soon as there was a photo op, they want you there. Externally, if there are partners or partner organizations, especially if there were people that could give us money, they're pushing all the people of color to the forefront. But internally, they definitely wanted you to know who was in charge. Okay, you're supposed to just 100 percent shut up and do your fuckin job 100 percent. They were orienting to us, like, "We hired you for a job. If you don't do it, we will find somebody else, and you will get fired." And the pay—I was making just like 50 cents over minimum wage at that time—wasn't enough for them to be acting that way.

Nzinga's whole demeanor shifted as they recounted what it was like. Their shoulders slumped over; at moments, tears welled up in their eyes and they seemed to cower over the coffee they sipped. I tried to lighten the mood a bit by asking what their hopes and dreams were for the food situation in South Central. They told me about the work they were doing now, which was focused on wellness. They spoke of their deep love for community, for connection, for loving one another. "I just want to create spaces of love, like a hug, for these hood babies," Nzinga said. They shifted back to thinking about the past. "I just found myself in the middle of these unnecessary power struggles." They paused and looked upward. I assumed they were trying to hold back tears again. We sipped our coffee, and Nzinga continued: "There's always just these groups of white people that are preying on Black and Brown folk and just people of color initiatives working towards becoming food-growing communities and food-providing communities. And so, see these people who come with their nonprofits and the capital that they already own, and they're like they are vultures. These so-called white allies need to check their homies. They need to stop."

To me, Nzinga was able to see the micro practices through which the power to shape the food justice movement was enacted. They could see how outsiders were able to shape the movement in ways that did not align with the values of people like them. What Nzinga saw as the "vulture" practices of "well-meaning" outsiders was a central force in undermining the possibility of multiracial coalition building, which in turn leaves justice undone. Like Nzinga, I turned my attention to how people withdraw from this cycle and turn toward other practices that allow them to move toward radical, liberatory organizing work.

EMERGENT STRATEGY AS A STEP TOWARD LIBERATION

For some people in the food justice movement, like Nzinga and Sarah Cunningham, their food work is connected to a larger liberation project. This approach to food justice is about working toward a world where people (often explicitly focused on Black, Indigenous, and other people of color who do not already experience full freedom) are genuinely free. This version of freedom is distinct from Enlightenment thinkers who did not imagine Black or Indigenous people as rational thinkers capable or worthy of liberty.[16] It is also distinct from the category of "free" that legal scholar Cheryl Harris articulates as fundamentally defined by whiteness.[17] Furthermore, these radical visions of freedom differ across groups, individuals, space, and time. However, some of the common dreams of freedom include a future where food systems are not profit-driven, where housing and land access are not profit-driven, where capitalism does not exist, where prisons and policing do not exist, where poverty does not exist, and where groups of people live in harmony with nature.

Imagining this kind of future is not easy. However, around 2015, I noticed that more and more people involved in the Los Angeles food justice movement were connecting movement work to a radical reimagining of the present and future. Given my long-term engagement with food justice, I could see that these approaches were quite different from most of what I had observed. Their work began to have synergies with abolition movements and Afro-futurism, both of which are about envisioning Black futures in ways that sometimes require speculation where science fiction and other art can offer inspiration.[18] In addition to *Emergent Strategy*, adrienne maree brown's broader work was particularly influential during this time. *Octavia's Brood: Science Fiction Stories from Social Justice Movements*, edited by brown and Walidah Imarisha, quickly made the rounds in LA organizing circles. After I noticed *Octavia's Brood* in the arms, backpacks, and on the desks of many of the people involved with the organizations I was studying, I picked up a copy. It is a collection of twenty "fantastical" short stories written by organizers, activists, and changemakers. The authors are mainly people involved in social change work, not professional writers. The chapters radically reimagine events of the past and present to envision an abolitionist future.[19]

The editors and many of the authors operated from the premise that "all organizing is science fiction," and "every time we imagine a world without capitalism, a world without prisons, a world without homophobia or transphobia, that's science fiction because we have never seen that world." They note that we must be able to imagine something in order to build it. Therefore "movements for social change absolutely need fantastical spaces like science fiction that not only allow us to throw out everything we are told is realistic and possible but demand that we do that." Organizing must start with "the question what is the kind of world that we want to live in and then how do we build that world into existence."[20] Just as these approaches are used in imagining a world without prisons or policing, they can be used to imagine a world without unequal distribution of food. These kinds of radical approaches to organizing were about shifting the power dynamics both within movements and in society at large. For me, brown's work was both an ethnographic object or data point that mattered deeply to my interlocutors and an analytical tool for understanding more radical approaches to social justice.[21]

Emergent Strategy was published in 2017, the same year brown launched a podcast with her sister, Autumn Brown, called *How to Survive the End of the World*.[22] Between the podcast, the book, and brown's personal connections with people in LA, her thinking had a significant influence on radical organizers in the city. In food justice planning meetings and conversations taking place while folks were carrying out projects, I started to hear people say that they needed "an emergent strategy" for their food justice work. It was time to envision the world in which *we* wanted to live. In a slight reframing of the us-versus-them divisions I described in chapter 2, brown emphasizes "we" as a collective and defines "emergent strategy" as "how we intentionally change in ways that grow our capacity to embody the just and liberated worlds we long for."[23] brown proposes a process of "creative ideation" as a process of "bursting new ideas," which is about "sharing in the process as early as possible."[24] She argues that collaborative visioning processes are essential for movement building and organizing, calling for a "disruption" of individualism.

In board meetings and in strategic thinking sessions, I heard people mention the need to think "parabolically," referencing Octavia Butler's *The Parable Series*, two postapocalyptic novels set in Los Angeles, and the moral lessons we take from our allegorical interpretations of the texts.[25] I also heard LA organizers begin to use the language of stewardship, shifting from seeing land from something to possess to seeing it as something to care for. This is a radically different take on power, which systematically shifts power away from individuals and into a collective. This works toward the type of food justice movement where an individual does not have the power to completely shift the approach of an intervention or project. Power is held instead in collective decision-making and group agreement.

For me, Butler's work opens the potential to envision radical change among a small subset of the food justice organizers that I worked with in Los Angeles. As anthropologist Priya Chandrasekaran argues, "for anthropologists, Butler is an interlocutor who opens spaces for thinking, writing, and coming to terms with some of the underlying questions in our field." Butler wrote in and of California in the 1990s, "a time of economic distress, anti-immigrant ballot initiatives, circulating narratives of 'stranger danger,' and urban divestment in neighborhoods of color. The police assault of motorist Rodney King that was captured on video, leading to mass racial unrest in Los Angeles, influenced Butler." Her protagonist, Lauren, a young Black teenager, survives an apocalypse and goes on to found the Earthseed religion, in which time is relational, and "it shapes and is shaped by social relationships and the material world."[26]

For food justice activists, drawing on Butler's parabolic thinking can "stitch a relational fabric among people and places . . . by slipping between the past, present, and future, or the future-past, the future-present, and the future-future, it."[27] Thus, thinking parabolically became a way for people to understand solidarity across space and time.[28] The work of aspirational emergent strategy requires constant attention, revisiting, and focused effort to transform thinking, stay on course with it, and not slip back into status quo orientations to the work. I started to see how adrienne maree brown and the thinkers she is in conversation with were part of the pull in food justice toward a broader understanding of liberation, which shifted understandings of how people are in relation to land and place. While some organizers held such beliefs as the foundation of their earliest work, others came to these logics over time and through the influence of authors like brown. Approaches like brown's were divergent from what many had been taught as undergraduates and in graduate programs that focus on working to *reform* the existing food system. In approaching their work parabolically, they had to relearn their methods. This approach harnesses the collective power to hold space for the seemingly impossible or incommensurable visions of food justice. It prioritizes opening up and cultivating reflection within movement organizing. As the activists I worked with latched on to and built upon brown's work, I started to see the emergent strategy approach as key to any possibility of multiracial coalition building toward radically different futures.

TOWARD TRANSFORMATIVE RELATIONSHIP BUILDING

I met Hyejin Kim during a task force meeting for a large food justice organization when she was a master's student at a nearby university. She came off as eager and excited to be there, willing to volunteer for tasks, and somewhat naïve about how long and difficult it would be to make changes to the food landscape of Los Angeles. In 2009, after we both attended a food justice event, we sat down together at a nearby Peet's Coffee for our first interview. Hyejin grew up in the Valley, went away to college, but had moved back to LA for her master's program. She decided to live in Koreatown because the rents were lower, it was convenient to school and areas like Downtown and South Central, and it was a chance to reconnect with her Korean heritage. Growing up in the 1980s, Hyejin's parents had shunned their Korean background, encouraging the children to learn English, and become "more American" to fit in at school.

But after college Hyejin felt she had accomplished the outcomes her parents sought and now had earned the ability to become reacquainted with her Korean-ness. A few years earlier, Hyejin had participated in a *kimjang*—the traditional group process of making kimchi, spicy fermented vegetables that accompany most Korean meals. The *kimjang* was located in an area that had been a central location of violence and standoffs between Black and Korean Angelenos during the 1992 uprisings. Many of the elders who participated in the *kimjang* had been there for the uprisings. The *kimjang* had a massive impact on Hyejin. After hearing stories from local Koreans who were still traumatized and processing the racialized violence and tensions they experienced then and now, Hyejin was determined to find a way to connect her passion for food, food justice, racial justice, and healing.

As part of her master's degree requirements, Hyejin completed a project for a local food justice organization where she was subsequently hired. I had several occasions to observe Hyejin in action. She often served in the role of translator for Korean elders and community activists, many of whom were corner store or restaurant owners in Koreatown, just adjacent to South Central. Although I do not speak Korean, in different settings I watched as Hyejin seized every opportunity to talk to Korean community members about race and racism in the ways that they relived the trauma of 1992 through their food-related businesses. There was still fear, resentment, and anger among many who lived through the destruction of their businesses, but Hyejin was unrelenting in her efforts to alleviate and ameliorate that trauma to move toward racial healing. This meant intervening in racist or racializing conversations with the Korean community members she worked with as well as others in her life who might racialize or stereotype other groups of people. Although not formally trained in psychology or counseling, Hyejin seemed to have developed an approach similar to motivational interviewing on her own, emphasizing listening closely but also intervening directly.[29]

Hyejin's vigilance around this had a palpable sense of urgency. She invited Korean elders working in food-related settings and corner store owners to join organizing events in South Central. In turn, she facilitated ways to showcase and share Korean food and culture with Black and Latinx groups in the area. Collaborating with a group of Korean youth outside of work, Hyejin organized a series of Black-Latinx-Korean *kimjang* events that brought community members together across racial lines. She wanted to make sure that everyone knew Latasha Harlins's story, that folks had the space to unpack different perspectives on it, and why ongoing racial tensions were still connected to food retail spaces in South Central. During these events Hyejin engaged the group in conversations to promote racial healing while sharing the art of kimchi making across race and cultural lines.

Years later, in 2019, when I heard that Hyejin had left the organization she had been working for and started working for herself, I called to see what had transpired. Here's what she told me:

> Well, you remember that I was about racial justice and healing. I was, and still am, really passionate about working with my community, with Koreans, to heal from the traumas of 1992 and the ongoing racial tensions we have with Black and Latinx, and also white people. So I was drawn to working in food justice because I was told that that is part of what they do—that they are doing the "justice" part. I think that that was what drew me to the program, to begin with, and I still believe that's a rich area for community building. . . .
>
> And so, it just didn't feel like there was attention and care being gauged to building trusting relationships with community members and advocat[ing] for some kind of larger plan for what we envision food and land work to be in LA. They didn't really . . . it felt like they were presenting [the group] as that, but not putting in the time to really do that ground-truthing except with the people who are already showing up for those spaces, who were usually the same kinds of people with the same ideas, not really members of the community at large. And because of that, the folks who were really on the ground and also the folks who are most impacted, didn't find the space to be accessible.

Hyejin realized that although the organization she worked for claimed to be "doing justice," in reality their everyday ways of operating were not grounded in the kinds of transformational practices that she felt were necessary to create systematic and long-term change. She specifically underscored the importance of spending time building relationships with the community, building trust, and spending time to collectively envision the future. Hyejin's orientation to organizing work was akin to the kind of work that brown advocates for in *Emergent Strategy*. Some of the principles that resonated with Hyejin's vision include the imperative to "trust the people. If you trust the people, they become trustworthy." And to "move at the speed of trust. Focus on critical connections more than critical mass—build the resilience by building relationships. Less prep, more presents. What you pay attention to grows."[30] Hyejin decided to leave the food justice organization because she was deeply committed to racial healing and justice. The organization did not value the links between racial justice and food justice as she did. She could not stay in line with her values and move the speed of the mainstream food justice movement and its drive from quick outcomes to please funders and board members. She refused to participate in that kind of power structure. For the organization that Hyejin worked for, and many others in my research, defining the scope of their work was an ongoing problem. This group did not see racial healing in the Korean community as essential and instead preferred to stay focused on what they understood as the needs of Black and Latinx communities. Staying true to her commitments, Hyejin left so that she could do work that aligned with those values, like the multiracial *kimjang* events she helped to organize. Her logics aligned with brown's understanding that collaboration and shifting organizing work toward the needs of diverse and evolving communities was part of an emergent strategy. Rather than shift toward the dominant approaches, Hyejin trusted the value of her commitment to Korean-Black racial reconciliation as fundamental for moving toward a more just and liberated local food system.

Hyejin reflected further on leaving the organization:

> But yeah, by the time that I was transitioning out it felt like . . . I mean, I didn't feel like there was really . . . I didn't feel that I had the capacity to steward that role in the relation . . . in the program with . . . without more mentorship and . . . Because I'm not like . . . I'm not a transformative justice facilitator. I don't have the experience, and it just . . . I was also very ill-equipped to play either the relationship holding role or the mediating role or the role of supporting with the actual tangible skill building that folks wanted out of the program. And there was also . . . we were being told not to focus so much on Koreans. But it also . . . again, because of my language and culture background, it kind of diminishes my usefulness in that program because it goes to the Spanish speaking [participants] and so there were a lot of reasons why I felt like it was time to transition out of the program.

Hyejin said that her bosses felt that having a Korean employee focused on Koreans was not serving the mission of food justice that they envisioned, which was focused on Black and Latinx groups. I responded that I felt that focusing on healing the racial trauma of 1992 among Korean store owners was deeply about Black groups in South Central. But the focus on Koreans did not give "the look" that food justice groups wanted, Hyejin explained. I assumed that what they mean by "the look" was part of broader forms of racialization in the United States where Asians and Asian Americans are distinguished from other Black, Indigenous, or people of color, as "model minorities" or as highly successful and therefore not the population that a charity or social justice organization should be focusing on.

This is part of a broader political orientation to serving only those who are most in need, but it also illuminates the dimensions of racialization and perpetuation of difference that are part of this kind of social justice work. The organization's "look" they aimed to achieve frames those in need of help in a particular way, leaving the Korean community and Black-Korean relations beyond the bounds of intervention. Conversations between two Koreans in Korean about racial trauma did not offer a photo-op or sound bite that would resonate with wider communities and funders. This was especially true given how few people working in food justice understood the history of Black-Korean relations in South Central and the connections to the 1992 uprisings. Furthermore, conversations alone did not offer a tangible outcome that could be moved toward or accomplished. These conversations took time, and there was no way to measure their effectiveness. In the end, this work toward racial healing was not part of the tasks that the food justice organization explicitly paid Hyejin to do.

Although Hyejin felt that these tasks were connected and that most of the racial healing work she was doing with the Korean community was in her free time, the organization felt that she was spending too much time invested in one thing. In building relationships with a small group of people, they felt it was not a good use of her time when there was a need to scale things up and move on to new projects. Therefore, Hyejin was told to stop doing that work and to focus more broadly on the group's food justice programming in South Central. While her deep commitment to racial healing across Black and Korean communities was important work, it did not fall neatly within the vision or desired outcomes of the organization that she worked for and so it was cast aside. Hyejin saw that the organizations' commitment to crafting certain optics and images of their work—centered on helping those most "in need"—was about maintaining their power within the hierarchies of the food justice movement.

In addition to feeling disappointed with the thinness of the organization's racial justice engagement, Hyejin noticed that the organization itself had a lot of problems and tensions around race. As she explained:

> In general, that younger, queer folks of color who don't have as much academic pedigree or that kind of background that allows you to navigate these kinds of [nonprofit/organizational] spaces, they, we, get the short end of the stick. And are asked to stay in entry level roles for a really long time and asked to sacrifice on behalf of the organization more than others and eventually burn out or transition out I think that there isn't . . . there hasn't been a

really dedicated effort to address those issues internally by the leadership overall, including their board, but also that's a result of the way the history of how the movement was shaped too. It's kind of an elite space, and I was hoping to change the culture from the inside, but I think once people saw that, I was kind of shut out.

As the organization grew and hired more people, Hyejin's boss had trouble figuring out how to find the right people. Thus the organization defaulted to hiring people with a minimum of a master's degree because to them it seemed like an easy way to guarantee that people would have skills in writing, communication, and project execution. The degree programs had already indoctrinated these new employees into the existing approaches to nonprofit work, saving organizations time and effort in some ways. However, the minimum degree requirement meant that there were few applicants from South Central or with experience in South Central; instead, the organization ended up hiring people with little work experience straight out of local graduate programs. Hyejin was pointing to one of the ways in which whiteness can creep into social justice organizations. She explained that this really shifted the organization toward young, white, liberal professionals, with aspirations to eventually make more money than what most nonprofits could pay. This new cohort of food "justice" workers came in with a superficial understanding of the area and of racial and economic justice, and their work reflected that shallow level of understanding. They transitioned quickly to other jobs.

For Hyejin the organization started to feel like a revolving door of "fancy" master's graduates who never stayed long enough to do anything substantive in the community. She explained:

> The fact of the matter is that the food justice movement, or whatever you want to call it, is not really grassroots or radical. And so around the time I left the work, independently in my personal life, I was starting to become more informed around broader issues of US imperialism. And the relationship between the US military and white supremacist heteropatriarchy and our ability to have a relationship with land and food, and . . . just recognizing that these things directly impacted me, and are directly impacting my community, and these ongoing racial tensions. And so, I'm continuing to have conversations with folks who want to see more of that transformative relationship building happen and to support that between.

Hyejin left the organization to start her own community work centered on healing relationships with the land, antigentrification, land justice, and connections between land and food. All of the work of her new organization is tied to racial healing for all Angelenos, but specifically between Indigenous, Black, Latinx, and Korean people who experience shared historical racial traumas in the overlapping areas where they live.

Although Hyejin never mentioned his name, I knew that one of the bosses that she was referring to was Chase Bledsoe. She knew I knew him, and he had been a part of my research. I assume that not saying his name was about politely saving face. Still, I could not help but remember my very early conversations with Chase. I remembered how he described himself as "radical from a young age," citing his mother as inspiring him with her "white feminist" ethics. Back then, Chase had told me that the foundation of his activism was built on what he learned in college, "thinking a lot about the history of white supremacy and racism in the United States and what it means to be a white person in that context and what it means to be an ally in that context" and "really focusing on my piece of the puzzle in terms of the work of dismantling racism, white supremacy, and systems of oppression." I had seen him lose the ability to overtly grapple with whiteness as he rose through the ranks of food justice. Through Hyejin, I saw how Chase had become someone jockeying for the power to pull food justice in less radical, more status-quo directions. I was disappointed but not surprised at how much Chase had changed over time.

STRUGGLING FOR RADICAL FOOD FUTURES

Hyejin and her story reflect a general trend I observed in the food justice movement in the late 2010s. This involved envisioning a future that is entirely different from the present and the past, which included severing relationships or leaving organizations that were invested in building within the status quo rather than working toward a different kind of future. Instead of focusing their time on outputs for organizations that wanted to scale up and attract more funding, a growing group of people seemed to be turning away from the nonprofit approach toward other work that was either more grounded in community organizing or business-based approaches to food. This not to say, however, that all of these people were looking for liberation or abolition; in fact, many left to work for or create for-profit companies.[31] For Hyejin, by leaving the organization that would not allow her to work toward the kind of future that she wanted to see, she built on emergent strategy and fled the status quo approaches; she envisioned and built approaches to justice that she did not find to be possible within the more formalized food justice movement. Her moves align with anthropologist Elizabeth Povinelli's argument that liberal state projects shift power structures in favor of work that is feasible. Hyejin used her power to reject these structures and continue trying something different.

The need to leave or change existing organizations is part of the "emergent strategy" approach. As brown notes, "organizations are often rooted in masculine action culture," which she describes as "penetrative."[32] She writes of organizations that swoop into communities with interventions that are "grounded in spectacle" but lack real community engagement, and therefore instead of changing the power dynamics, the work of these organizations maintained status quo power hierarchies.[33] These same issues that brown found in her own organizing work were also present in the Los Angeles food justice movement. In part this is why Hyejin ultimately decided to leave the organization and, later, the food justice movement. As brown notes, these masculinist, institutional ways of orienting to labor are widespread, even in progressive nonprofits and organizing circles. In fact, to do things differently, most people and organizations will find that they must constantly remind themselves to shift away from what they have been taught and socialized into. That kind of change would involve fundamentally rethinking ties to land and ideas of private property; it would involve relearning the histories we were not taught in school. Such an approach would mean shifting from the desire for quick results and tangible outcomes to slow, long-term solutions and the faith that change will come eventually.[34]

While Hyejin and others point to the kinds of logics that our education systems indoctrinate us into, which include systems of racial capitalism and whiteness, we know from other examples in this chapter how such inclinations seep into various aspects of organizing work. This applies even in organizations that eschew higher education and specifically seek to employ those whose knowledge comes from lived experience. Building on her explicit engagement with brown's work, Hyejin chose to leave the organization because she was trying to be in right relationship with the communities that matter most to her. She viewed this as fundamentally important to improving food access and equity in Los Angeles. Hyejin's *kimjang* collective was part of a liberatory praxis to create spaces for herself and others to think about and pave paths forward that are not confined by dominant structures of the nonprofit world that her job had placed upon her.

LABORS OF LOVE?

Sunny, the executive director of Food for All, and I worked side by side, filling bags with fresh produce for the program's small list of community-supported agriculture (CSA) subscribers. Sunny circled back to a conversation we had a few weeks earlier. She had told me the organization tried not to hire people with degrees but instead to hire members of the community, who statistically were less likely to hold a degree. I think she could tell that I was confused by that statement, so she brought it up again that day: "See, we don't need someone with a BA or an MA to fill grocery bags. We need someone who is willing to do the work and doesn't think they are too good for it. In our experience, people who get degrees at any kind of school somehow think they are above doing this kind of labor. They have a sense of entitlement, ideas that they should somehow be more important than people without a degree, and we really can't have that kind of attitude in our space." We loaded the bags into the organization's van, and another staff member drove them to the pick-up site. Not only was Sunny trying to avoid hiring people who felt they were above the work or deserved more compensation, but she also valued knowledge acquired through experience in the community over knowledge from the classroom.

Later in an interview, Sunny returned to the education issue, wondering if she had offended me, as someone with a BA, MPH, or MA, working toward a PhD at the time. "It's not just that people with degrees tend to always feel that they are above the work that we need to do," Sunny explained, "but also they have been indoctrinated into the system, into white supremacy, heteronormativity, into all of the things that we are trying to undo here." For people like Sunny, degrees (especially expensive MA degrees) could be understood not only as a proxy for wealth and entitlement but also as an endorsement of these broader ideological systems, including whiteness and racial capitalism, and as part of a capitalistic fetish of higher education and social status. Sunny was thinking of people who become their work, who become "the institution" and wield forms of institutional power through their work and personal identities, like other food activists who have been detailed in this book. It was not that everyone with an education was this way, she offered, giving the example of a longtime friend and community member.

> [This person] had actually become an attorney. His sister had been killed by the California highway patrol, and through the organizing to get justice for his sister, he'd become interested in the law and became an attorney. And so,

FIGURE 15. Grocery bags with fresh produce. Photo by the author.

he began to use his legal knowledge to actually engage in community economic development.

So, through his law, he specialized in criminal law and community economic development. And so, he began to use [his degree to help a local nonprofit become an official 501c3] and to really provide fiscal status for grassroots agencies to help a lot of agencies that people in LA.

Sunny cited him as an example of someone who really combined his knowledge "from the streets" with what he learned in school. This person had organized meetings between the Bloods and the Crips to try to curb violence in the area.[35] Both gangs trusted and respected him. Despite his law degree, Sunny used him as an example of someone who was motivated to improve the everyday lives of people in South Central and willing to dedicate their entire lives to that cause.

Like Hyejin, Sunny highly valued the skill of working *with* people to overcome conflict. To Sunny, the purpose of her friend's degree was to enable this work, not to achieve status or make money. Those were the kinds of people that Sunny looked to hire. She elaborated further:

> So, we don't want to become this 9-to-5 organization where people just come to collect a salary. And so, one of the things we decided was, and now that we're beginning to get money and we can actually pay people, we want to lose that spirit of just wanting to make this happen. So, one of the things we decided was, everyone who's on staff has to put in volunteer time. So, just everybody does that. And I mean, the level of commitment has really seriously been there because there was one year where we literally ran out of money, it was that same year where loads of nonprofits closed their doors. The summer following that we were waiting on a number of grants we'd applied for. We had run out of all our money and all of our staff were willing to be unemployed for three months and keep doing the work that had to be done until the money came in. And I don't know of any other organization that can say that.

Sunny emphasized the desire to operate in a different way from a standard job, to attract staff who are so passionate about their work that they would do it for free. However, there are clear drawbacks to this approach; given that this organization has a strong preference to hire local people from South Central, the erratic pay structure and irregular access to benefits created instability and may impoverish their own staff, assuming they did not have savings or another household salary to fall back on. It is puzzling how the values of supporting local community and the insistence that employees be willing to go without pay align. It is not clear how *not* compensating staff is part of the kind of abolitionist framework that Sunny embraces. Given that her reflections on payment came up after we had discussed the problem with overeducated staff, to me Sunny is implying that people with BA, MA, and PhD degrees, who she assumes are saddled with debt, are not the kind of people who take on this work because they feel a need to earn more money for a variety of reasons.

Of course, this characterization of some people with degrees in higher education as "good" and doing acceptable work, while others are driven to make money and accumulate social capital, is highly subjective and Sunny's personal opinion. However, her sentiments capture a broader feeling among food justice organizations that many volunteers come to these organizations claiming to want to help, but in the end they do not show up, do not put in much effort, but still receive accolades for their good will and virtue signaling. Sunny and food justice leaders like her find this pattern frustrating and harmful to their work. She explained: "But the difference, I think, with us is that when we have the money, we compensate our staff really well. So just now, we just got this big grant, and we're about to have the best medical, we've never had medical insurance for staff before, but we're about to have the best medical insurance that anybody I know I've had."

Sunny moves back and forth between a narrative of envisioning a world in which earnings and benefits are not the only motivation for work, a world in which she attracts the staff she would like to have through additional benefits, like better medical insurance than other area employers. These fluctuations between thinking outside of the status quo, envisioning alternative orientations to labor and community, while also needing to reasonably support people in an increasingly expensive city is exemplary of the kind of ideological pivoting that many food justice workers have had to do over the years of this research. Though there is certainly a way of reading Sunny's approach as exploitative, in a subsequent conversation she explained her position regarding willingness to work without pay vis-à-vis the lessons of the INCITE! Women of Color Against Violence collective.[36] In *The Revolution Will Not Be Funded*, the collective offers insights into how many groups across the globe are undertaking critical organizing work and community support on shoestring budgets. Grounded in this kind of ethos, Sunny and Food for All must constantly toggle back and forth to find the place where their approaches to the work are moving beyond the past and present ways of doing things to try to get to real systematic change. Still, at the same time, they must operate within the existing nonprofit structures and societal expectations for labor and compensation.

Similar tensions are at play in Sunny's reflection on how the organization got started:

> We had been doing a lot of work around trying to because at that time, I don't know if you remember, but there were also a lot of issues with Black and Brown violence, both in the prisons and in the schools. These things happen in spurts, and around that time, there was a lot of this stuff going on, a lot of shootings, a lot of killings in the prisons that were spilling over into the streets in South LA. And so, we were also doing some organizing through [the organization] around that to bring the Black and Brown communities

together and we were doing different things. . . . We were organizing rallies in parks that were really aimed around the Black and Brown issue, really talking about "Why are we killing each other?" [And] really going back to some of that really grassroots organizing. And as part of that, that developed into a program that we called "Education for Us" as an afterschool program.

And really the program was designed to really get at the heart of, "Why is it that our kids are killing themselves and each other?" With all these problems that we have going on. And really our understanding of it was and is that they were doing that and are doing that still because they basically have no idea of who they are. They don't have any understanding of their place in history, who they are, who each other is and as like Frederick Douglass said, and many others have said in different ways, but if you don't know your past, how can you possibly understand presently where you are at. And the schools weren't teaching any . . . So we designed this program that was really meant to get to the heart of this . . ., which was based around the teachings of Paulo Freire. So we really immersed ourselves in Freire and pedagogy in terms of how we would engage with young people in this program.

But what we experienced in implementing that program was that the kids we were working with were not nourished; they would come after school, and they would have all kinds of behavioral issues. And as we began to really look at it and think about it, we were realizing that this is really a result of the fact that these kids have had sugar, sugar, and sugar in some form or the other for the whole day. And they've actually had no real nourishment. So we began to just try different things with them. We began to get them to keep food diaries and to document when they got into trouble at school, and they themselves began to see how drinking a soda at a certain point was connected to when they would do something crazy at school that they—later on—couldn't even explain and this kind of stuff.

Reflecting on the beginnings of her organization, Sunny recalled her own moment of seeing the links between racialized violence in the community and the foods that children were consuming. Like Hyejin and other food justice organizers, Sunny views racialization and inadequate food access as inextricably linked. She sees how food access and race are tied to various other problems in the community, from young kids getting in trouble in school to incarceration rates to killings in prisons. Sunny sees these connections and thinks through how to create programs to address the problems at the root. She begins with curricular innovations that reimagine the history and ideologies children learn in school.[37]

While Sunny's approach to reeducating South Central kids was an attempt to begin to imagine the world otherwise, unfortunately the use of food diaries and accounting for daily food consumption practices with the kids can serve to reify the understanding that problems with food consumption stem from and can be rectified through individual consumptive behavior rather than systematic change.[38] This approach is another example where, despite Sunny's radical orientations, she falls into mainstream, neoliberal logics in her processes of trying to get outside of the neoliberal, nonprofit industrial complex. This illuminates the complexities and tensions of doing this kind of radical work despite the impossibility of completely getting outside of the status quo systems that keep organizations funded and legible. Sunny was coming up against the impossibility of sustaining an incommensurate world with the radical possibility of producing something otherwise.[39]

A few weeks after my March 2014 interview with Sunny, she emailed and invited me to a "brainstorm" about food justice organizing in South LA and what had been happening recently. "The first step is a brainstorm to create the perimeters and essential questions of this project," she wrote, "and we would be honored to have you be part of this process. Please join us." When I arrived at Food for All's headquarters for the brainstorm, Sunny greeted me at the door and led me to a long table with large dishes of freshly prepared food that she and the team had made for the meeting. She guided me through the food line, and I fixed a plate for myself. She explained why we had gathered that day:

> We're doing a project right now, a research project—actually that we got a little bit of money for—specifically around this issue. We're looking at how much money has there been in food justice work in food work in LA over the last ten years, where has that money been spent. What are the projects that have had longevity? What has happened to most of these projects after the money's gone? What are organizations who claim to be doing justice actually doing? Because "food justice" is now the prevalent term, just like "farmers markets" were the big thing. All these organizations who claim to be doing food justice work, what actually is going on in their organizations, how many people of color do they have? How many people of color do they have beyond a certain level, or who's their leadership who's on their board?
>
> So we're actually doing some research, we're about to start doing this project right now to look at that because— [sic]. And in my opinion, unfortunately, most nonprofits, especially bigger corporate nonprofits, they're pimps. They're poverty pimps, whether the people in there, and I'm not trying to say here that everybody involved with them are intentionally doing that, that's not what I'm trying to say. Because most of the people who work in those organizations are good people, they're, well-intentioned, they're well-meaning, that simply by the logic of the system itself.

The purpose of the brainstorm was not only to sketch out the landscape of food justice organizations—who they hired, where they got their funding, and the work they were doing—but also to lay bare the elements of others' work that Sunny saw as problematic and to determine how not to fall into that way of doing things. Although she was certainly pitting her organization against others in terms of fundamental divergences in the ideologies behind their approaches, she wanted the same funding they were getting and viewed them as sucking up funding that should be going to organizations like hers.

Unfortunately, I never heard what the results of Sunny's research revealed, but I know that the fact that she set aside time to reflect and engage in a strategic visioning process allowed her to assess and reorient the work of Food for All. With the brainstorm Sunny was trying to get the lay of the land so that she could continue to develop her own emergent strategy and vision for systematic change both in everyday work of her organization and in the food system more broadly. The practice of stepping back to assess and reaffirm the group's vision was rare among the food justice organizations that I studied. It was often too complicated, took up too much time, or could leave the group feeling ungrounded and vulnerable. Sunny's insistence on this praxis was essential to opening the possibility for this organization to orient toward their work in an abolitionist way, envisioning a possible future that is not yet known.

In their process of reflecting on the work of Food for All through the analysis of other food justice organizations, Sunny and her team decided to add new programs that were geared toward overall wellness and well-being. They added regular free yoga, meditation, Tai Chi, and Zumba classes to their weekly schedule. Sunny noted that these programs weren't about food, but they were about well-being and creating space to bring community members together. These are the kinds of programs that many other organizations would eschew as unrelated to their mission, but Food for All sees their work as fostering overall well-being rather than a narrow focus on healthy eating. They have incorporated these programs into their funding and loan applications, arguing that their food justice work is ultimately serving a broader goal of wellness for residents of South LA. These programs addressed needs among the community members Sunny's organization served that were not likely to be supported by granting agencies focused on individual behavioral change related to food. For Sunny and Food for All, creating these opportunities to build community and practice wellness, to get outside of and away from the evaluation structures of the nonprofit world, was a practice of liberation.

MOVING ON, MAKING SPACE

By 2020 some of the people I had first interviewed or observed in the early years of my research had moved on to other things. Hyejin created her own organization, and Sunny moved on to work for a national organization and turned Food for All over to a new executive director. In late 2020, I got wind that Federico was stepping down from a prominent organization's board. I interviewed him over Zoom about his tenure in the food justice movement and the reasons he was departing. He reflected on his thirteen years working in food justice. Looking back, Federico felt like he was a young kid when he began. I had watched him during those years; many others had looked up to him. He stood out as a clear leader in the movement. The best part of the movement was working with the other people in it, he told me. "It's just—it's a deep connection," he said. "When I think about my career, I think about like, 'Wow, if I change jobs or went somewhere else, that means I can't go to the [group] meetings.' You know what I'm saying. It's like, 'Wow, this is something that's important to me.'" Given how important this work was to him, I asked Federico why he stepped down from the board. He said:

> I think there's other people that can be leaders, and I think it's important for us to step up and to step back. So I think it was time for me to step down. I feel like [Sarah Cunningham], for example. [Sarah] just stepped down, and she wrote a long email about why she is stepping down and it was just really, it was about creating space for others. But she had other things that she wanted to pursue, but she's still kind of part of the family still. For me, it was like I had other things on my plate. And the other thing too that's important about these things is that you have to be aware enough where you realize that you may not be adding the most value, then maybe there's someone else that could do a better job because they have more space. And that's really important, which is something that I think [Sarah] was implying too.

Sarah Cunningham had also recently left food justice to focus on building a new food-related public benefit corporation. She had shared with Federico the idea that at a certain point organizations need to make space for fresh ideas and new ways of thinking about problems. Both Federico and Sarah saw that over time their thinking was less nuanced, and they offered less to the organization in terms of innovative thinking and creative energy. Federico continued:

There's like, I mean, we have to build the bench. Don't you think? You can't just rely on the same people. That's why I always get worried when they see an organization had the same people for twenty years. It's like, "Come on, dude. How are you building the next generation?" And so I just . . . I don't think it's like the founders are the movement, and then the movement's done. It's like, "No, it's changing, it's growing." I'm even thinking of like just veganism and vegetarianism and plant-based living and stuff like that, it's changing now. Whereas, like ten years ago, it's like, "You're tripping. What is that? These are just some weird people doing that thing." Now it's changing. There's more people in the next generation who are thinking, like, "No, we got to think about how we control our food and where it comes from."

Although Federico was in his late thirties, some people would put him in the same generation as Nzinga or Ronica, the young food justice organizers from South Central. Federico recognized his tendency to be stuck in ways of thinking that were common ten years ago. He saw ideologies moving even if he was not moving with them, such as, for example, the shift toward promoting "plant-based living" instead of vegetarianism or veganism. Nzinga and Ronica were, incidentally, plant-based. Rather than viewing himself as older and wiser, Federico's recognition of the shift signaled to him that it was time to move on and make space for new ways of thinking and living.

Given that Federico's departure coincided with both the COVID-19 lockdowns and the 2020 Black Lives Matter uprisings, I asked how those two things influenced his work and decision to step down.[40] He replied:

Well, I mean, I think that the people that we work for and with are people that are really vulnerable and have always been living on the edge, meaning, economically. And so the pandemic has really pushed people too, just like it's been disastrous to a lot of people. And there's a lot of people that are hungry, and I know that a lot of people in the food system are struggling . . . the entrepreneurs are, as we talked about, but then also our friends that are distributing food are also at capacity, and it's hard.

And I think, it's hit us in many different ways, and I think my feelings about the pandemic from a political standpoint is that while it's been really a disaster, the crisis has also revealed, well, we've known for a long time that the things that we had longed for were actually really possible even when they said that they weren't. That you can close down public facilities and house people, that you can give people cash, that you can legalize eating on the sidewalk overnight. They told us that it was not possible before, but the pandemic showed us that it really is. What was missing was the will to do it. So, to me, it gives me personally a lot of like, "Dude, this is just getting going," because they showed us that it is possible, and they just didn't want to do it before. So that's kind of a little bit of the optimism in the pandemic.

Federico paused and looked at me on the Zoom screen. I assumed he was studying my reaction to see if mentioning something positive coming out of a devastating pandemic would upset me. I was not upset. I agree that many good lessons were learned during the pandemic. He continued:

> The movement for Black Lives . . . that *worked* for us. I think it hit us in different ways. I think it's emotional for us. Certainly, my team at work we're really emotional about it, specifically the murder of George Floyd. And I think that the demands of Black Lives Matter and other activists are things that, like, "Yeah, dude, we've been needing those things, and we support them." And I think that it really calls into question how we can do more and how we stepped up in different ways to support them. . . . And so, we started to think about like, "Well, what *is* our role?" Right. We're not researchers and analysts that are involved in abolition and police reform. That's not our thing, but we are good at certain things, but we do have expertise in these things, and how do we instill these values in that work. And so the team began to talk about anti-Blackness. So that was one way we began to incorporate these things of like, "This is our role. We have a role to play, and we see a lot of anti-Blackness in the [community]." We're also going to be like, "Bro, we need you to read this zine that we wrote about how do you combat anti-Blackness in your family?" And so those are certain things that I think we have a role to play, and I don't know.

In yielding the floor, these leaders intentionally make space in the movement for younger people with fresher ideas. Federico and Sarah were enacting brown's principle of "radical honesty," which brown views as central to the development of "liberated relationships." This involves "acknowledging the dynamics" and determining how to keep growing once grounded in the existing power dynamics.[41] For brown, the essential praxis involves "being in the complexity" of the existing power dynamics across age, race, class, gender, ability, and so forth "while evolving beyond them through relationships."[42] In my analysis Federico clearly espouses this approach of radical honesty, acknowledging one's place in an organization and adjusting accordingly to allow the organization to grow. This contrasts with orienting to work to better oneself or to build one's career. While Federico and Sarah both moved on to do different things careerwise, they did not commandeer or hold hostage their organizations to do so; instead, they yielded space to others in those organizations.

Federico adjusted his work following the changing needs of the COVID-19 pandemic when he developed an extensive campaign to give cash cards at first to those who were not eligible for unemployment or the stimulus payments and then to anyone who had been working with his organization and needed money to stay afloat. Giving away large sums of cash, Federico circumvented formal COVID-19 stimulus programs, which did not work for his participants, and he leveraged his power to create a system that could address immediate needs effectively. Federico said he "was just doing what he needed to do." However, I read his work to distribute cash as a radical move that went beyond the bounds of institutional frameworks and boundary setting, liberating funds from the system, and getting cash into the hands of the people.

EMERGENT STRATEGY, COLLECTIVE VISIONING, AND REASSESSMENT

Even as people like Sunny and Hyejin attempt to move away from or *get outside of* dominant paradigms and approaches to organizing work, there are many ways that they are sucked back into the mainstream approach to nonprofit work. The radical, liberatory approach that they aspire to requires constant attention and work, both within themselves and with their collaborators. The attention that these liberatory aspirations require is on top of very demanding work schedules that are oriented toward producing outcomes and appeasing funders in a timely manner. The temporalities of their day-to-day work make it difficult to find time to step back, pan out, and understand the ways in which the daily work and its effects align with their broader ideological desires for the work that they do. To ground their work, these organizers use a lexicon of emergent strategy and root their orientation to the work in grassroots, community-based needs and desires.

The ability to track the links between an overarching ethos and the day-to-day tasks is a difficult skill to hone; it is rarely taught in school, and if it is developed at all, it is most often found in mentoring or apprentice relationships. Those relationships, approaches, and ways of thinking are examples of aspirational emergent strategy. Hyejin intuitively sought such strategies in her work but found them to be missing from the organization she worked for, and Sunny intentionally tried to cultivate such approaches regularly, including the brainstorm. While these skills were learned over time, higher-education programs instead focused on the skills necessary for day-to-day work—for example, managing budgets, creating reports, conducting assessments, and so forth. To people like Chase Bledsoe, the skills learned in MA programs were understood as necessary for nonprofits that want to sustain and grow their reach. However, as people like Chase and Nzinga highlight, higher education in and of itself it not the problem; instead, particular ideologies that are commonly found in higher education encourage students to maintain status quo differences and uphold the logics of the liberal state. There is also the broad-scale encouragement of students to undertake hasty projects in "the community" without understanding historical circumstances or developing relationships with local residents.

In addition, it is the material effects of higher education—such as educational debt necessitating high earnings or hierarchies produced by degree types—that create tensions within organizing circles. The tensions between needing the skills of people with degrees in higher education and the hierarchies that these degrees reproduce tend to revolve around money and issues related to finances. People like Hyejin and Nzinga were struggling to find the right micro practices that would allow them to subvert these neoliberal logics to mobilize more radical social justice projects. As people like Hyejin and Sunny continually reassess their commitments and their work, their moves in new directions within social justice work are still ongoing, and their successes are not entirely clear. However, their methods and approaches offer great potential.

The writer-activist adrienne maree brown frames "being in the complexity" as the way to evolve beyond and through relationships.[43] The liberatory practice enacted here becomes one way that food justice activists who aspire toward radical praxis may work through the problems inherent in the structures of their work. This practice is about constantly working to get outside of the dominant frameworks that have created the problems and will continue to entrench problems like patriarchy and white supremacy more deeply. Getting outside of these ideologies is an extremely difficult task that requires constant work. Part of the work being done is to remain committed to the place, to further emplace oneself within the area of the city or within the work that one is committed to ideologically. As food justice activists are pulled into mainstream organizing practices, they must constantly work to move away from the status quo. This work is part of the system of jockeying for forms of power within movement spaces, and this group of more radically oriented activists may need to do more to jockey for power in this space because their ideologies and frameworks are not aligned with various kinds of dominant systems.

There is a lot at stake in these types of practices. They offer the possibility of a future where patriarchal hierarchies and white supremacy are not the ideologies structuring our organizations and infrastructures. Radical, liberatory approaches to food justice are part of a broader refusal to participate in practices that ultimately serve to uphold the status quo with respect to power structures. To change the structures that create and maintain inequality in our food system, we must get outside of the logics of these structures and imagine other ways of being that produce different outcomes. However, as the norms of the non-profit world and the individual needs and desires of activists to live more stable, middle-class lives increasingly come into play, those with abolitionist desires for the food movement struggle to maintain their vision. The space in which abolitionist praxis can exist feels increasingly narrow and challenging to locate. As activists struggle to stay within that liberatory, abolitionist orientation to their work, often leaving formal positions and finding or creating new ways to engage in social justice work becomes the most common solution. As abolitionist practitioners grapple with these tensions, they struggle to build the relationships, organizations, institutions, and future world where we can achieve the dreams of freedom and healthy, flourishing Black and Brown communities.

The activists and organizers featured in this chapter show that time and time again, it proves impossible to actually conduct their operations outside of dominant paradigms, including whiteness and racial capitalism. In my analysis the actual state of "being outside" that these groups aspire to is not the most important takeaway for those who want to understand how to do this work in more radical ways. Instead, these organizations and leaders show that the process of constantly stepping back to do the work of revisioning and reorienting toward organizational and community values is the most valuable takeaway. The process of continually reassessing how the organization's various projects, partnerships, and other day-to-day work aligns with its vision and values has even more strength when paired with a similar process of collaborative visioning and reassessment with the community that the organization is working with or intervening on. This collaborative visioning with the community is essential for building and maintaining trust, which Hyejin laments so few organizations take the time to establish.

Conclusion

The End(s) of Food Justice

On February 13, 2022, Super Bowl LVI was played at the new SoFi Stadium in Inglewood, California, the shared home of National Football League (NFL) teams, the Los Angeles Rams and the Los Angeles Chargers. To date, it is the most expensive stadium in the world, with a $5.5 billion construction cost. A crucial site for opening and closing ceremonies, as well as football, archery, and swimming events of the 2028 Los Angeles Olympics, the stadium is located next to South LA.[1] Along with federal, state, and city-based investments in area infrastructure and private development, the SoFi Stadium is creating new housing projects and retail spaces, which have the potential to generate investments in places like South LA.[2]

When I began this project in 2008, many food justice activists and residents I spoke to, including my own family members and friends in the area, wanted significant reinvestment in South Central. Some really wished that there was a Whole Foods Market closer to them. Whole Foods became a symbol of food apartheid, therefore having one in the area might make the food system feel more equal. On August 21, 2022, a brand new 51,413-square-foot Whole Foods Market opened on La Cienega Boulevard in Culver City. Just south of the 10 freeway, it is close enough to *feel* adjacent to South LA for many people. Amazon Fresh opened a brick-and-mortar location in Ladera Heights, just east of South LA. In early 2020 a Smart and Final opened in the new Jordan Downs Plaza across the street from the seven-hundred-unit Jordan

FIGURE 16. SoFi Stadium. Photo by the author.

Downs Housing complex in Watts, an area adjacent to South LA also known for the absence of larger grocery stores. The Koreatown-based development firm Archeon Group was approved in 2020 to build a seven-story building with 180 apartments and a grocery store in a city-owned vacant lot on South Broadway in South LA proper.[3] Rumors circulated that Aldi would be the store in the development. These grocery stores all help to relieve the burden of overcrowding in existing South LA markets. In some ways these stores might be part of the solution people called for beginning in the early 2000s, but in other ways these stores are part of a different, burgeoning issue of rapid development and displacement. It remains unclear whether higher-end grocery stores are part of the solution, or if they will become part of the problem.

These projects are not the result of community organizing, place-making, or the food justice movement. While some people will welcome more retail and new food markets in the area, as Sarah Cunningham noted, these development projects bring different benefits and burdens to the broader area. In June 2020 protestors gathered near the SoFi Stadium.[4] Although the City of Los Angeles has pledged $160 million to

FIGURE 17. A new housing complex with Whole Foods Market on the ground floor. Photo by the author.

improve community parks and local sports facilities, local activists say this is little compared to the billions going toward new sports facilities, which have already created traffic problems, noise, and air pollution.[5] However, their main grievance is that sports-related projects attract developers and drive up already high housing costs.[6] Even before the stadium project began, expanding the Expo Line and adjacent mixed-use housing and retail complexes brought new food retail to the area, which coincided with significant increases in housing costs. According to Redfin, the median sale price for a home in South LA was $740,000 in June 2022, and sales prices increased by 14.7 percent year after year. Prices continued to rise.[7] By July 2023 the median price for a home in Los Angeles hovered over $1 million.[8] Approximately 75 percent of South LA residents are renters. In 2022 the average rent for a two-bedroom in South LA was $2,500, up 5 percent from 2021.[9] Multiple residents have told me they stopped answering their landline phones altogether because of the number of people calling to try to convince them to sell. One resident who lives close to SoFi told me people knock on her door daily wanting to purchase her home.

As these new developments bring food retail and higher housing costs to the area, many food justice activists have had to reflect deeply on what it means to do food justice work amid rapid development and change. The grocery chains some organizers called for years ago are now here, but who will the stores serve? As housing costs increase with development, Black and Brown residents are displaced by more affluent newcomers. These changes are leading some food justice leaders to question how food justice projects might have led to or exacerbated gentrification on more minor scales throughout South LA. In 2016, the same year SoFi Stadium broke ground, I met with two different food justice organizations coming together to help create a new healthy food market and adjacent gardening space. During the conversation one participant cautioned, "We have to be careful not to make it too nice." This participant feared that this project, which was also a beautification project, might be gentrification and attract developers or lead outsiders to purchase homes and drive up prices.

Fear that food justice work could be entangled with gentrification led Hyejin to start questioning the value of some food justice projects entirely. She reflected on one corner store conversion project, telling me that the "troubling thing was that that particular store owner was obviously wanting to survive gentrification, which is understandable but also in such a way where he . . . I don't know. It was really unclear if he was invested in the existing customer base at all. He wanted to appeal to gentrifiers. That was really disheartening to find out three-quarters of the way through the transformation process. And I think a lot of that is the pragmatics of being a business owner and the political position that that puts you in." For Hyejin, the food justice work that sought to bring healthy food to the Black and Brown people of South LA and repair racial trauma between Black and Korean communities would all be in vain if it ultimately served to gentrify the area and established places where future newcomers or outsiders who are imagined to be white and at least middle class could access healthy food. For her, food justice was always about racial justice, but even among food activists who were not orienting their work around racial justice, the point was to serve Black and Brown people, not white middle-class people. Thinking about food justice over the long-term period of this research, to me, Hyejin is pointing to one of the central problems with this movement—the centering of outsider visions of idealized healthy food retail and consumption had played a role in the beginnings of gentrification and displacement.

In addition to Hyejin and Jamarcus's explicit reflections, my sense was that the cascade of stadium development projects caused a fundamental shift in how many food justice practitioners were thinking about their work. For some food justice practitioners, the arrival of Whole Foods and other stores, imagined to be a solution to the food apartheid problem back in 2008, indicated that their work was no longer necessary. For other practitioners, development created new problems and challenges the nature of their work. To them, the addition of a few high-end grocery stores at the periphery of South LA was not a solution to a food access problem at all, and they saw the influx of development projects conceived by outsiders as failing to account for local needs. From their point of view, these projects did not serve the community, despite city and private entities touting development as "helping" South LA. They knew that large-scale development projects would likely lead to an influx of new-comers—now arriving not to initiate nonprofits or justice programs but to live. Gentrification could ultimately displace the low-income Black and Brown people they set out to serve, leading many to recalibrate the mission of food justice work in South LA and redefine what success might look like.

Jamarcus stepped down from Rooting Change in 2020. Before that, he started to move some of the food-related programs he had created in different directions. In a follow-up interview with me, he reflected on why he had made those changes. Jamarcus said that he developed a "growing understanding that the problems were not being solved by these interventions." As he put it:

> Because we needed to remember that the folk that we serve are Black and Brown folk, and we deliberately target or program to those folk and we work in census tracks where folk are economically vulnerable, and so we . . . we work with a population of folk that—where the average median income is $22,000 a year. The overall city's average median income is like $44,000 or $45,000. So we're actually focusing on targeting them. And so, we said, "Nope, we need to shift our program to *actually serve* folk." And that's really hard for a lot of, I think, nonprofits to do unless you start a program, [people are like] "Yeah, we've got to continue it at all costs." No, no, we don't do that. We take a step back. We evaluate, we have an annual retreat every year, we evaluate our program, and we see what's working, what's not working, and then we make decisions to move forward or to not move forward certain things. So we're not wedded to doing things a certain way. We're wedded to serving the community based upon *their* needs.

For example, after one annual retreat and reflecting on their program-ming, Jamarcus explained, Rooting Change decided to end their com-munity garden and community-supported agriculture (CSA) program:

Because the people who we were serving with our CSA program could afford fresh fruits and veggies and could afford to go to Whole Foods and Trader Joe's. Members of the community who were more affluent were taking advantage of the program and the people that we intended to serve, which were economically vulnerable residents, couldn't even afford the $10-a-month box. And we were subsidizing that, at first, but we also shut it down because it was really expensive to run that program. All the staff that we needed every week, and we had a full-time staff person plus five other staff members maintaining all these gardens, aggregating food, redistributing that food, all the supplies, all the time, all the transportation to bring this subsidized box to a population that could already afford this kind of food at the store. . . . So, in communities like this where land is at a premium, where an acre of land is $3 million, because I spent $3 million to grow it over in the damn garden, it's only going to bring you in maybe $40,000–$50,000 a year, right? Like that just economically doesn't make sense.

Jamarcus and his organization utilize their regular time for program reflection to truly ask themselves if and how their work is serving the community that they intend to serve. They are better able to understand whether they are actually serving the needs of the community because they are members of the community and they are in constant dialogue with the diverse group of residents that they serve. They have a much deeper understanding of the ways in which poverty impacts residents in broad and dynamic ways, and they constantly reassess their work to make sure that the food justice initiatives they have are in line with the broader forms of economic justice that they seek. As Jamarcus pointed out, it takes a lot of courage and work to discontinue a launched project once it becomes clear it is not serving the most vulnerable populations. He was able to make changes to his programming because he had already established trust with his funders, his board, and other local institutions that were key partners to his organization, allowing it to adapt and thrive. To me this was one of the most fundamental lessons that I took away from my research: social justice programs will only succeed if they are intimately in touch with the community they serve and take time to constantly reassess their programming in relationship to community needs.

While people like Jamarcus, Hyejin, and Federico are moving away from food justice toward organizing around more urgent problems for residents of South LA and East LA, other practitioners will stay in the fight to build more equitable food systems. For instance, Food for All remains committed to food equity work, and its former director, Sunny, went on to work on food issues at the national level. Many of these community-oriented organizations are still committed to working on food issues but adapt practices and projects to the needs and desires of the residents they serve. For instance, some programs launched emergency food assistance during and after the COVID-19 pandemic because their clients faced dire circumstances and needed immediate access to free or low-cost food.

REFLECTING ON THE LOS ANGELES FOOD JUSTICE MOVEMENT

From the beginning of this research project, I was overwhelmed by the sheer volume of people working on food justice and related issues in Los Angeles. Beyond the organizations I focused on, there were hundreds of others working to improve food and the food system. It was hard to see a cohesive movement or shared values, as each person and group seemed to have a different motivation, approach, and goal. From organizers focused on labor issues to activists concerned about the environment or animal rights, every part of the unequal and imperfect food system had a passionate advocate for change. Although I could not systematically study all of the organizations and people involved with LA food justice work, I observed, over more than a decade, a general lack of understanding of the complexities of the food system. This was a problem that plagued every organization in one way or another. Many people were passionate about their work after being exposed to it through popular media—film, television, online articles, and books— and rallied around a particular problem. However, little popular media on food framed food justice problems within the larger historical and structural systems that produce inequality in the first place. It was easy for people to become passionate about a tiny issue without recognizing that they were approaching only the tip of the iceberg, so to speak. A superficial understanding of the problem is part of what led to ineffective or problematic attempts at solutions.

In addition, many people engaged in food justice work held utopic beliefs that did not map to reality. Among the organizations that I studied, leaders and activists commonly believed that food should not be a commodity sold for profit, and by extension, grocery stores should have a social and moral obligation to sell high-quality food to residents regardless of income. This idealization of food as a right outside of capitalism ignored the nature of grocery as a for-profit industry deeply embedded within a global, industrial system of food production and distribution that is fundamentally driven by corporate profit.[10] The proposed solutions to add more grocery stores, particularly higher-end grocery stores, ignored the core problems of the grocery industrial complex—corporate consolidation, monopoly control, niche consumer profit–driven models that cater to shareholders—that fueled food access inequality in the first place. The complexity of the current food systems, including the realities of logistics and distribution, was overlooked, therefore organizations created simplified solutions that were unsustainable.

Furthermore, a lack of awareness of race, racism, and the historical and ongoing conditions of racial inequality impeded the success of food justice projects, although this was not the case with everyone. In general, the organizations included in this study fell on a spectrum that ranged from total disinterest in the structural and historical factors facing the area to a genuine understanding of the structural complexity and historical practices that created food apartheid in the first place. Regardless of where they landed along this spectrum, most organizations lacked the skills or expertise to address structural problems in their programming. People were uninformed or misinformed about the relationship between food apartheid and the histories of racist policy and racialized geographic development in South LA. Even those aware of the deep structural problems fell back on programming that focused on individual behavior change, sometimes with a vague hope that their work would educate and inspire future leaders from South LA. In other words, although they had an awareness of structural issues, they lacked competency and the ability to articulate and imagine structural interventions.[11]

Despite the good intentions of many organizations, the food justice interventions outlined throughout this book tended to revert to individual behavior change solutions that placed the burden of "healthy eating" on the people of South LA. Disappointingly, none of the organizations and projects I observed conducted rigorous and up-to-date research on what people living in South LA actually ate, or whether the foods they were eating could be called "healthy." In practice, the label "healthy" was associated with fresh fruits and vegetables and not "ethnic" cuisine, and yet the definition of "healthy snacks" or "healthy meals" promoted by these organizations became increasingly unclear. In many instances the "healthy food" concept became an empty signifier, used to mean whatever people needed it to mean in the moment, or part of a racialized language of social justice. In other words, to promote "healthy food" is to hold the shared understanding that the way South LA residents eat is not healthy and therefore must be changed. Healthy food interventions are often based on a set of logics that "enframe" the external reality to make sense of it, whether it is real or not.[12]

Enframing places like South LA as unhealthy, or food deserts, works alongside forms of late liberal statecraft that seeks to "change," "fix," and "help" people of color, and (intentionally or not) ultimately works to make people in these communities into idealized healthy, productive citizens grounded in white norms that maintain present-day social hierarchies. The mobilization of the "healthy food" concept became an extended form of "food shaming," which promoted a conceptual leap that there was no healthy food at all, nor any possibility of being healthy, in a place like South LA.[13] From my perspective this is simply not the case, but it begs us to interrogate the meaning of "healthy" and the meaning of "food" across these communities. Nevertheless, like Ronica, some South LA residents who participated in food justice programs and projects took up a moralized message that "social justice" somehow translated into their individual eating habits and health status, rather than the political education that programs like the Black Panther Party's Free Food Program engaged. Still, there were many residents who strategically used the resources of programs and simply ignored what was intended to shift their behaviors.

The oversimplification of the food access problem through "food desert," "food swamp," and "food mirage" imaginaries naturalized a structural problem and created a sense that there is a "crisis" that demands immediate intervention. The invention of crisis (or "crisisification") allows for a justification of quick, sloppy work with little or no planning for long-term sustainability. The naturalization of the problem and the crisis narrative gave the impression that the Black and Brown people who live in places like South LA are either helpless or somehow incapable of self-regulation and therefore require outside intervention. The sense of urgency around a problem opens the possibility that anyone with any level of expertise can and should "help" solve the problem. This logic gives outsiders license to intervene and a sense that bringing "justice" to South LA is always virtuous—a practice that scholars have described as "white virtue."[14] When a critical mass of food justice work is motivated by this framework, the projects they enact are white racial projects. Food justice interventions that are white racial projects implicitly assume of the value of whiteness. This is most often mobilized in the food justice space through the promotion of "healthy food" as something that can and should be extended to

Others. By focusing on individual behavioral change rather than structural interventions, the blame is placed on Black and Brown communities when food justice interventions fail—and they often do fail. In other words the narrative of Black and Brown deficiency is bolstered, while racial hierarchies and white privilege are reinforced.

Therefore, food justice interventions sometimes operate as ideological projects that can serve to further entrench status quo differences, sustain racial stereotypes, and block potential for collaboration and dialogue. The cooking workshops I attended as part of this research were spaces where I consistently felt the tension between different kinds of racial projects. Many cooking workshops used recipes that were created by the outsiders who developed the intervention. None of the workshops that I observed were created by people with any expertise in food or nutrition (not that that would have necessarily made them more successful). The recipes planned were based on *assumptions* about the eating habits, knowledge, capabilities, needs, and desires of South LA residents. Most of the time cooking workshop attendees were Black and Latinx women who cooked meals for their families most nights of the week. In other words, these women had a great deal of cooking experience. Food justice interventions run counter to common understandings that within many Black and Latinx households, cooking and food consumption are revered cultural and social practices. Cooking the dishes that our mothers and grandmothers cooked, sharing food with family and friends, and understanding eating as pleasurable and social is a familiar relationship to food among Black and Latinx households.[15]

For households in South LA the conditions of food apartheid may have presented barriers and difficulties to consistently cultivating valued food traditions. Women in the community might have attended a cooking workshop hoping it would provide help overcoming structural barriers. But when presented with a recipe for kale salad with nutritional yeast—an ingredient that is expensive and not readily available in the area—the workshop wasted people's time and achieved nothing. This kind of cooking workshop is an example where the white racial project of "healthy" eating was often at odds with Black and Latinx orientations to food as cultural, familial, social, and pleasurable. This kind of tension was also present in the K–12 lessons that I observed where students shared stories of foods that were important to their families, foods that were culturally and socially significant. Yet food justice interventions that just focused on getting students to eat more vegetables ignored or misunderstood the social significance of the foods students ate at home.

A lack of understanding of everyday lives and the actual practices of food acquisition and consumption within South LA households was an issue that cut across most of the organizations I studied. In some ways this makes sense because none of the people involved in the projects I observed were experts in cultural foodways, nutrition, or related topics. Instead, many who intervened in South LA drew on training in undergraduate and advanced degree programs. These programs often emphasize technical solutions and tools to break down complex problems into attainable goals that are specific, measurable, achievable, relevant, and time-bound (SMART). The SMART framework eschews factors beyond the scope of the project, which leaves little space for attending to cultural foodways, racial inequality, histories of redlining, or supply chain factors that might lead to project sustainability issues down the line.

Nevertheless, food justice leaders would often bracket off the complexity of these problems, rallying behind concepts like "justice" and "placemaking," and their drive to be helpful, good people who were "willing to get their hands dirty." They wanted to help others as a way to give back to society and to feel connected. They also wanted to share their "expertise" and "experiment" with their skills. A general desire to "get things done" quickly meant that few took the time to develop deep understandings of what it is like to live in South Central, and few engaged in collaborations or even dialogued directly with residents. Instead, confident that they understood the problem and knew how to devise a solution, they were quick to act on their visions of what "bringing justice" or "facilitating placemaking" might look like. Although many people intervened with the good intentions to empower residents of South LA, they often did it without taking the time to build trust in the community and understand what residents actually wanted and needed. As Hyejin lamented, "it just didn't feel like there was attention and care being gauged to building trusting relationships with community members and advocate for some kind of larger plan for what we envision food and land work to be in LA."

Over the course of my research some of the organizations that I worked with became attuned to some of the problems I have outlined here. As they identified problems, each organization developed a different approach to moving forward. Some changed their projects and cautioned that there could be negative repercussions that were not well understood yet. In the end, though, many shifted away from food justice toward other things that they understood as more salient to the needs of the community. Increasingly, as big development projects flank

South LA, raising rents and potentially displacing the community, this has meant a shift toward thinking about land, property, and housing justice.

JOCKEYING FOR POWER IN THE FOOD JUSTICE MOVEMENT

Throughout this book I have sought to illuminate the potential for radical political organizing within the food justice movement across different kinds of social justice organizations. I have analyzed the power dynamics within food justice spaces with the goal of understanding how the actions of particular individuals or groups shifted the conversations in those spaces either toward the status quo or more radical future possibilities. I have focused on particular moments or types of gatherings where approaches to food justice might collide or conflict and analyzed the types of conversations or tactics that pulled the resulting work in a particular direction over others. In addition, I have uncovered some of the deeper structures and systems that facilitate certain forms of power. Structures like whiteness and racial capitalism are critical to bolstering the power of particular individuals or groups of people to leverage specific narratives and ideologies that sculpt or destroy radical possibilities within food justice organizing spaces. The systems, ideologies, and practices that shape these forms of power are complex and difficult to identify; they are inscribed through "signs that are often hard to notice even for the social actors who use and impose them."[16]

Different actors have shaped the definition of food justice, and those with the greatest power to do so rely on a moralized language of justice, health, and virtuosity. This effectively buries the structures of race and racism behind food access inequality, couching the work in more benign language of "health," "healthy food," "justice," "placemaking," and "empowerment." These slippery signifiers have uneven understandings and have been used in the food justice movement to push particular agendas by leaning on the presumption of a shared political perspective tied to terminology. By ignoring how racism is foundational to the problem of food access, food justice activists legitimate their power within the movement in a way that is beyond reproach. In turn, the work serves to perpetuate the racialized power dynamics that created inequality in the first place, which have always shaped multiple historical and contemporary systems, including the food system, within the United States. Although there was opportunity for change in some food justice organizing spaces, ultimately the food justice movement organizers in my research relied on the same forms of sovereign power that made South LA what it is and that continues to shape the future possibilities of Black and Brown people who live there.

Beyond draining money and resources that could be more productively used by South Central residents, there are several broad and long-term negative impacts caused by the superficial and problematic projects detailed throughout this book. Foremost is the co-optation of terms like "justice," "placemaking," "empowerment," or "health." Feckless initiatives warp the meaning of these powerful words both semantically and practically, and in turn undo the radical potential of organizing under these banners. A large group of outsiders doing so-called food justice work has the effect of undoing justice in two ways: they dilute and warp the meaning of justice as a concept, and they compete with radical grassroots efforts to improve the lives of the most vulnerable. Undoing justice in this way has the result of increasing distance between outsider and community members, withering the future possibility of multiracial collaboration, and diluting community members' faith that well-meaning allies can aid in their pursuit of a better future.

(RE)TURNING TO OUR ROOTS

For those organizations that remain committed to food justice and are able to disentangle themselves from these dominant power structures that only serve to perpetuate the same kinds of problems, the question of how to orient their work around community needs is still essential. Beyond the organizations that I studied in South LA, across the United States there are thousands of groups organizing for food justice and more equitable food systems through different frameworks and approaches to their work. In October 2018, I attended the Black Urban Farmers & Growers (BUGS) conference in Durham, North Carolina.[17] For me, this conference offered insights into some of the larger food, agriculture, and land access questions that Black communities across the United States face. This conference featured many grassroots organizations that were driven by the needs and desires of their communities, with members of those communities driving the programs and projects devised to solve those community-based needs.

The conference theme was "Roots and Resilience: Preserving Black Land, Reclaiming Self-Determination." Leah Penniman and Dr. Monica White were the two keynote speakers. The conference was not about presenting findings; instead, participants were focused on sharing approaches, networking, and genuinely learning from one another. After the Friday evening kickoff reception, over two full days the conference brought together urban and rural farmers, students, chefs, food product makers, herbalists, nutritionists, consumers, policy makers, educators, activists, and organizations from across the country. Through the participatory panels, networking sessions, and hands-on workshops, I observed this group of majority-Black farmers collectively think through what a liberated food future would look like in their respective communities. These farmers wanted to discuss Black food sovereignty, reclaiming Black cultural foods, Black land loss and reclamation, and Black ancestral knowledge of farming and food production. Sunday was set aside as a Black-only space to think through what work needs to be done to holistically rebuild Black communities. For me, these were just the kinds of spaces and conversations that could be part of an emergent strategy in a future food justice movement.

From the vantage point of the BUGS conference participants, I saw approaches to food justice in a completely different light from how it has been framed by many scholars, activists, and those I had been studying in Los Angeles. From the perspectives of these Black growers, the roots of food justice could be traced back to the Black Panther Party, to Ida B. Wells, to recuperating the five hundred years of the knowledge and practices taken from African diasporic people. Their origin stories did not trace food justice as a movement that rose out of environmental justice. That food justice movement, which was what most of the leaders and organizations that I had worked with in Los Angeles traced their work to, was an entirely different one from the lineage that these Black organizers followed. One clear lesson from my research is that knowing the roots of the problem is essential for devising solutions. From the BUGS conference participants I realized that knowing the roots of the solutions matters deeply to how solutions are enacted. If, in asking the question, "What does a just food system look like?" we begin with radical roots, traced back to Black organizers like Ida B. Wells and the Black Panther Party, then the question of how we know we have succeeded or of what a successful intervention looks like is quite different.

In reflecting on what kind of food work he would do in the future, Jamarcus told me:

> We realized in the midst of all of this and we're like, okay now we're growing food, but people don't know what to do with this food anymore. Our cultural traditions have been lost; our food tradition has been lost. . . . When

I grew up, my grandmother had her own garden; we used to grow corn and stuff in my backyard, and I realized as a kid growing up, I realized I was like, Oh, I've always been connected to food in this way because my grandmother, she [had a] lemon and an orange tree, and these really sweet and sour tangerine tasting lemon oranges in the back. Then she bought the avocado tree, and she would just stand there—she would have to water the avocado tree. She picked the avocados, and we go in the house and make avocado salad, right? With vinegar, salt and pepper, and other spices she would add. She would grow bell peppers in the back and then she'd take it out and she'd make stuffed bell peppers for dinner, right? And I would be in the kitchen with her all the time as a kid growing up just watching her cook, and she would chop the pickles for the potato salad and she would pickle her cucumbers under the kitchen sink, right? She would make her own pickles. So I grew up with those food traditions. So when the kids, when we came back to this, it was almost, in some ways it was for me, it felt like a natural fit. I was like, Oh, I know how to grow food, I didn't know how to grow food, but I knew how to grow food. I knew how to experience food in that way.

Following the orientation of Jamarcus to the deep roots of Black community and ancestral knowledge of food production and preparation, along with the varying efforts of the Black growers at the BUGS conference, it is clear that there is an abundance of knowledge and skill about growing and preparing food within these communities. But Jamarcus did not think of his own ancestral connections to food at first; it took him years of working on Rooting Change and collaborating with others in the food justice movement to see the problems with many approaches to food justice. Instead, what he needed was to return to his own roots, community, and ancestral knowledge.

Over time, Jamarcus came to see much of the work that fell under the framework of food justice as part of a broader liberal fantasy. At the same time, he retained hope for the possibility of liberation by turning away from a deficit model of understanding problems facing places like South LA and instead turning inward toward abundance, community, and ancestral visions of self-reliance. After leaving food justice, he sought an elected position in city government. Through the years of listening to and watching Jamarcus make different kinds of moves, I saw that not only was he insistent on his vision of liberation for South Central. He was also incredibly savvy at navigating the local nonprofit and political worlds in the service of that vision. Jamarcus was drawing together radical visions with more centrist or liberal stances, and he had been very effective. He was shifting the "us" and "them" divides between the Westside and South Central, between radical and liberal, and shifting both sides toward a "we" that works together toward a common goal. I started to see Jamarcus's quiet work to bring together everyone who wanted to make South Central a better place as some of the most productive work that I witnessed in food justice. I realized that coming together across these arbitrary lines would be necessary for the social movement to continue and thrive.

When I started this research, both food justice activists and local residents dreamed of a Whole Foods Market in the area, but food justice activists were also convinced that more gardens for growing food would solve food access issues, imagined that converting liquor stores and corner stores into healthy food markets would mean residents would shop for fresh produce within walking distance of their homes, and believed that teaching residents about "healthy eating" would change their behaviors and lower obesity rates. I have seen these ideas and aspirations enacted in different ways by food justice organizations. These interventions have not facilitated the food justice dream of creating equal access to healthy food in South LA. Instead, many food justice activists leveraged their work to move on to other causes, and development and demographic changes have reshaped regional concerns in the area. While these kinds of projects have the effect of undoing justice, other activists remain dedicated to the work, however it is labeled, pivoting and adjusting as community needs shift.

Yet many residents of South Central, like Journee and Ronica, who recognize the ways in which many of these programs work against the radical possibility for justice, are still there, facing multiple struggles and without equal access to healthy food. Some residents were never too concerned about their access to fresh fruits and vegetables, and instead sought affordable, convenient food that is nourishing and fulfilling. And still, some residents will turn toward other paths to reimagine food futures that reckon with the roots of injustice at the foundation of food apartheid and draw on community-based knowledge and needs to devise innovative solutions for collective and collaborative organizing. The process will be long and messy, it will slow down, speed up, and sometimes feel like all progress has been lost, but in looking to other kinds of centuries-long struggles as examples, I believe that grassroots initiatives can, with time, enact radical, liberatory change.

Acknowledgments

I am deeply indebted to the organizations and people that allowed me to study their work. Although I cannot name them here, this project would not have been possible without them. When I first started to conceptualize this project, many people at UCLA inspired and supported the work. There I worked closely with Carole Browner, Linda Garro, C. Jason Throop, Akhil Gupta, and Robin Derby. Advice and inspiration came from Jessica Cattelino, Hannah Appel, Kyeyoung Park, and Jemima Pierre. I thank the late Dr. Leo Estrada, professor of urban planning at the UCLA Luskin School of Public Affairs, who helped pave the way for a lot of this research. Professor Estrada was a pivotal force in understanding why the uprisings of 1992 erupted, unearthing the problems with how policing functioned in LA, and, perhaps most important, he used his skill as a researcher to understand the role of historical and structural factors to help reform policing and other problems in Los Angeles. I drew inspiration from his steadfast dedication to working for slow, impactful social change.

While I was a University of California President's Postdoctoral Fellow in the Department of Anthropology at UC Irvine, my mentor Leo Chavez was the one who convinced me to write this book. While there, I benefited from the support and advice of George Marcus, Keith Murphy, Damien Sojoyner, Valerie Olsen, Belinda Campos, Raul Fernandez, and Kris Peterson. I also learned a lot from a research collaboration and friendship with practicing anthropologist Michael Powell.

During my first faculty appointment at UC San Diego, colleagues in the Department of Anthropology and beyond offered helpful advice on this research and the early stages of writing. I thank Joe Hankins, Dredge Kang, Nancy Postero, Suzanne Brenner, and David Pedersen as well as (then) graduate students Belinda Ramirez, Alicia Wright, and James Crawford.

Under the Woodrow Wilson Career Enhancement Fellowship, I was mentored by Deborah Thomas, who offered indispensable career and life advice. I am immensely grateful for her support and the research and writing time that fellowship afforded.

At Princeton I thank my colleagues in the Department of Anthropology—João Biehl, John Borneman, Elizabeth A. Davis, Julia Elyachar, Agustín Fuentes, Rena Lederman, Ryo Morimoto, Serguei A. Oushakine, Ikaika Ramones, Beth Michelle Semel, Amelia Frank-Vitale, and Jerry C. Zee. The advice of Heather Paxon, Alyshia Gálvez, Karla Slocum, Aisha M. Beliso-De Jesús, and Carolyn M. Rouse during a book workshop was vital. I am grateful for all of the important work of our staff—in particular, Patty Lieb and Joseph Capizzi. Laurence Ralph, who facilitated a book workshop for this manuscript, has read and reread it, offering sage advice that drastically improved the book.

At Princeton, I am deeply appreciative of my food studies colleagues Tessa Desmond, Allison Carruth, Anne Cheng, Andrew Chignell, Jonathan Conway, Shamus Khan, Daniel Rubenstein, and Gina Talt. J. Kēhaulani Kauanui, Ruha Benjamin, Keeanga-Yamahtta Taylor, Matt Desmond, Rachel Price, Reena Goldthree, Filiz Garip, Betsy Levy-Paluk, and Fred Wherry have offered inspiration and priceless advice. I thank Julian Ibarra for proofreading.

My writing group was fundamental in the development of this book. I thank Lee Cabatingan, Mrinalini Tankha, Erin V. Moore, Saiba Varma, and Malavika Reddy for their close readings and comments on many versions of different chapters over the years. I am also grateful to Ashanté Reese, Mara Buchbinder, and Keith Murphy for comments on early drafts. I am very thankful for comments from members of the Nutrire Colab—in particular, Megan Carney, Maggie Dickinson, Alyshia Gálvez, Jessica Hardin, Hiʻilei Hobart, Ariana Ochoa Camacho, Natali Valdez, and Emily Yates-Doerr.

Early in the process my sister, Sara Garth, helped with transcription. My mother-in-law, Phyllis Morrison, offered free childcare, which was essential to carrying out the research and writing. I thank Natasha Gordon-Chipembere for developmental editing and copy editing. At UC Press, I am so grateful to Kate Marshall for seeing the potential in this project and for sticking with it through the ups and downs. I thank Chad Attenborough, Natalie Gomez, and the entire production team for shepherding it through production.

This project was funded by the Woodrow Wilson Foundation, the UC Consortium for Black Studies in California Research Grant, the UCSD Social Sciences Divisional Research Grant, the UCSD Faculty Career Development Program, and the UCSD Black Studies Project Faculty Fellowship.

I have delivered talks on this research at UC Irvine, UCLA, Occidental College, University of South Florida, SUNY Binghamton, City University of New York, The New School, University of Arizona, American Mock World Health Organization (AMWHO), University of Toronto, Northern Illinois University, Toronto International Festival of Authors (TIFA), Rhodes College, Cornell University, the University of Minnesota, Fordham University, and the University of Southern California. This book has benefited tremendously from the questions and comments of the audience members at each of these talks.

I am grateful to my partner, Christel Miller, for giving me some excellent notes and for all of her support, and to my kids who have willingly or not-so-willingly attended many food justice events and spent long stretches of time in Los Angeles in the years since we moved away.

Finally, I thank my parents for their support and the many ways in which they raised me to be able to see the kinds of subtleties of racism and injustice that are foundational to this work. In December 2019, while in the middle of conducting research for this book, I received a call from my sister that my dad had passed away. I miss him every day and am thankful for everything he taught me. This book is dedicated to him.

Notes

1. Julie Guthman has noted that the positive feelings around getting one's hands dirty tend to be associated with whiteness. As a nonwhite person, I experience positive emotions and feelings of calm when working in the garden, my hands directly in the earth. Guthman, "Bringing Good Food to Others."

2. While I did not conceptualize this work as "studying up," I saw the people I was studying as peers and thought of this more as studying *laterally*. Karen Ho's insights (in *Liquidated*, 19) into "studying up" offer some fruitful ways of understanding this kind of ethnographic research. Ho characterizes her work as needing to explore and combine "multiple sites for fieldwork"; she draws upon what Hugh Gusterson ("Studying Up Revisited," 116) has called "polymorphous engagement," which involves "interacting with informants across a number of dispersed sites, not just in local communities, and sometimes in virtual forms; and it means collecting data eclectically from a disparate array of sources in many different ways."

3. On the "anthropology of the good," see Robbins, "Beyond the Suffering Subject,"447–62; Ortner, "Dark Anthropology and Its Others," 47–73. On "horizoning," see Petryna, *Horizon Work*.

4. Ortner, "Dark Anthropology and Its Others," 49.

5. Keane, "Self-Interpretation, Agency, and the Objects of Anthropology," 223.

6. Shange, *Progressive Dystopia*.

7. Thomas, *Political Life in the Wake of the Plantation*, 19.

8. For the complexity of the idea of insider/outsider and Other in anthropology, see Narayan, "How Native Is a 'Native' Anthropologist?," 671–86.

9. Logan, *Scarcity Slot*; Trouillot, "Anthropology and the Savage Slot," 17–44.

10. Much of what is offered in the interludes comes from ethnographic research I carried out with South Central households from 2021 on. That research will form the basis of a future book on food and everyday life in South Central.

INTRODUCTION

1. With the exception of some public events and comments, throughout the book I use pseudonyms and, if necessary, change details about the people and organizations involved to protect their identity, in accordance with standard ethnographic conventions. This research was approved by an institutional review board (IRB). Over the course of this work I was affiliated with three different academic institutions, and there was wide variability in how those institutions interpreted the need for human subjects' protection. Under the first IRB, I was to anonymize the research participants, scrub my data of identifiers, and use pseudonyms in publication. Under the next IRB, participants could request to be anonymized or have their names and the names of their organizations published. During that period many of the people I worked with opted in to having their names shared. I talked and wrote about public figures using their real names during that period. However, under the third IRB, I was required to anonymize and deidentify my data. In all future publications, I anonymized participants.

2. Damien Sojoyner ("Another Life is Possible," 515) has theorized policed schools as "enclosed places" that are part of "the brutal system of punitive containment and curricular evisceration" in urban public schools. Schools can be sites of "multiple forms of violence central to education as enclosed places" and "state-governed projects that attempt to adjudicate normative constructions of difference through liberal tropes of freedom and democratic belonging." Working in a school in the San Francisco Bay area, anthropologist Savannah Shange builds upon Sojoyner to point out that even progressive, liberal charter, and alternative schools can perpetuate similar forms of anti-Blackness. Shange (*Progressive Dystopia*, 15) theorizes the concept of "carceral progressivism" "to illuminate the paradoxical dynamic in which social reform practices, particularly those that target inequities in communities of color, can perpetuate anti-black racism even as they seek to eliminate it."

3. At the time I did not see that by limiting my focus to organizations working on "food justice" in South LA, I was not systematically studying the many organizations doing the work of getting good food to the community—from churches to mosques to women's groups and many others. Those organizations did not label their work as food justice, but they were still part of a much larger group of organizations that support the community. These organizations often saw their work as just serving the needs of the community—which sometimes meant doing cooking workshops and giving away bags of free produce—but it was tied to other kinds of missions and goals. Although these organizations were not the focus of this research, over time I saw what an important role they play in community food security and building community. My subsequent research among South Central households beginning in 2021 has looked at the

role these groups play in the everyday lives of residents, and I plan to include these organizations in a future book about that research.

4. Shange and Liu, "Solidarity-as-Debt."

5. Nathan McClintock and Michael Simpson ("Stacking Functions," 19–39) found six main motivational frames that guide urban ag practice: "entrepreneurial, sustainable development, educational, eco-centric, DIY secessionist, and radical." They link the following motivations together under the category "radical": social justice, food justice, food sovereignty, reclamation of the commons and alternative economy/anti-capitalist exchange. They position "radical approaches" as distinct and distant from "eco-centric" and "entrepreneurial." With respect to the "radical frame," McClintock and Simpson categorize these participants as driven to undermine or move away from the "corporate food regime" and to focus a larger goal of "systematic changes to capitalist and imperialist structures such as property regimes and global markets." They note that this group is concerned about "race-, class-, and gender-based oppression." For McClintock and Simpson "explicit attention to underlying structural inequities lies at the heart of the Radical frame." See McClintock, "Radical, Reformist, and Garden-Variety Neoliberal," 147–71; McMicheal, "Food Regime Genealogy," 139–69; Ramírez, "Elusive Inclusive," 748–69; Sbicca, "Growing Food Justice," 455–66.

6. McClintock and Simpson, "Stacking Functions," 19–39. See also Garth, "Blackness and 'Justice,'" 107–30; Holt-Giménez and Shattuck, "Food Crises, Food Regimes and Food Movements," 109–44. Activist Hank Herrera has critiqued the proliferation of scholarship focused on defining aspects of the food movement as part of an individualized, careerist orientation to this work. See Bradley and Herrera, "Decolonizing Food Justice," 97–114.

7. Heynen, "Bending the Bars of Empire," 406–22.

8. Hassberg, "Nurturing the Revolution," 82–105.

9. While there are other groups that have emphasized healthy eating, like the Black Nationalists, I did not find their ideas to be as prominent as the BPP in the community-based organizations that I worked with.

10. I believe Andrés was referencing geographer Ruthie Wilson Gilmore's definition of racism as death dealing displacement of difference into hierarchies that organize relations within and between the planet's sovereign political territories." Gilmore, "Fatal Couplings of Power and Difference," 15–24.

11. Naa Oyo Kwate ("Fried Chicken and Fresh Apples," 32–44) argues that "race-based residential segregation is a fundamental cause of fast-food density in Black neighborhoods," showing the historical and ongoing conditions of segregation that give rise to the conditions that "increase the likelihood that Black neighborhoods in urban environments will bear a disproportionate burden of fast-food restaurants." My research reveals similar patterns of logic that Kwate is trying to write against.

12. Washington and Penniman, "You Belong to the Land." See also Brones, "Karen Washington."

13. Curtis, Ferguson, and Gupta, "Anthropologies of Development and Non-Governmental Organizations."

14. As anthropologist and political scholar Mahmood Mamdani (*When Victims Become Killers*) reminds us, the language of liberation was central

to the Hutu justifications for killing and raping Tutsi people in the Rwandan genocide.

15. The organizations involved in this research were all developing or involved in programming that intervened in South LA. Part of the inclusion criteria for the research was that the organizations had to have at least one project that intervened in South LA. Many also had projects in East LA, which were included in the research. Some people include the Watts area within the bounds of South LA, and a smaller proportion include the City of Vernon, Huntington Park, South Gate, Lynwood, and Compton. For my research I consider these to be adjacent areas.

16. Complete population profiles on South LA are somewhat difficult to find as population is often broken down by district or the smaller neighborhoods that make up the broader South LA area. According to the *Los Angeles Times*'s Mapping LA project, which defines LA spatially in a very similar way to how I have defined it here, in 2000 the population of South LA was 749,453, and according to Point2Point, a real estate site, in 2020 the population was 818,043 people. Other sources estimate the population to be closer to between 150,000 and 300,0000. No matter how the lines are drawn, South LA includes portions of CD 8, CD 9, CD 14 and CD 15, all of which are categorized as having very high or high-low census response and thus categorized as a "hard-to-count population." See *Los Angeles Times*, "South L.A."; LA Census 2020, "Low Response Area Report."

17. The Los Angeles–Long Beach statistical area and the Los Angeles–Anaheim–Riverside statistical area are two other ways that people bound the broader metro area; see US Census Bureau, "Census Urban Land Area List."

18. Lipsitz, *Progressive Investment in Whiteness*, 251. As Darnell Hunt has noted, Los Angeles in general is only vaguely imagined as a Black place; his work seeks to "situate black-identified places" like Baldwin Hills (in his case) and South LA (in my case), "within the context of a much broader space" thought of as Black Los Angeles. Hunt and Ramón, *Black Los Angeles*; see also Hunt, "American Toxicity," ix–xviii.

19. For a personal account of what life was like in South Central during the 1980s and 1990s, see Benjamin, *Viral Justice*.

20. Other media portrayals include *Blackish*, *Grownish*, *Insecure*, and *All American*. For instance, Hunt and Ramón (*Black Los Angeles*) write of BET's *Baldwin Hills*, viewed in one million Black homes across the United States, as attempting to create a counternarrative to "a more dominant narrative that placed black people in the ghetto, their children at constant risk of being swept up by drug and gang culture, and their dreams for a 'better tomorrow' permanently on hold." Hunt and Ramón underscore that even this show on a "black-oriented cable network" was designed to cater to "white sensibilities," playing on tropes and erasing the real history of places like Baldwin Hills. The show features the upper-middle-class Black neighborhood in Southwest Los Angeles, which borders South Los Angeles. However, Hunt and Ramón point out that the area just adjacent to Baldwin Hills, called Baldwin Village formally, is informally known to locals as "The Jungle" and was featured in the film *Training Day* starring Denzel Washington.

21. In addition, because of the age of the film, these references positioned the food justice practitioners within the generation sometimes referred to as X-enniels, those just on the cusp of Generation X and Millennials. My research supports Ruth Wilson Gilmore's finding ("In the shadow," 44–47) that among social justice activists in Black communities, both donors and recipients "acted on assumptions about each other and about the possibility for social change, which regardless of intent, reinforced the very structures groups had self-organized to dismantle."

22. *Los Angeles Times*, "South L.A." This demographic shift from a majority Black area to an increasingly Latinx area is common across California. Some reports show even lower numbers of Black residents. See Kun and Pulido, *Black and Brown in Los Angeles*; Pulido, *Black, Brown, Yellow, and Left*; Zamora, *Racial Baggage*.

23. SCOPE, "New Economy for South Los Angeles—SCOPE."

24. *Los Angeles Times*, "South L.A."

25. See Desmond, *Evicted*; Desmond, *Poverty, by America*.

26. Azuma et al., "Food Access, Availability, and Affordability."

27. The Los Angeles Food Policy Council estimated that there were ninety-one grocery stores in South LA, but they did not delineate the specific area they were referencing. The City of Compton drew the lines of South LA somewhat differently from how I have outlined above, including portions of Huntington Park, South Gate, Lynwood, and Compton to the south and east. Therefore, their population estimate for South LA is 1.3 million. Assuming people shop where they live, those sixty stores serve 1.3 million residents. Thus each store in South LA serves approximately 22,000 people. LAFPC, *Good Food Zone*.

28. Compton Chamber of Commerce, "Target Region."

29. Bassford, Galloway-Gilliam, and Flynn, *Food Desert to Food Oasis*.

30. Compton Chamber of Commerce, "Target Region."

31. On cross-cultural trends that push vegetable consumption as the best approach to healthy eating, see Trapp, "Performing Vegetable Nutrition," 120–31; Hardin, "Life before Vegetables," 428–57; Garth, "Food, Taste, and the Body," 5–22.

32. Coulombe, *Becoming Trader Joes*.

33. Vallianatos, "Food Justice and Food Retail in Los Angeles," 186–94.

34. Reese, *Black Food Geographies*, 3. Katherine McKittrick ("On Plantations," 947, 951) reflects on Black geographies as "not solely inhabited by black bodies, [that] are classified as imperiled and dangerous, or spaces 'without'/ spaces of exclusion, even as those who have always struggled against racial violence and containment populate them."

35. Kwate et al., "Retail Redlining in New York City," 632–52. In 1948 a Supreme Court decision challenged the legality of racially restrictive covenants. However, in practice race-based restrictions of ownership were still included in deeds across the United States after this date. As Darnell Hunt (in Hunt and Ramón, *Black Los Angeles*) notes, the original 1953 deed for the home he would later purchase in Baldwin Hills included the following:

> 1. No part of any said realty shall ever be sold, conveyed, leased, or rented to any person not of the white or Caucasian race.

2. No part of any said realty shall ever at any time be used or occupied or be permitted to be used or occupied by any person not of the white or Caucasian race, expect such as are in the employ of the resident owner or resident tenants of said property.

36. Garth and Reese, *Black Food Matters*; Reese, *Black Food Geographies*, 9.

37. Twitty, *Cooking Gene*, 6.

38. Here I disagree with Pollan and instead believe that culture or various cultural influences continue to shape how we eat, whether we eat a salad from vegetables grown in our own garden, tacos from a food truck, a McDonald's Happy Meal, or a Snickers chocolate bar. Pollan's understanding of culture appears to be linked to an idealized understanding that the way humans ate in the past is how people today should be eating—this is a misguided interpretation of culture and the ways that human culture continues to shift and influence food consumption in new and different ways.

39. The literature I read during this period included Bower, *African American Foodways*; Carney, *Black Rice*; Harris, *Beyond Gumbo*; Opie, *Hog and Hominy*; Rodriguez, "Invoking Fannie Lou Hamer," 231–51; Smart-Grosvenor, *Vibration Cooking*; Williams-Forson, *Building Houses out of Chicken Legs*.

40. Poppendieck, *Breadlines Knee Deep in Wheat*; Poppendieck, *Sweet Charity?*.

41. Poppendieck, *Sweet Charity?*; De Souza, *Feeding the Other*; Dickinson, *Feeding the Crisis*.

42. At the time of writing, SNAP was administered by the United States Department of Agriculture, and benefits were distributed to specific programs in each state. Dickinson, *Feeding the Crisis*.

43. Dickinson, *Feeding the Crisis*.

44. Julier, "Political Economy of Obesity," 462–79; Greenhalgh, "Weighty Subjects," 471–87.

45. Julier, "Political Economy of Obesity"; Greenhalgh, "Weighty Subjects."

46. In 2008 a ban on opening new fast-food restaurants was implemented in South Los Angeles as a way to combat obesity, which was rising at disproportionately high rates.

47. In 2015 the nonprofit research think tank RAND released a report showing that after the 2008 fast-food ban there was not a decline in obesity rates but rather that both fast-food consumption and rates of overweight and obesity increased. In 2007 an estimated 63 percent of South LA's seven hundred thousand residents were overweight or obese, and by 2011 this figure had increased to 75 percent. In addition, I found that in general South Central residents were angry about the ban and felt that they were being treated unfairly as other parts of the city continued to have newly built fast-food establishments. Sturm and Hattori, "Diet and Obesity in Los Angeles County," 205–11.

48. White House Archive, "Obama Administration Details Healthy Food Financing Initiative."

49. These food desert imaginaries are written into many of the documents used by food justice organizations. See Robbins, "From Food Deserts to Food Oases"; McLaughlin, "This Millennial Is Eliminating Food Deserts."

50. As Andrés suggested in his talk (quoted at the outset of this chapter), landscape metaphors can problematically lead people to see these as natural states rather than results of structural processes. Others have conceived of the problem with variations on landscape metaphors, including the "food swamp," as an area inundated with fast food and other unhealthy food retail, or the "food mirage," where the dispersal of healthy food was uneven and found in surprising places like small corner stores or independently owned markets. Short, Guthman, and Raskin, "Food Deserts, Oases or Mirages?," 352–64; Cooksey-Stowers, Schwartz, and Brownell, "Food Swamps Predict Obesity Rates," 1366.

51. Gottlieb and Joshi, *Food Justice*, 6.

52. Allen, *Together at the Table*; Guthman, "Fast Food/Organic Food," 43–56; Hinrichs, "Practice and Politics of Food System Localization," 33–45; Guthman, Morris, and Allen, "Squaring Farm Security and Food Security," 662–84; Guthman, "'If They Only Knew,'" 387–89; Allen and Guthman, "From 'old school' to 'farm-to-school,'" 401–15; Slocum, "Anti-racist Practice and the Work of Community Food Organizations," 327–49; Slocum, "Whiteness, Space, and Alternative Food Practice," 520–33.

53. Slocum as referenced in Guthman, "Bringing Good Food to Others," 434. See also Guthman, foreword, xv; Guthman, "'If They Only Knew,'" 387–89; Slocum, "Anti-racist Practice and the Work of Community Food Organizations," 327–49; Slocum, "Whiteness, Space, and Alternative Food Practice," 520–33; Slocum, "Thinking Race Through Corporeal Feminist Theory," 849–69; Slocum and Saldanha, *Geographies of Race and Food*.

54. For a related discussion of anthropology and white supremacy, see Beliso-De Jesús, Pierre, and Rana, *Anthropology of White Supremacy*.

55. Black, "Abolitionist Food Justice," 1.

56. Shange, *Progressive Dystopia*, 24; Povinelli, *Cunning of Recognition*.

57. Povinelli, *Cunning of Recognition*.

58. Povinelli, "Radical Worlds," 326.

59. The conditions of food access inequality can be understood as what Elizabeth A. Povinelli (*Economies of Abandonment*) calls "cruddy" quasi-events that are not quite a crisis. This is how most residents that I have spoken with understood things, especially in relation to other problems in their everyday lives that seem much more urgent. However, tethering food access inequality to obesity allows for food justice activists to make the problem into a crisis that impacts us all. When speaking with residents, obesity is rarely mentioned in relation to food access; in fact, many residents worry instead about malnutrition and not having enough food.

60. McKittrick, *Dear Science and Other Stories*, 41; Davies, *Left of Karl Marx*.

61. Guthman, *Problem with Solutions*.

62. Povinelli, "Radical Worlds," 319–34, 326.

63. Trouillot, "Anthropology of the State in the Age of Globalization," 125–38.

64. Didier Fassin (*Humanitarian Reason*, 3) has asked similar questions in his analysis of humanitarian reason at global scales. Ruha Benjamin (*Viral Justice*) asks similar questions at the scale of South Central Los Angeles.

CHAPTER 1. HISTORY

1. This location would become a Superior Grocers, after they bought out Numero Uno Market in 2022. Superior is one of the largest independently owned grocery store chains in Southern California. *Shelby Report*, "Big Deal In SoCal."

2. Chadburn, "Destructive Force of Rebuild LA."

3. Park, *LA Rising*.

4. Allison, dir., *A Love Song for Latasha*.

5. Davis, *City of Quartz*, 18.

6. See Robinson, *Black Marxism*; Garth, "Violence of Racial Capitalism," 649–50.

7. Lloyd, "Brief History of LA's Indigenous Tongva People."

8. The Tongva people utilized a path along the Sepulveda Canyon to enter the area that is now Los Angeles, and their footpath is said to be the original route that expanded into the 405 freeway. See Masters, "How Sepulveda Canyon Became the 405."

9. Torres-Rouff, *Before L.A.*

10. Robinson, "Race, Space, and the Evolution of Black Los Angeles," 19–59; Kun and Pulido, *Black and Brown in Los Angeles*.

11. Kun and Pulido, *Black and Brown in Los Angeles*.

12. Davis, *City of Quartz*, 25.

13. Davis, *City of Quartz*, 25.

14. Molina, *Fit To Be Citizens*.

15. Davis, *City of Quartz*, 25.

16. In the early years, people of Chinese, Mexican, and Japanese descent were scapegoated as threats to the character and health of the city; see Molina, *Fit To Be Citizens*. These forms of racialization and health were also found in the Bay Area; see Shah, *Contagious Divides*.

17. Molina focuses on anti-Chinese and anti-Mexican rhetoric as it was connected to concepts of health and modernity in early Los Angeles. She notes that 1879 Chinatown was labeled "a rotten spot," a way of demarcating both the area and the people within it as "antithetical to the 'legitimate' residents of Los Angeles, namely, white Americans, many of whom themselves were recent transplants." See Molina, *Fit To Be Citizens*, 12.

18. Molina, *Fit To Be Citizens*, 12.

19. Molina, *Fit To Be Citizens*, 12. Race-based discrimination was also extended to Chinese launderers in the late 1880s, who were ousted from Pasadena after a white mob threatened to lynch them and other Chinese residents. Hormann, "'No Chinese Employed' in Early Pasadena."

20. Stephens and Pastor, "What's Going On?" 1–32.

21. Wilkerson, *Warmth of Other Suns*.

22. By 1930 there were 46,425 Black people in LA County (2.2 million total population); see Robinson, "Race, Space, and the Evolution of Black Los Angeles."

23. Stephens and Pastor, "What's Going On?" 1–32.

24. Sides, *LA City Limits*.

25. Sojoyner, *First Strike*.

26. The post-Moynihan logics that Black urban areas were "underdeveloped" because of flaws in Black family structure or individual behavior are part of a narrative fiction. See Moynihan, *Negro Family*.

27. Rosas, *South Central Is Home*.

28. Rosas, *South Central Is Home*.

29. Hondagneu-Sotelo and Thompson-Hernandez, "Latino Identity in South Los Angeles"; Vargas, *Catching Hell in the City of Angels*.

30. Stephens and Pastor, "What's Going On?"

31. Taylor, *From #BlackLives Matter to Black Liberation*; Vargas, "*Los Angeles Times*' Coverage of the 1992 Rebellion."

32. Vargas, "*Los Angeles Times*' Coverage of the 1992 Rebellion," 39.

33. Hubler, "*Los Angeles Times* Rebuilding the Community."

34. Kolb, *Retail Inequality*.

35. For a more nuanced take on leveraged buyouts and shareholder benefits, see Ho, *Liquidated*.

36. Cotterill, "Food Retailing."

37. Stark and Kennedy, *Vons Grocery Company*.

38. Coulombe, *Becoming Trader Joe*.

39. Coulombe, *Becoming Trader Joe*.

40. The original company was called Frontier Foods. Song founded it with James Oh and her sister Marie. In 2022, Song was inducted into the Food Industry Hall of Fame. *Shelby Report*, "CEO Song Honored."

41. Nogales as quoted in *LA Business Journal*, "Numero Uno Markets Sold."

42. Silverstein and Brooks, "Shoppers in Need of Stores."

43. Cho, "Korean Americans vs. African Americans," 196–214.

44. Ong and Hee, "Los Angeles Riots/Rebellion and Korean Merchants."

45. Ong and Hee, "Los Angeles Riots/Rebellion and Korean Merchants."

46. In addition to the predominantly Korean-owned smaller stores, The Boys Supermarkets and affiliated Food 4 Less, Viva, and ABC supermarkets continued to operate in South LA. Although The Boys store group was praised for operating in South LA when others would not, they were also accused of excessive price gouging, sometimes up to twenty times that of other stores. Regional chains such as Luckys, Alpha Beta, and Ralphs did not have a single store in South LA by the early 1990s. In addition to these larger stores, the area had many smaller, independently owned markets. These smaller stores were reputed to have higher prices and lower-quality products since they did not have the purchasing power to buy in bulk and did not turn over items as quickly as larger stores. Silverstein and Brooks, "Shoppers in Need of Stores"; Chang, "Los Angeles Riots," 10–11; Yu, *Black-Korean Encounter*.

47. "El Super."

48. Vargas, *Catching Hell in the City of Angels*. Vargas notes that due to the city's proximity to drug cartels, LA area gangs are heavily involved in the drug and weapons trade. I presume Vargas is referring to cartels located south of the US border in Mexico and Central America. This is not a matter of drugs and violence simply coming from Mexico and Central American into the United States. It is instead a complex system where groups south of the border are

responding to increasing demand for illicit drugs in the United States. More weapons are smuggled out of the United States into Mexico and Central American than are smuggled in. For more on this, see Jusionyte, *Exit Wounds*.

49. Los Angeles ABC7 report as cited in Stallworth and Manthey, "Homicides in Los Angeles Reach Highest Level."

50. CDC, "Firearm Mortality by State."

51. Fieldstat, "Murder Map: Deadliest U.S. Cities."

52. In 2021, however, Los Angeles recorded the most homicides they have had in the city since 2006.

53. Wikipedia, "Crime in Los Angeles."

54. Horne, *Fire This Time*.

55. Vargas, "*Los Angeles Times*' Coverage of the 1992 Rebellion."

56. Taylor, *From #BlackLivesMatter to Black Liberation*.

57. Taylor, *From #BlackLivesMatter to Black Liberation*, 39.

58. Kaba, *We Do This 'Til We Free Us*.

59. Das Purkayastha, "Feeding the Inner City."

60. Miranda, "Of the 63 People Killed During '92 Riots."

61. Fritsch, "Los Angeles Police Differ Sharply."

62. Matheson and Baade, "Race and Riots."

63. Lazzareschi and Stewart ("Riot Job-Loss Figure Is Halved") found that approximately twenty thousand jobs were lost because of the uprisings.

64. Hunt, "American Toxicity," xi, xvii.

65. Tsing, *Mushroom at the End of the World*, 2.

66. White, "Riot Impact Worse Than Predicated."

67. White, "Riot Impact Worse Than Predicated."

68. White, "Riot Impact Worse Than Predicated."

69. Rivera, "Food Crisis a Measure of Suffering." Despite massive loss, some grocery chains like Food 4 Less pledged to keep "more than 1,000 workers at its closed stores on the payroll with the help of a new agreement with the grocery workers' Union." During this time Food 4 Less did not pay into the employee health-care fund, and it used that savings to pay the salaries while employees still had full health-care coverage. The backing of the United Food and Commercial Workers was essential for brokering this deal. See Lazzareschi and Stewart, "Riot Job-Loss Figure Is Halved."

70. Desmond and Emirbayer, *Race in America*.

71. After the uprising, the LA area gangs Crips and Bloods came up with a "Plan for the Reconstruction of Los Angeles." The gangs came to the table with a set of demands. First, they asked that every burned and abandoned structure would be gutted, that the city would purchase the property and build community centers, counseling centers, or recreational areas. They demanded that the Department of Transportation repave sidewalks and create pedestrian walkways, noting that they would point out areas especially in need of pedestrian protection. The organizations asked for increased lighting in all neighborhoods, including alley lights installed by homeowners. They asked that area trees be trimmed and maintained, and new trees planted to "increase the beauty of our neighborhoods." They requested that vacant lots be cleaned up, that pest control was implemented in the area, and that the city should help facilitate neigh-

borhood cleanups where residents are responsible for maintaining their own blocks. These demands represented a strong stance from the people about what was needed to improve the area, and clear requests for assistance from local government. The organizations made specific requests about education, human welfare, law enforcement, and economic development. The demands of the Bloods and Crips were nothing like the projects implemented by RLA. "Crips' and Bloods' Plan for Reconstruction of Los Angeles," GangResearch.

72. Oh, "Rebuilding Los Angeles"; Zilberg, "Troubled Corner."

73. Chadburn, "Destructive Force of Rebuild LA."

74. Chadburn, "Destructive Force of Rebuild LA."

75. Brooks and Weinstein, "19 of 68 Firms Question Listing by Rebuild L.A."

76. Chadburn, "Destructive Force of Rebuild LA."

77. Zilberg, "Troubled Corner." In addition, the RLA board was accusing of bloating the salaries of RLA leadership and staff, while underpaying and maintaining poor working conditions for their subcontractors—e.g., "the Justice for Janitors campaign put Rebuild LA on their 'Top Trash List' for refusing to sign a workers' bill of rights." See Chadburn, "Destructive Force of Rebuild LA."

78. The LACCD received RLA's cash assets, computer hardware and software, and all its active records. LACCD planned to link industries with classroom programs through its Community Development Technologies Center. The new agency called itself LA Public Resource and Occupational Support Program for Economic Revitalization, or LA PROSPER Partners. The remainder of RLA's records was transferred to Loyola Marymount University's Center for the Study of Los Angeles Research Collection.

79. Chadburn, "Destructive Force of Rebuild LA."

80. My research reveals that most food justice activists do not know the story of RLA.

81. We were not able to systematically categorize and document these stores, which are difficult to locate GIS as they are often mislabeled or do not appear.

82. Although food justice activists and planners may not see these stores as suitable for purchasing food, many residents prefer to shop at dollar stores because of the low prices. Further exacerbating food access issues in April 2024, the 99 Cents Only store announced that it would close all 371 stores effective immediately. Chang and Darmiento, "99 Cents Only to Close All 371 Stores."

83. Molina (*Fit To Be Citizens*) argues that from its very inception the role of the health department in regulation food retail has been an institutionalized racial practice.

84. Many of these experiences of racism are not overt and difficult to identify and explain. However, clear indications of racist sentiment frequently come to light. The 2022 racist comments by Los Angeles City Council president Nury Martinez are one such example. See Reuters, "Los Angeles Council President Steps Down."

85. Democracy Now, "Police Forcibly Shut Down South Central L.A. Urban Farm."

86. Chang, "Antidevelopment Protesters Are Arrested."

87. The pink slime clip eventually went viral and became ubiquitous when referencing cheap chicken nuggets or chicken fingers. It was so impactful that McDonald's changed its formula for chicken nuggets in 2016, removing many of the forty artificial ingredients that the old recipe contained. Changes to the McNugget included "frying oil that does not contain the preservative tert-Butylhydroquinone" and removing sodium phosphates. See Rahoumi, "McDonalds Is Changing Its Chicken McNugget Recipe"; Calderone, "McDonalds To Serve Chicken."

88. Broad, *More Than Just Food*.

89. White House Archive, "Obama Administration Details Healthy Food Financing Initiative."

90. Wright, "Interactive Web Tools Maps Food Deserts." The funding to create the USDA Food Desert Locator was part of the Obama administration's $400 million Healthy Food Financing Initiative, which aimed to "bring grocery stores and other healthy food retailers to underserved urban and rural communities across America." White House Archive, "Obama Administration Details Healthy Food Financing Initiative."

91. Wright, "Interactive Web Tools Maps Food Deserts."

92. Barnes et al., "Do People Really Know What Food Retailers Exist?"; Bridle-Fitzpatrick, "Food Deserts or Food Swamps?," 142; Caspi et al., "Local Food Environment and Diet"; Donkin et al., "Mapping Access to Food at a Local Level"; Kelly, Flood, and Yeatman, "Measuring Local Food Environments"; Wilkins et al., "Using Geographic Information Systems."

93. Kolb, *Retail Inequality*.

94. US Census Bureau, "American Community Survey."

95. Lipsitz, *Progressive Investment*, vii.

96. Ferguson, *Anti-politics Machine*, 56.

97. In Greenville, South Carolina, Kolb (*Retail Inequality*) found that although residents wanted better food retail and access to the same kind of foods as people living in more affluent parts of the city had, in reality food costs were most important to them.

98. Molina, *Fit To Be Citizens?*, 179; see also Douglas, *Purity and Danger*.

99. Slocum et al., "Properly, with Love, from Scratch," 187.

100. I have heard this in reference to Black vegans and vegetarians as well as stereotyped all-natural hippies who prefer organic, locally grown food.

CHAPTER 2. JUSTICE

1. The LAFPC has been central to the Los Angeles food justice movement. Initially established in 1992 after the rebellion, the organization was reinvigorated when former Los Angeles mayor Antonio Villaraigosa announced the creation of the LAFPC Task Force in September 2009 as part of the thirtieth anniversary celebration of the first official farmers market in Los Angeles County. The task force convened in November 2009 and was charged with developing a Good Food policy agenda for Los Angeles, with the goal of ensuring that the local food system was healthy, affordable, fair, and sustainable. The early phase involved intense research on the Food Policy Council model as it had been used

in other cities, including Toronto, New York, San Francisco, and Detroit. It was coupled with ten months of meetings and listening sessions with stakeholders in Los Angeles, through approximately July 2010. The task force brought together stakeholders from across the spectrum of LA, including from the City Council, LA County, the Department of Public Health, the Farm Bureau, local corporations, and nonprofits. The twenty people on the task force came from city, county, and state-based organizations; food, agriculture, and health-related nonprofits; as well as educational institutions from all over the region. The LAFPC became a formalized independent nonprofit in 2011 and was only loosely connected with the Office of Los Angeles Mayor Eric Garcetti until 2015. According to Clare Fox, the executive director of the LAFPC until 2019, "a food policy council is a body that brings together stakeholders and leaders from across the entire food system, from farm to fork and beyond so that we are talking across sectors and silos and through that process coming up with holistic policy and systems solutions." See Fox, "Food Policy Councils," 12.

2. Mayor Garcetti located himself as a resident of LA, neglecting to mention that he lives in Ryu's district because that is where the Getty House is, a 6,000-square-foot house with a 22,000-square-foot lot that has been used as the LA mayor's residence since 1977.

3. On the "lower-middle class" category, see Jefferson, "'Not What It Used To Be,'" 310–25.

4. In March 1892 a series of racist events surrounding the People's Grocery in Memphis, Tennessee, culminated in the lynchings of the store's Black owner, Thomas Moss, and two Black store employees, Calvin McDowell and Will Stewart. Moss was said to be an upstanding member of the Black community. "A family man, he delivered mail by day and ran the People's Grocery by night," offering a much-needed service to his community. The People's Grocery was successful; it was a community gathering place and a source of pride for the Black community. Moss and his employees were lynched because the success of People's Grocery was a threat to the area's white businesses—and in particular to a store owned by a white grocer named William Barrett. These lynchings are remembered not only for the commonplace forms of white violence against successful Black people, but also for inspiring the work of anti-lynching activist, teacher, and journalist Ida B. Wells. The lynching of a Black grocer is one clear reminder that the US food system has long been racialized and anti-Black. While it is often easier to see racism and anti-Blackness in the food systems of the past, forms of racialization continue to impact the disparities in the food system today. Barnes, "She Was a Twin," 49–60. See also Garth and Reese, *Black Food Matters*.

5. De Souza, *Feeding the Other*.

6. Borneman, *Settling Accounts*, vii–viii.

7. At the height of the food justice movement, bus tours had become a way for outsiders to be introduced to both the poor conditions of food access in the area and the programs that had been established to improve them. I participated in several such tours, and this was much like the ones I had already experienced. One example of a funder's bus tour has been written up in Lui, "Transforming Food Deserts."

8. Using the term "articulate" in reference to Black people is often racially loaded. In 2007 then Senator Joseph Biden referred to then Senator Barack Obama as "the first sort of mainstream African American [presidential candidate], who is articulate and bright and clean and a nice-looking guy." The use of the terms "clean," "bright," and "articulate" are positioned as surprising, distinct, and exceptional for a Black person. This implies that most Black people are *not* those things, which negatively racializes Black people in opposition to these positive attributes. See *New York Observer*, "Biden Tapes"; Clemetson, "Racial Politics of Speaking Well"; Alim and Smitherman, *Articulate while Black*.

9. While this particular set of meetings was not explicitly billed as doing food "justice" work, emails and fliers about the gathering used the language of "fairness," "fair food access," and "equitable food systems," and during the meetings the word "justice" was often used interchangeably with "fairness." Thus a "justice" approach was implied. In the small group breakouts there was a wide range of competing discourses and opinions about the best way forward. In my analysis the ways stakeholders framed their concerns were around their own relationships to the community, usually linked to the "us" versus "them" logics discussed throughout this chapter. Stakeholders also had different understandings of what the problems were, competing approaches to tackling the problem, and a wide variety of different forms of expertise coming to the table with each person operating from their own deeply entrenched positions.

10. In the early twentieth century the concept of social justice was closely tied to dignity and the right of citizens to be treated ethically. Social justice increasingly became about the equal application of the law and political rights under the law. The concept of social justice remained tied to the Latin concept of "dignitas," literally meaning "worthiness"—that is, those who are worthy or virtuous are deserving of equality under the law. Although people can often recite this definition and will say it is about equal distribution of both benefits and burdens, in practice their articulations and actions around "justice" neglect the idea of the equal distribution of burdens, and instead focus on "helping" Others. This desire is linked to this understanding of justice. Indeed, Plato's conceptualization of justice was about "order" and "duty." It was about "harmonious strength" and the moral obligation to be a "good person" but also to account for the harmony of society as a whole. "Helping Others" could easily be understood as a necessary part of being a "good person." However, like the definition above, Socrates's conceptualization of justice was linked to the notion of the "social contract"—an idea later taken up by John Locke—and the understanding that those who accept the benefits of society must also accept responsibility for the burdens of society. Although "social justice" often went undefined by the people using the concept in the food justice movement, in my research there was a general understanding that "social justice" refers to the equal distribution of the burdens and benefits of society. Here Rawls's understanding (in *Theory of Justice*) that a society founded on justice cannot take away rights, privileges, and benefits from one group to share with another group is in direct contradiction to how many people in the food movement understand food justice as sharing the "benefits and burdens" of the food system. Instead, by drawing on Rawls's def-

inition of "fairness," there is a general understanding that the people working in the food movement can share the benefits of the food system without necessarily taking on the burdens. In some ways this logic is akin to the "separate but equal" approach of Jim Crow America.

11. Rawls's specific understanding of justice and the notion that "justice denies that the loss of freedom for some is made right by a greater good shared by others" allows for an interpretation of social justice where no one loses any benefits of society or takes on burdens, but greater good can still be achieved. See Rawls, *Theory of Justice*, 3.

12. Rawls, *Theory of Justice*, 3–4; Rawls's stance is in opposition to utilitarianism. His arguments are based on the imaginary conditions of the "original position" (Rawls used this as opposed to the "state of nature" used by Hobbes). The "original position" assumes that individuals make choices about society from behind a "veil of ignorance" where they do not know their social status, ethnicity, race, gender, or what their idea of how to lead a good life might be. Here the "veil of ignorance" and the "original position" are supposed to simulate an impartial condition. While these simulations allowed Rawls to overcome some of the flaws of the "state of nature" in philosophy, a central problem is that all his social theory was based on these ideal conditions when in reality we are increasingly aware that we cannot completely remove our biases, prejudices, or put ourselves in the shoes of the other, relinquishing our knowledge of our own social position and characteristics. Those involved in the food justice movement attempt to do something akin to the "original position," as they imagine that they are in a neutral position and go about envisioning the ideal conditions for a good life for people in places like South LA.

13. Shange, *Progressive Dystopia*.

14. Laclau, *Emancipation(s)*; see also Austin, "Plea for Excuses," 1–30.

15. Harvey, *Brief History of Neoliberalism*, 6.

16. Harvey, *Brief History of Neoliberalism*.

17. McChesney, introduction.

18. Frey et al. observe that "social justice is not done when 'we' in our largess donate some of our disposable resources to 'them,' it is done when we act on our recognition that something is amiss in a society of abundance if some of us are well off while others are destitute" (Frey et al., "Looking for Justice in All the Wrong Places," 36–37, as cited in De Souza, *Feeding the Other*, 111). Ironically, many people in the food justice movement eschew charity, as "reinforc[ing] social distance and hierarchy between givers and receivers, us and them" (Frey et al., "Looking for Justice in All the Wrong Places," 35).

19. Alkon and Agyeman, *Cultivating Food Justice*.

20. De Souza, *Feeding the Other*, 44.

CHAPTER 3. WHITENESS

1. Garth, "Blackness and 'Justice.'"

2. Garth, "Blackness and 'Justice,'" 108.

3. See, for instance, the works of Psyche Williams-Forson (*Building Houses out of Chicken Legs*; "Other Women Cooked for My Husband"; *Eating while*

Black), Rafia Zafar (*Recipes for Respect*), Tony Whitehead ("In Search of Soul Food and Meaning"), Jennifer Jensen Wallach (*Dethroning the Deceitful Pork Chop*; *Getting What We Need Ourselves*), Michael Twitty (*Cooking Gene*), Toni Tipton-Martin (*Jemima Code*), Vertamae Smart-Grosvenor (*Vibration Cooking*), Ashanté Reese ("We Will Not Perish"; *Black Food Geographies*), Kimberly Nettles-Barcelón ("California Soul"), Frederick Opie (*Hog and Hominy*), Adrian Miller (*Soul Food*), Edna Lewis (*Taste of Country Cooking*), and Jessica B. Harris (*Beyond Gumbo*; *High on the Hog*). In addition to these texts, television series like *Delicious Miss Brown*, *New Soul Kitchen*, Netflix's *Street Food* series season three, which focused on the United States and starred several Black cooks, and more recently Stephan Satterfield's *High on the Hog: How African American Cuisine Transformed America*, all feature the love and history that goes into cooking Black cultural dishes and cuisines.

4. Laclau, *Emancipation(s)*.

5. In addition, as sociologist Sabrina Strings (*Fearing the Black Body*) has documented, historical links between fatphobia and anti-Black racism persist in contemporary US idealizations of body type. Strings notes that in the late-nineteenth-century United States, while slender figures were praised, "round-ness" was acceptable. However, fatness was thought of as "menacing" and "gross." During this time slender figures came to be associated with moral goodness and the habits of European elites, while corpulence was associated with Black "savages." During the time that fatness came to be negatively associated with Blackness, it also took on an association with sinfulness.

6. Strings, *Fearing the Black Body*, 87. Like the ways in which food justice practitioners operate within the food desert imaginary as they develop and implement interventions, anthropologist Arturo Escobar (*Encountering Development*) has pointed out how development operates as a discourse in which "certain representations become dominant and shape indelibly the ways in which reality is imagined and acted upon." Similarly, in her work in Sierra Leone, Adia Benton (*HIV Exceptionalism*) has found that "the persistent cultural significance of AIDS in the global imagination" has continued to influence the work of development organizations and local practitioners even though there has been a sustained decrease in prevalence rates and there is no "obvious link between HIV/AIDS and conflict."

7. Trechter and Bucholtz, "White Noise," 5.

8. Frankenberg, "Mirage of Unmarked Whiteness."

9. For many activists this form of whiteness as part of their work ethos is like what Karen Brodkin ("Comments on Discourses of Whiteness," 147) observed among union activists in Los Angeles where there was an "ambivalence about the costs and benefits of what they embrace and what they devalue" as part of the system of whiteness.

10. Sociologist Ruth Frankenberg (*White Women, Race Matters*) defined whiteness as (1) a location of structural advantage, of race privilege; (2) a standpoint or place from which white people look at (them)selves, at others, and at society; and (3) a set of cultural practices that are usually unmarked and unnamed. Frankenberg saw whiteness as a structural position. Anthropologist Karen Brodkin (*How Jews Became White Folks*, 148) understands whiteness as

"white folks' unacknowledged participation in the reproduction of their structured social privileges." See also Beliso-De Jesús, Pierre, and Rana, *Anthropology of White Supremacy*.

11. Lipsitz, *Progressive Investment in Whiteness*.

12. This research largely took place prior to Trump's first presidency and therefore before a period when overt contemporary racists in the United States were incited to voice their positions. The forms of overt racism linked to the US right under Trump are things that most of the people in this study would stand against; they are not overt racists.

13. Anthropologist John Jackson (*Racial Paranoia*) has categorized the many phases of how Americans talk about and understand racism as "de jure," "de facto," and "de cardio." De jure racism was the era when racism was "codified and sanctioned by law." De facto racism began as certain forms of racism and discrimination were becoming illegal beginning with *Brown v. Board* in 1954. De cardio racism developed after legal discrimination and segregation were outlawed, and it becomes taboo to express racist views and hold racial biases in public. For Jackson this means "explicit racism has gone underground, at least partially, relegated to people's hearts and inner thoughts."

14. Unlike the early civil rights movement, when it was expected that white racism was a direct cause of Black disenfranchisement and poverty, the rise of color-blind racism and the idea of a postracial society have manifested a situation where many people are not able to talk about race and racism and therefore cannot adequately address the roots of the problems that they intervene on. Bonilla-Silva, *Racism without Racists*, 2.

15. Bonilla-Silva, *Racism without Racists*.

16. These logics also deny the specificity of anti-Blackness in favor of a more multicultural approach in the terminology of "people of color."

17. Reynolds and Cohen, *Beyond the Kale*.

18. Mills, *Racial Contract*. Similarly, Ruth Frankenberg (*White Women, Race Matters*, 21) defines whiteness as "a dominant cultural space with enormous political significance, with the purpose to keep others on the margin." Sara Trechter and Mary Bucholtz ("White Noise," 8) define the whiteness as an "ideological pivot, the usually unmarked term in a series of hierarchically arranged racialized binaries"; they specifically note that it is "largely through language itself that racialized binaries come to be produced and reproduced." See also Mills, "White Ignorance."

19. DiAngelo, "White Fragility," 54–70; Du Bois, *Philadelphia Negro*; Combahee River Collective, "Combahee River Collective Statement"; Cooper, *Eloquent Rage*; Oluo, *So You Want To Talk About Race*; Kendi, *Stamped from the Beginning*; Coates, *Between the World and Me*.

20. This invisibility may be increasingly impossible for white food justice activists as more and more public scholarship has taken up the concept in the post–George Floyd moment. However, at the time of this research, most of which took place before the racial reckonings of 2020, food justice activists still seemed to lack an understanding of whiteness as a status or property. See Chang and Martin, "Summer of Racial Reckoning: The Match Lit"; Chang and Martin, "Summer of Racial Reckoning: The System"; Chang and Martin, "Summer

of Racial Reckoning: The Way Forward"; Soon-Shiong, "The *Times'* Reckoning on Race."

21. Food critical scholars Rachel Slocum and Julie Guthman have documented the "whiteness problem" within the alternative and community food movements, which Slocum attributes to "the invisibility of whiteness" and "the resistance within the movement to embrace an anti-racist practice for fear of offending allies." Guthman (foreword, xv) adds that "white idioms, sensibilities and histories pervaded the movement, to the extent that its goals, major strategies, and representations seemed off putting to 'people of color.' For example, the adopted idioms of 'putting your hands in the soil' and 'knowing where your food comes from' seemed insensitive to the thoroughly racialized agrarian economy of the US, just as the infatuation with food localism as a strategy for change seemed to best suit already existing privileged communities." However, many food scholars and activists saw the problem of whiteness as confined to alternative food movements and the call for more organics, while they looked to food justice as the more radical space that was not ideologically based in whiteness. See Black, "Abolitionist Food Justice." See also Guthman, "'If They Only,'" 97; Guthman, "Bringing Good Food to Others," 425–41; Slocum and Saldanha, *Geographies of Race and Food*; Slocum, "Anti-racist Practice," 327–49; Slocum, "Whiteness, Space and Alternative Food Practice," 520–33; Slocum, "Thinking Race Through Corporeal Feminist Theory," 849–69.

22. Hartigan, "Establishing the Fact of Whiteness," 498. Although the logics of whiteness are rooted in specific historical contexts, including European colonial expansion, the emergence of capitalism, and even Europe's formation (e.g., Romans versus Barbarians), whiteness is not merely a thing that white people did or thought in the past. Whiteness is an integral part to larger processes of racialization, not something that is a separate feature that can be abolished on its own; ignoring and negating whiteness will not make it disappear. Drawing on the work of coauthors Pierre Bourdieu and Loic Wacquant (*An Invitation to Reflexive Sociology*), sociologists Matthew Desmond and Mustafa Emirbayer (*Race in America*, 5) categorize people of color who internalize prejudice "unintentionally contributing to the production of racial domination" as suffering from "internalized racism" or "internalized oppression." They label this as a form of "symbolic violence" or "violence which is exercised upon a social agent with his or her complicity." See Robinson, *Black Marxism*; Smedley, *Race in North America*; Roediger, *Wages of Whiteness*.

23. While I am focusing here on the term "liberal" to denote political party affiliation in the United States, I also understand this as a part of an anthropology of late liberalism as anthropologist Elizabeth Povinelli (*Cunning of Recognition*, 6) defines it—that is, "the colonial and postcolonial subjective, institutional, and discursive identifications, dispersions and elaborations of the enlightenment idea that sociality should be organized on the basis of rational mutual understanding." Povinelli asserts that "a core obligation of liberalism is to decide public matters on the basis of autonomous, reasonable, and rational subjects or "private persons," bracketing the social differences that exist among themselves and presenting to their fellow citizens the most robust, true, sincere, and legitimate argument they can muster." This kind of bracketing was a cen-

tral feature of the work done by food justice activists. The scholar Savannah Shange (*Progressive Dystopia*, 14) also builds upon Povinelli, noting that the forms of progressivism that she observed in San Francisco could also be understood as "a sort of 'cunning' of multi racial liberalism, whereby the acknowledgement of systemic injustice serves as an alibi for the retrenchment of that very system." Here again, I see similar trends within the food justice movement, which I elaborate throughout the book.

24. The idea that people who are food insecure lack valued traits of US individualism further reinforces the idea that people who are food insecure are fundamentally different from the kinds of "good" citizens who engage in volunteer and aid work. See also Dickinson, *Feeding the Crisis*, 20; Poppendieck, *Breadlines Knee Deep in Wheat*; Poppendieck, *Sweet Charity?*; De Souza, *Feeding the Other*.

25. Bourdieu, *Logic of Practice*; Broad, *More Than Just Food*.

26. Winant, "White Racial Projects," 97.

27. Omi and Winant, *Racial Formation in the United States*.

28. Winant, "White Racial Projects," 106.

29. Tuck and Yang, "Decolonization Is Not a Metaphor," 1.

30. Halvorson and Reno, *Imagining the Heartland*.

31. Beliso-De Jesús, Pierre, and Rana, *Anthropology of White Supremacy*, 3.

32. Benjamin, *Viral Justice*, 44.

33. Gordon, "On Neofascism."

34. Harris, "Whiteness as Property," 1707–91.

35. Harris, "Whiteness as Property," 1726.

36. Harris, "Whiteness as Property."

37. Social Enterprise Alliance, "About."

38. Through the [aid organization] and teaching abroad, Josh had worked with "outsider" organizations that used their own tools and methods for determining what the communities that they were intervening in needed. This might have been established with a systematic needs assessment tool or rubric coming out of US-based, or international public health, education, or development organizations. These assessment tools had been used dozens or hundreds of times and were therefore understood to be the best way of understanding what a community needs; they were even better at determining community needs than the community members themselves. They were understood as "validated instruments."

39. Josh went on to tell me of a local "African" leader in the community who insisted that the schools needed televisions in the classrooms, so that they could play educational videos allowing children to continue learning while teachers had prep time or one-on-one time with students. Josh responded to this request saying "No, you just want to bring that home so you can watch [movies]." He played the role of arbiter of goods in this case, using his own moral valences on what was appropriate to determine who received things and who did not. He noted other community requests that he and his organization had deemed more practical, telling me that "other people were like, 'We need a heater for our school,' and you realize okay, well, that's actually very viable the way you look at the budget and you see like there's all this money and where is this money going to. . . . So you realize that they have identified that the school does need

this particular project, it needs a heater especially in the winters, so they get their heater, but they thought 'Hey, we might as well make the most of, exploit this need.'" In this case, even when the outside organization agreed with the community about needs and priorities, Josh understood the community as trying to exploit the NGO and get something out of them.

40. Escobar, *Encountering Development*; Ferguson, *Anti-politics Machine*.

41. Research by Alexander Ortega and colleagues ("Substantial Improvements Not Seen in Health Behaviors") found that corner store conversions in two Latino food swamps had "limited effectiveness" on improving health behaviors. A study by M.R. Lent et al. ("Randomized Controlled Study of a Healthy Corner Store Initiative," 2494–500) found "healthy corner store initiatives did not result in significant changes in the energy content of corner store purchases or in continuous or categorical measures of obesity."

42. Like what anthropologist Lisa H. Malkki (*Need To Help*) has found among Finnish international volunteers, many of the people involved in the food movement are compelled to do their work to fill a "need" or void in their own lives. In the eighteenth and nineteenth century in Europe, this need was called ennui—it was the result of having too much wealth and essentially being bored.

43. The inclination toward offering technical fixes through design also related to the commonly held view among white Americans that the government is ill-equipped "to help the poor" although most white Americans think it should be the job of the government to do so. The inclination toward technical fixes aligns with the view that charities and nonprofits are also not well-equipped to solve these problems. See Johnson, "Urban Precariat," 445–75.

44. Li, *Will To Improve*. See also Guthman, *Problem with Solutions*.

45. For an extended anthropological critique of the concept of "capacity building," see West, *Dispossession and the Environment*.

46. Although some of these concepts—white supremacy, in particular—are associated with conservative values and right-leaning politics, what I have observed in Los Angeles is that these particular forms of whiteness are linked to the other side of the political spectrum ranging from more centrist liberal-democratic views to very left-leaning politics.

47. Winant, "White Racial Projects," 100.

48. Beliso-De Jesús and Pierre, "Introduction," 65–75. Their analysis underscores the ways that anthropology as a discipline is rooted in a critical examination of racism, eroticization, and fetishizing "the Other" as the ethnographic subject, the "Other" almost always having been a nonwhite, non-Western subject. It is increasingly clear that the ways in which anthropologists have exoticized and fetishized the Other can contribute to racialization and racist ideals, despite intentions to do otherwise. Although it is usually not made explicit or clear in any way, most anthropological work has framed the "Other" in opposition to an unstated white, Western norm. So, while this chapter and this book are about how various forms of whiteness and power operate in the food justice movement, it also seeks to understand the relationship between whiteness, power, and Othering within anthropology and the social sciences more broadly. Despite many years of scholarship on whiteness that expand the concept, for many Americans the concept of white supremacy conjures up images of right-

wing groups, such as the Ku Klux Klan or Neo-Nazis, and while those groups would be included under the umbrella of white supremacy, it is also the broader understanding and social processes through which whiteness and white people are understood as superior to others.

49. Beliso-De Jesús, Pierre, and Rana, *Anthropology of White Supremacy*.

CHAPTER 4. PLACEMAKING

1. Oldenburg, *Great Good Place*.

2. Freire, *Pedagogy of the Oppressed*.

3. Molina, "Importance of Place and Place-makers," 71.

4. Molina, *Place at the Nayarit*.

5. Reese, "In the Food Justice World," 46; Langwick, "Politics of Habitability," 415–43; Povinelli, *Economies of Abandonment*, 116.

6. Carter, "Valued Lives in Violent Places," 239–61.

7. During this period there were also crackdowns and police raids on street food vendors, raids that specifically targeted undocumented vendors. See Rosales, "Survival, Economic Mobility and Community" 697–717.

8. In December 2022 street food vendors like Alejandra's mom took to the streets protesting the "no vending zones" that were written into the law legalizing street food vending. It took over a year of fighting before the city council voted to eliminate no-vending zones. Miller, "City Street Food Merchants Sue."

9. Based on my conversations with several people who worked on the project or in other roles at the organizations involved, there were several factors that contributed to why this store was not offered ongoing support. First, it was understood as a pilot or experiment with a new way of converting corner stores and thus was not always thought of as officially a full-fledged project. Second, the consulting work on the project was pro bono and only offered for a short period of time. Third, once the project was under way, the organizations realized how much labor would be involved in completing the project alone, therefore ongoing support was viewed as too much of a strain on the already limited labor force of the organizations. And finally, there was an understanding that because labor and resources were finite, it was better to have an impact on more stores and "hand off" the project to the store owner after the conversion rather than investing in long-term support.

10. Ferguson, *Give a Man a Fish*.

11. West, *Dispossession and the Environment*, 65; Ferguson, *Give a Man a Fish*.

CHAPTER 5. LIBERATION

1. The word *sangha* is a Pali or Sanskrit word that means "community." It is used in the United States to refer to a group of people who meditate together or a Buddhist community.

2. This experience was one among many where groups emphasized being outside, as connecting to the earth by sitting or placing bare feet directly on the soil or grass was a way to be in relationship with the land.

3. The sentiment here is from Octavia Butler's *Parable of the Sower*. It is the foundation of her character Lauren's Earthseed.

4. This attests to the ways in which the "research" and "data collection" for this book were so deeply entangled with my everyday life that it was often difficult to draw lines of distinction between "work" and "life."

5. brown uses lowercase letters for first, middle, and last name.

6. Reese and Carr, "Overthrowing the Food Systems' Plantation Paradigm."

7. Black, "Abolitionist Food Justice"; Kaba, *We Do This 'Til We Free Us*.

8. This inability to recollect speaks to the nature of this kind of fieldwork that was so immersed in my everyday life that it was unclear if an object or event was "fieldwork" (which I would record and take fieldnotes on) or life (which I would treat much more ephemerally). My own experience in the moment was likely to be what I valued most, and recording or taking notes might detract from my ability to experience my own life.

9. Reese and Carr, "Overthrowing the Food Systems' Plantation Paradigm."

10. McGranahan, "Theorizing Refusal: An Introduction," 319–20.

11. McGranahan, "Theorizing Refusal: An Introduction," 320 (emphasis in the original).

12. Simpson, "On Ethnographic Refusal," 67–80; Simpson, *Mohawk Interruptus*.

13. Simpson, *Mohawk Interruptus*, 515; Garth and Reese, *Black Food Matters*.

14. Shange, *Progressive Dystopia*, 4.

15. Erewhon is an upscale grocery chain that took off in Los Angeles after the Beverly Hills location was purchased by new owners in 2019 and a private equity firm purchased a minority stake. In 2022 the chain significantly expanded in the Los Angeles area. Beginning in 2023, Erewhon became the cultural symbol of elite food consumption in Los Angeles.

16. Stoval, *White Freedom*.

17. Harris, "Whiteness as Property," 1707–91.

18. Afro-futurism generally refers to science fiction or historical fiction that address the intersection of race and technology as part of a critical exploration of Black life. Coined by Mark Dery in 1993, the term was popularized by Alondra Nelson in the late 1990s.

19. Imarisha, *Octavia's Brood*. For example, one chapter is set in 1959 in a Black nation in the Southern states, which reimagines a past where John Brown's 1859 rebellion at Harper's Ferry had been successful. In another chapter an author is processing her emotional response to prison hunger strikes in Guantanamo Bay. Another author imagines her granddaughter living in the apocalypse in the flooded remains of the San Francisco Bay area. Her granddaughter teams up with all our granddaughters to interact with and heal planetary existence.

20. Imarisha, "Octavia's Brood."

21. Here I see overlap in many ways with the forms of activism and social justice that Beliso-De Jesús saw in "brujxing." Beliso-De Jesús, "39. Brujx," 528–38.

22. Creating a consistent space for this kind of envisioning, the sisters created "a podcast about learning from apocalypse with grace rigor and curios-

ity." The pilot episode opens with a famous quote from Octavia Butler's *Parable of the Sower*: "All that you touch you change, all that you change changes you, the only lasting truth is change, God is change." The episode focuses on thinking about "what do we need in order to survive and what do we need our kids to know" to survive the apocalypse. The podcast builds on Butler's character Lauren Olamina's declarative affirmation "I aim to survive." See Brown and brown, "Trailer: This Is How To Survive," 2017.

23. brown, *Emergent Strategy*, 3.

24. brown, *Emergent Strategy*, 158.

25. Butler, *Parable of the Sower*; Butler, *Parable of the Talents*.

26. Chandrasekaran, "Thinking Parabolically."

27. Chandrasekaran, "Thinking Parabolically.".

28. Chandrasekaran, "Thinking Parabolically."

29. Carr and Smith, "Poetics of Therapeutic Practice," 83–114.

30. brown, *Emergent Strategy*, 42.

31. As Nathan McClintock and Michael Simpson ("Stacking Functions," 35) note, "funding appears also to play a role in the embrace of the Radical frame, as well as the specific motivations therein. Organizations invoking food justice and social justice as primary motivations tended to receive the majority of their funding from private foundation grants. Those invoking food justice and food sovereignty were also less likely to operate using government funding sources. These trends suggest the political sensitivity of such terms, in contrast to the relative freedom of foundations to fund more explicitly equity-oriented projects."

32. brown, *Emergent Strategy*, 61.

33. brown, *Emergent Strategy*, 61.

34. brown, *Emergent Strategy*, 49.

35. The Bloods and the Crips are two different long-standing rival gangs with territories in and around South LA. Both gangs began more than fifty years ago. Anthropologist Damien Sojoyner ("You Are Going To Get Us Killed," 659) has argued that the Coalition Against Police Abuse (CAPA), and its founder Michael Zinzun, former member of the Los Angeles chapter of the Black Panther Party, have been essential to showing how "the organizational structure established by the Crips and the Bloods was crucial to the building of a multilayered liberation struggle." CAPA's organization of the gang truce was "inspired by the Black Panthers' ten-point platform" and "also focused on political economy (such as job programs) and the right of communities to protect themselves via communal organization (such as autonomy over community resources granted via the city and state)."

36. INCITE! Women of Color Against Violence, *Revolution Will Not Be Funded*.

37. This is akin to what Akhil Gupta attempted to do for US anthropology in his AAA presidential speech in which he reimagined the canon for the discipline. See Gupta and Stoolman, "AAA Presidential Address."

38. Here I am intentionally slipping back and forth between South Central and South LA, as Sunny does when speaking about the place. To me, Sunny moves back and forth between seeing the place as residents do (South Central)

and framing it as outsider activists do (South LA). For further explanation of this usage, see the prologue and introduction.

39. Povinelli, *Economies of Abandonment*.

40. For more on these events, see Garth, "2020 Los Angeles Uprisings."

41. brown, *Emergent Strategy*.

42. brown, *Emergent Strategy*, 143.

43. brown, *Emergent Strategy*.

CONCLUSION: THE END(S) OF FOOD JUSTICE

1. In 2026 the stadium will be among the US venues for the World Cup, and it will be a central venue for the 2028 Olympic and Paralympic Games. With these massive international events and all the development projects attached to them, Inglewood and the surrounding areas have already begun to completely transform. "Close to 4 billion people—more than half the world's population—have tuned in for each Olympic Games since 2004." Mahoney, "Environmental Justice Fight."

2. As part of the hosting deal, the City of Los Angeles will receive funding from the International Olympic Committee (IOC) and the US federal government to invest in development projects, including expanding transit lines to the area (Measure M) and renovating the Los Angeles International Airport, just three miles from the stadium. To the north, the Expo Line will be expanded; to the south, the Green Line will reach from Redondo Beach to Norwalk; and a completely new "Crenshaw Line" will connect the Expo Line to the airport's "people mover" system. In 2019 planning began for the proposed Vermont transit corridor, which would finally bring a rail line into the heart of South LA. Projected to open between 2028 and 2030, the line would go from the Los Feliz area beginning at Sunset and Vermont, pass through an area near USC, continue through South LA, and end just south of the 105 freeway. The near-term purpose of this transit is to provide visitors with access to Olympic events. If funding continues, the line will go all the way to San Pedro by 2060. In addition to transportation, the stadium is linked to the massive Hollywood Park development, which, when finished, will have twenty-five hundred homes in two residential communities—The Crosby, dubbed as "a mid-century-modern mood-maker," and the Wesley, "a brilliantly colorful residence in the heart of LA's hottest creative scene."

3. The development will lease office space and 500,000 square feet of "lifestyle retail at the center of a creative resurgence," a twelve-screen cinema, and a 20,000-square-foot public grocery market called Woodhouse.

4. TRD Staff, "Archeon Group to Join 180 Apartments and Grocery Store."

5. Mahoney, "Environmental Justice Fight."

6. LA officials can technically claim no-fault for two reasons: "First, the bulk of this construction has taken place in Inglewood, a city within Los Angeles County nestled between two different LA city limits. Second, the stadiums are privately owned. While both of these things are true, the effects on local residents and the environment are much the same as they would be if the city had undertaken construction within its own boundaries." Mahoney, "Environmental Justice Fight."

7. Redfin, "South LA Housing Market."

8. Palm, "Median Listing Price for Homes in Los Angeles."

9. Zumper, rental listing.

10. The idea that profit is immoral is not necessarily a given, although many of the food justice activists I interacted with felt strongly that no one should profit off goods or services that were basic human needs. The link between money and morality is complex. Religion is also central to the complexity underlying the links between morality and money. David Graeber (*Debt*, 319–23) recounts how money and religion collided at some point during the Middle Ages all around the world. Graeber argues that it is a central feature of modern capitalism to think of corporate profit as a moral imperative and that the drive to profit is a moral obligation to shareholders. This is integrally linked to power, and for Graeber "money as a political instrument."

11. Metzl and Hansen, "Structural Competency."

12. Mitchell, *Colonizing Egypt*, 28.

13. Williams-Forson, *Eating While Black*.

14. Halvorson and Reno, *Imagining the Heartland*.

15. Garth and Reese, *Black Food Matters*; Williams-Forson, *Eating While Black*.

16. Gal, "Semiotics of the Public/Private Distinction," 79.

17. For more information about the Black Urban Farmers & Gardeners (BUGS) conference, visit https://BUGS.nationalbuilder.org.

Bibliography

Administration for Children and Families (ACF). "Obama Administration Details Healthy Food Financing Initiative." *ACF* website. February 19, 2010. www.acf.hhs.gov/archive/media/press/2010/obama-administration-details-healthy-food-financing-initiative.

Agnew, Julie. "Michael Pollan: Love Him? Hate Him? Both?" *St. Louis.* May 13, 2013. www.stlmag.com/dining/Michael-Pollan-Love-Him-Hate-Him-Both/.

Agyeman, Julian, Caitlin Matthews, and Hannah Sobel, eds. *Food Trucks, Cultural Identity, and Social Justice: From Loncheras to Lobsta Love.* MIT Press, 2017.

Alim, Samy, and Geneva Smitherman. *Articulate while Black: Barack Obama, Language, and Race in the US.* Oxford University Press, 2012.

Alkon, Alison H. *Black, White, and Green: Farmers Markets, Race, and the Green Economy.* University of Georgia Press, 2012.

Alkon, Alison H., and Julian Agyeman. *Cultivating Food Justice: Race, Class, and Sustainability.* MIT Press, 2011.

Alkon, Alison H., and Theresa Mares. "Food Sovereignty in US Food Movements: Radical Visions and Neoliberal Constraints." *Agriculture and Human Values* 29, no. 3 (2012): 347–59.

Allen, Jafari Sinclaire, and Ryan Cecil Jobson. "The Decolonizing Generation: (Race and) Theory in Anthropology since the Eighties." *Current Anthropology* 57, no. 2 (2016): 129–48.

Allen, Patricia. *Together at the Table: Sustainability and Sustenance in the American Agrifood System.* Pennsylvania State University Press, 2004.

Allen, Patricia, and Julie Guthman. "From 'old school' to 'farm-to-school': Neoliberalization from the Ground Up." *Agriculture and Human Values* 23 (2006): 401–15.

Allison, Sophia Nahli, dir. *A Love Song for Latasha.* 2019. Netflix.

Anderson, Carol. *White Rage: The Unspoken Truth of Our Racial Divide.* Bloomsbury, 2016.

Appadurai, Arjun. *Modernity at Large: Cultural Dimensions of Globalization.* University of Minnesota Press, 1996.

Armstrong, Franny, dir. *McLibel. Documentary.* 2005. Spanner Films.

Aspen Institute. "Conversations on Food Justice: The Racial Origins of Free Breakfast and the Food Justice Movement." YouTube. October 29, 2020. Accessed October 9, 2023. www.youtube.com/watch?v = nzOD4o1uF3Q&t = 1113s.

Associated Press. "Daryl Hannah Arrested after Garden Protest." *Today.* June 13, 2006. www.today.com/popculture/daryl-hannah-arrested-after-garden-protest-1C9432760.

Associated Press. "L.A. OKs Moratorium on Fast-Food Restaurants." *NBC News.* July 29, 2008. www.nbcnews.com/id/wbna25896233.

Associated Press. "McDonald's Phasing Out Supersize Fries, Drinks." *NBC News.* March 2, 2004. www.nbcnews.com/id/wbna4433307.

Associated Press. "6 Hurt in Shooting at South Los Angeles Grocery Store." *US News.* December 31, 2021. www.usnews.com/news/best-states/california/articles/2021-12-31/6-hurt-in-shooting-at-south-los-angeles-grocery-store.

Associated Press. "West Virginia Town Shrugs at Being Fattest City." *NBC News.* November 17, 2008. www.nbcnews.com/health/health-news/w-virginia-town-shrugs-being-fattest-city-flna1c9466073.

Austin, J. L. "A Plea for Excuses: The Presidential Address." *Proceedings of the Aristotelian Society* 57, no. 1 (1957): 1–30. https://doi.org/10.1093/aristotelian/57.1.1

Azuma, Andrea Misako, Susan Gilliland, Mark Vallianatos, and Robert Gottlieb. "Food Access, Availability, and Affordability in 3 Los Angeles Communities, Project CAFE, 2004–2006." *Preventing Chronic Disease* 7, no. 2 (2010): A27.

Barnes, Riche J. Daniel. "She Was a Twin: Strategic Mothering, Race-Work, and the Politics of Survival." *Transforming Anthropology* 24, no. 1 (2016): 49–60.

Barnes, Timothy L., Bethany A. Bell, Darcy A. Freedman, Natalie Colabianchi, and Angela D. Liese. "Do People Really Know What Food Retailers Exist in Their Neighborhood? Examining GIS-based and Perceived Presence of Retail Food Outlets in an Eight-County Region of South Carolina." *Spatial and Spatio-temporal Epidemiology* 13 (2015): 31–40. https://doi.org/10.1016/j.sste.2015.04.004.

Barris, K., A. Kinney, L. Wilmore et al. (writers); P. Chatmon, S. Caple Jr., T. Biermann, K. Bray, M. Cunningham, J. Fortenberry, S. Meghie, A. Y. Rubin, E. D. Seaton, S. Tree, and S. K. Tsuchida (directors); and A. Anderson, K. Barris, J. Bean, E. B. Dobbins, L. Fishburne, H. Sugland et. al (producers). *Grown-ish.* 2018. Freeform (ABC Family).

Barris, Kenya, Michael Petok, Vijal Patel, Gail Lerner, Corey Nickerson, Lindsey Shockley, Peter Saji et al. *Black-ish. The Complete First Season.* 2015.

Bassford, Nicky, Lark Galloway-Gilliam, and Gwendolyn Flynn. *Food Desert to Food Oasis: Promoting Grocery Store Development in South Los Angeles.* Community Health Councils Inc., 2010.

Benjamin, Ruha. *Viral Justice: How We Grow the World We Want*. Princeton University Press, 2022.

Beliso-De Jesús, Aisha M. "39. Brujx: An Afro-Latinx Queer Gesture." *Critical Dialogues in Latinx Studies: A Reader*. Edited by Ana Y. Ramos-Zayas and Mérida M. Rúa. New York University Press, 2021.

Beliso-De Jesús, Aisha M., and Jemima Pierre. "Introduction: Special Section Anthropology of White Supremacy." *American Anthropologist* 122, no. 1 (2020): 65–75.

Beliso-De Jesús, Aisha M., Jemima Pierre, and Junaid Rana. "White Supremacy and the Making of Anthropology." *Annual Review of Anthropology* 52 (2023): 417–35.

Beliso-De Jesús, Aisha M., Jemima Pierre, and Junaid Rana, eds. *The Anthropology of White Supremacy: A Reader*. Princeton University Press, 2025.

Benton, Adia. *HIV Exceptionalism: Development through Disease in Sierra Leone*. University of Minnesota Press, 2015.

Black, Sarah Thomas. "Abolitionist Food Justice: Theories of Change Rooted in Place- and Life-Making." *Food and Foodways* (2022): 1. https://doi:10.1080/07409710.2022.20309422022.

Blair, April. *All American*. 2018. The CW.

Bonilla-Silva, Eduardo. *Racism without Racists: Color-Blind Racism and the Persistence of Racial Inequality in America*. Second edition. Rowman and Littlefield, 2006.

Borneman, John. *Settling Accounts: Violence, Justice and Accountability in Post Socialist Europe*. Princeton University Press, 1997.

Bourdieu, Pierre. *The Logic of Practice*. Translated by Richard Nice. Stanford University Press, 1990.

Bourdieu, Pierre, and Loic Wacquant. *An Invitation to Reflexive Sociology*. University of Chicago Press, 1992.

Bower, Anne, ed. *African American Foodways: Explorations of History and Culture*. University of Illinois Press, 2007.

Bradley, Katharine, and Hank Herrera. "Decolonizing Food Justice: Naming, Resisting, and Researching Colonizing Forces in the Movement." *Antipode* 48, no. 1 (2015): 97–114.

Bridle-Fitzpatrick, Susan. "Food Deserts or Food Swamps?: A Mixed-Methods Study of Local Food Environments in a Mexican City." *Social Science & Medicine* 142 (2015):202–13. https://doi.org/10.1016/j.socscimed.2015.08.010.

Broad, Garrett. *More Than Just Food: Food Justice and Community Change*. University of California Press, 2016.

Brodkin, Karen. "Comments on Discourses of Whiteness." *Journal of Linguistic Anthropology* 11, no. 1 (2001): 147–50.

Brodkin, Karen. *How Jews Became White Folks and What That Says About Race in America*. Rutgers University Press, 1998.

Brodkin, Karen. *Power Politics: Environmental Activism in South Los Angeles*. Rutgers University Press, 2009.

Brones, Anna. "Karen Washington: It's Not a Food Desert, It's Food Apartheid." *Guernica online*. May 7, 2018. www.guernicamag.com/karen-washington-its-not-a-food-desert-its-food-apartheid/.

Brooks, Nancy Rivera, and Henry Weinstein. "19 of 68 Firms Question Listing by Rebuild L.A." *Los Angeles Times*, November 18, 1992. www.latimes.com /archives/la-xpm-1992–11–18-mn-495-story.html.

brown, adrienne maree. *Emergent Strategy: Shaping Change, Changing Worlds*. AK Press, 2017.

brown, adrienne maree, and Autumn Brown. "Trailer: This Is How To Survive the End of the World." November 7, 2017. *How To Survive the End of the World* podcast. Produced by Zak Rosen, Apple Podcasts.

brown, adrienne maree, and Walidah Imarisha, eds. *Octavia's Brood: Science Fiction Stories from Social Justice Movements*. AK Press, 2015.

Brown, Kardea, series host. *Delicious Miss Brown*. 2019. Food Network.

Bureau of Street Services. "Commonly Asked Questions." 2022. Accessed July 14, 2022. https://streetsla.lacity.org/vending-questions.

Butler, Octavia. *Parable of the Sower*. Seven Stories Press, 1993.

Butler, Octavia. *Parable of the Talents*. Four Walls Eight Windows, 1998.

Cadena, Marisol de la. "Matters of Method; Or, Why Method Matters toward a Not Only Colonial Anthropology." *HAU: Journal of Ethnographic Theory* 7, no. 2 (2017): 1–10. https://doi.org/10.14318/hau7.2.002.

Calderone, Julia. "McDonald's To Serve Chicken Raised without Certain Antibiotics Worldwide." *Consumer Report*. August 23, 2017. www.consumerreports .org/antibiotics/mcdonalds-to-serve-chicken-raised-without-antibiotics/.

Campt, Tina. "Black Feminist Futures and the Practice of Fugitivity." Helen Pond McIntyre '48 Lecture at Barnard College, October 7, 2014. http:// bcrw.barnard.edu.

Carney, Judith. *Black Rice: The African Origins of Rice Cultivation in the Americas*. Harvard University Press, 2001.

Carr, E. Summerson, and Yvonne Smith. "The Poetics of Therapeutic Practice: Motivational Interviewing and the Powers of Pause." *Culture Medicine Psychiatry* 38 (2013): 83–114.

Carter, Rebecca Louise. "Valued Lives in Violent Places: Black Urban Placemaking at a Civil Rights Memorial in New Orleans." *City & Society* 26, no. 2 (2014): 239–61.

Caspi, Caitlin E., Glorian Sorensen, S. V. Subramanian, and Ichiro Kawachi. "The Local Food Environment and Diet: A Systematic Review." *Health & Place* 18, no. 5 (2012): 1172–87. https://doi.org/10.1016/j.healthplace.2012.05.006.

Center for Disease Control (CDC). "Firearm Mortality by State." *CDC*. Accessed November 8, 2022. www.cdc.gov/nchs/pressroom/sosmap /firearm_mortality/firearm.htm.

Center for Good Food Purchasing. Good Food Purchasing. 2017. Accessed July 14, 2022. https://goodfoodpurchasing.org/.

Center for Good Food Purchasing. "The Good Food Purchasing Program: A Roadmap for the Post-Pandemic Food System We Need." Good Food Purchasing. Accessed January 23, 2021. https://goodfoodpurchasing.org/good-food-roadmap/.

Chadburn, Melissa. "The Destructive Force of Rebuild LA Curbed Los Angeles, April 27." *Curbed LA*. April 27, 2017. https://la.curbed.com/2017/4/27 /15442350/1992-los-angeles-riots-rebuild-la.

Chandrasekaran, Priya. "Thinking Parabolically: Time Matters in Octavia Butler's Parables." *Theorizing the Contemporary, Fieldsights*. December 18, 2018. https://culanth.org/fieldsights/thinking-parabolically-time-matters-in-octavia-butlers-parables.

Chang, Ailsa, and Rachel Martin. "Summer of Racial Reckoning: The Match Lit." *Weekend Edition Sunday*. NPR. August 16, 2020.

Chang, Ailsa, and Rachel Martin. "Summer of Racial Reckoning: The System." *Weekend Edition Sunday*. NPR. September 8, 2020.

Chang, Ailsa, and Rachel Martin. "Summer of Racial Reckoning: The Way Forward." *Weekend Edition Sunday*. NPR. September 24, 2020.

Chang, Andrea, and Laurence Darmiento, "99 Cents Only to Close All 371 Stores and Wind Down Its Business." *Los Angeles Times*, April 4, 2024.

Chang, Cindy. "Antidevelopment Protesters Are Arrested at Farm Site in Los Angeles." *New York Times*. June 14, 2006. www.nytimes.com/2006/06/14/us/14garden.html.

Chang, Edward T. "The Los Angeles Riots: A Korean American Perspective." *Korean and Korean-American Studies Bulletin* 4, no. 3 (Summer/Fall 1993): 10–11.

Cho, Sumi K. "Korean Americans vs. African Americans: Conflict and Construction." In *Reading Rodney King/Reading Urban Uprising*. Edited by Robert Gooding-Williams. Routledge, 1993.

City of Los Angeles. "Health Atlas for the City of Los Angeles." 2013. Accessed July 28, 2022. http://planning.lacity.org/cwd/framwk/healthwellness/text/HealthAtlas.pdf.

City of Los Angeles. "Los Angeles County (South Central)—LA City (South Central/Watts) PUMA, CA." *Census Reporter*. Accessed July 1, 2024. https://censusreporter.org/profiles/79500US0603751-los-angeles-county-south-central-la-city-south-centralwatts-puma-ca/.

City of Los Angeles. "South Los Angeles Demographics." Department of City Planning Report. 2017.

Clancy, K., Janet Hammer, and D. Lippoldt. "Food Policy Councils-Past, Present, and Future." In *Remaking the North American Food System: Strategies for Sustainability*. Edited by C. Clare Hinrichs and Thomas A. Lyson. University of Nebraska Press, 2008.

Clemetson, Lynette. "The Racial Politics of Speaking Well." Week in Review. *New York Times*. February 4, 2007.

Coates, Ta-Nehisi. *Between the World and Me*. Spiegel & Grau, 2015.

Collins, Keith. *Black Los Angeles: The Maturing of the Ghetto, 1940–1950*. Century Twenty One Publishing, 1980.

Combahee River Collective. "Combahee River Collective Statement." 1977. Library of Congress. Accessed March 12, 2023. www.loc.gov/item/lcwaN0028151/.

Community Services Unlimited, Ltd. (CSU). "Community Services Unlimited, Ltd." Accessed July 11, 2022. http://csuinc.org/.

Compton Chamber of Commerce. "Target Region: Greater Compton Area." 2021. Accessed July 1, 2024. www.comptonchamberofcommerce.org/compton-nutrition-demographics.

Cooksey-Stowers, Kristen, Marlene B. Schwartz, and Kelly D. Brownell. "Food Swamps Predict Obesity Rates Better Than Food Deserts in the United States." *International Journal of Environmental Research and Public Health* 14, no. 11 (2017): 1366.

Cooper, Brittney. *Eloquent Rage: A Black Feminist Discovers Her Superpower.* MacMillan, 2018.

Cotterill, Ronald W. "Food Retailing: Mergers, Leveraged Buyouts, and Performance." Food Marketing Policy Center Research Report 14. University of Connecticut, 1991.

Coulombe, Joe. *Becoming Trader Joe: How I Did Business My Way and Still Beat the Big Guys.* Harper Collins, 2021.

Cox, Aimee. *Shapeshifters: Black Girls and the Choreography of Citizenship.* Duke University Press, 2015.

Crapanzano, Vincent. "The End—The Ends—of Anthropology." *Paideuma: Mitteilungen zur Kulturkunde* 56 (2010): 165–88.

"Crips' and Bloods' Plan for Reconstruction of Los Angeles." 1992. Accessed November 9, 2022. http://gangresearch.net/GangResearch/Policy /cripsbloodsplan.html.

Curtis, Jennifer, James Ferguson, and Akhila Gupta. "Anthropologies of Development and Non-Governmental Organizations. Interview." *PoLAR: Political and Legal Anthropology Review Online.* March 10, 2012. http://polarjournal .org/2012/03/10/interview-with-james-ferguson-and-akhil-gupta.

Das Purkayastha, Jayanta Kumar. "Feeding the Inner City: Geographies of Food Retailing in South Los Angeles." PhD diss., University of Southern California, 1996.

Dave, Naisargi N. "What It Feels Like To Be Free: The Tense of Justice." Correspondences, *Fieldsights*, June 29, 2018. https://culanth.org/fieldsights /what-it-feels-like-to-be-free-the-tense-of-justice.

Davis, Angela. "Let Us All Rise Together: Radical Perspectives on Empowerment for Afro-American Women." In *Women, Culture, and Politics*. Random House, 1989.

Davis, Angela. "Radical Frameworks for Social Justice." Keynote Lecture Regis University. Denver Colorado Women's Studies Program, February 21, 2008. Accessed December 1, 2023. www.youtube.com/watch?v = FS9_vnfxWB0.

Davis, Angela. *Women, Race & Class.* Penguin Random House, 1981.

Davis, Mike. *City of Quartz: Excavating the Future in Los Angeles.* Verso, 1990.

Davies, Carole Boyce. *Left of Karl Marx: The Political Life of Black Communist Claudia Jones.* Duke University Press, 2007.

De Certeau, Michel. *The Practice of Everyday Life.* University of California Press, 1984.

De Lara, Juan D. *Inland Shift: Race, Space, and Capital in Inland Southern California.* University of California Press, 2018.

Democracy Now. "Police Forcibly Shut Down South Central L.A. Urban Farm, 40+ Protesters Arrested." June 14, 2006. www.democracynow.org/2006 /6/14/police_forcibly_shut_down_south_central.

Desmond, Matthew. *Evicted: Poverty and Profit in the American City.* New York: Crown Publishers, 2016.

Desmond, Matthew. *Poverty, by America*. New York: Crown, 2023.

Desmond, Matthew, and Mustafa Emirbayer. *Race in America*. W.W. Norton and Company, 2016.

De Souza, Rebecca. *Feeding the Other: Whiteness, Privilege, and Neoliberal Stigma in Food Pantries*. MIT Press, 2019.

DiAngelo, Robin. "White Fragility." *International Journal of Critical Pedagogy* 3, no. 3 (2011): 54–70.

Dickinson, Maggie. *Feeding the Crisis: Care and Abandonment in America's Food Safety Net*. University of California Press, 2020.

Dimock, Michael R. "The Los Angeles Food Policy Council: A Model for the Nation." *Roots of Change Blog*. Accessed April 19, 2023. www.rootsofchange .org/blog/the-los-angeles-food-policy-council-a-model-for-the-nation/.

Djang, Jason. "The Story of the White House Garden." Obama White House Archives, August 31, 2009. https://obamawhitehouse.archives.gov/blog/2009 /08/31/story-white-house-garden.

Donkin, A.J., E.A. Dowler, S.J. Stevenson, and S.A. Turner. "Mapping Access to Food at a Local Level." *British Food Journal* 101, no. 7 (1999): 554–64. https://doi.org/10.1108/00070709910279054.

Douglas, Mary. *Purity and Danger: An Analysis of Concepts of Pollution and Taboo*. Praeger, 1970.

Du Bois, W.E.B. *The Philadelphia Negro: A Social Study*. Gin and Company, 1899.

Du Bois, W.E.B. *The Souls of Black Folk*. Bantam Classics, 1989.

Edelman, Marc, and Angelique Haugerud, eds. *The Anthropology of Development and Globalization: From Classical Political Economy to Contemporary Neoliberalism*. Blackwell Publishing, 2004.

Equitable Food Oriented Development (EFOD). Website. Accessed July 11, 2022. https://efod.org/.

"El Super." 1997. *El Super*. Accessed January 19, 2023. https://elsupermarkets .com/.

Elyachar, Julia. "Neoliberalism, Rationality, and the Savage Slot." In *Mutant Neoliberalism: Market Rule and Political Rupture*. Edited by William Callison and Zachary Manfredi. Fordham University Press, 2020.

Environmental Protection Agency (EPA). "Environmental Justice: Basic Information." 2021. Accessed July 11, 2022. www.epa.gov/environmentaljustice /learn-about-environmental-justice.

Escobar, Arturo. *Encountering Development: The Making and Unmaking of the Third World*. Princeton University Press, 1995.

Estabrook, Barry. *Tomatoland: How Modern Industrial Agriculture Destroyed Our Most Alluring Fruit*. Andrews McMeel Publishing, 2011.

Fairfax, Sally K., Louise Nelson Dyble, Greig Tor Guthey, Lauren Gwin, Monia Moore, and Jennifer Sokolove. *California Cuisine and Just Food*. MIT Press, 2012.

Fassin, Didier. *Humanitarian Reason: A Moral History of the Present*. University of California Press, 2012.

Ferguson, Gillian. "KCRW Good Food." *LAFPC Origin* podcast. 2017. Accessed July 6, 2022. https://soundcloud.com/gillian-ferguson-1/lafpc-origin-podcast -mp3.

Ferguson, James. *The Anti-Politics Machine: Development, Depoliticization, and Bureaucratic Power in Lesotho.* Cambridge University Press, 1994.

Ferguson, James. *Give a Man a Fish: Reflections on the New Politics of Distribution.* Duke University Press, 2015.

Ferguson, James, and Larry Lohmann. "The Anti-politics Machine: 'Development' and Bureaucratic Power in Lesotho." *The Ecologist* 24, no. 5 (1994): 176–81.

Fieldstat, Elisha. "Murder Map: Deadliest U.S. Cities." *CBS News*, February 23, 2022. www.cbsnews.com/pictures/murder-map-deadliest-u-s-cities/.

Finley, Ron. "MasterClass: Ron Finley Teaches Gardening." Accessed July 13, 2022. www.masterclass.com/classes/ron-finley-teaches-gardening.

Finley, Ron. "Ron Finley: A Guerrilla Gardener in South Central LA." TED Talk. March 2013. 10 min., 29 sec. www.ted.com/speakers/ron_finley.

Foucault, Michel. *The Archaeology of Knowledge and the Discourse on Language.* Translated from the French by A.M. Sheridan Smith. Pantheon Books, 1972.

Fox, Clare. *Food Policy Councils: Innovations in Democratic Governance for a Sustainable and Equitable Food System.* Los Angeles Food Policy Task Force Report. 2010. Accessed March 17, 2025. https://goodfoodlosangeles.wordpress.com/wp-content/uploads/2011/01/fpc_final_dist-5-indd.pdf.

Frankenberg, Ruth. "The Mirage of Unmarked Whiteness." In *The Making and Unmaking of Whiteness.* Edited by B.B. Rasmussen, E. Klineberg, I.J. Nexica, and M. Wray. Duke University Press, 2001.

Frankenberg, Ruth. *White Women, Race Matters: The Social Construction of Whiteness.* University of Minnesota Press, 1993.

Freire, Paulo. *Pedagogy of the Oppressed.* Continuum, 1970.

Freshworks. "Client Stories: LURN-Los Angeles." *California Freshworks.* 2015. Accessed July 18, 2022. www.cafreshworks.com/clientstories/leadership-for-urban-renewal/.

Frey, Lawrence R., W. Barnett Pearce, Mark A. Pollock, Lee Artz, and Bren A.O. Murphy. "Looking for Justice in All the Wrong Places: On a Communication Approach to Social Justice." *Communication Studies* 47, no. 1–2 (1996): 110–27. https://doi:10.1080/10510979609368467.

Fritsch, Jane. "Los Angeles Police Differ Sharply with Prosecutors on Arrest Totals." *New York Times*, May 10, 1992. www.nytimes.com/1992/05/10/us/los-angeles-police-differ-sharply-with-prosecutors-on-arrest-totals.html.

Fuqua, Antoine, dir.. *Training Day.* 2001. Warner Bros.

Gal, Susan. "A Semiotics of the Public/Private Distinction." *Differences: A Journal of Feminist Cultural Studies* 13, no. 1 (2002): 77–95.

Galvez, Alyshia. *Eating NAFTA: Trade, Food Policies, and the Destruction of Mexico.* First edition. University of California Press, 2018.

Garcia, Deborah Koons. *The Future of Food.* Lily Films, 2004.

Garth, Hanna. "Blackness and 'Justice' in the Los Angeles Food Movement." In *Black Food Matters: Centering Black Ways of Knowing in the Wake of Food Justice.* Edited by Hanna Garth and Ashanté Reese. University of Minnesota Press, 2020.

Garth, Hanna. *Food in Cuba: The Pursuit of a Decent Meal.* Stanford University Press, 2020.

Garth, Hanna. "Food, Taste, and the Body: Ingestion and Embodiment in Santiago de Cuba." *Medical Anthropology Quarterly* 37 (2023): 5–22.

Garth, Hanna. "Toward Adequate Food Systems: Collaboration and 'Non-Sovereign' Food Futures." *Journal of the Anthropology of North America* 24, no. 2 (2021): 74–83.

Garth, Hanna. "The 2020 Los Angeles Uprisings: Fighting for Black lives in the Midst of COVID-19." In *Viral Loads: Anthropologies of Urgency in the Time of COVID-19.* Edited by Lenore Manderson, Nancy J. Burke, and Ayo Wahlberg. University College London Press, 2021.

Garth, Hanna. "The Violence of Racial Capitalism and South Los Angeles' Obesity 'Epidemic.'" *American Anthropologist* 122, no. 3 (2020): 649–50.

Garth, Hanna, and Ashanté Reese, eds. *Black Food Matters: Racial Justice in the Wake of Food Justice.* University of Minnesota Press, 2020.

Gary Gray, F., dir. *Friday.* 1995. New Line Cinema.

Gary Gray, F., dir. *Straight Outta Compton.* 2015. Universal Pictures.

Gilmore, Ruthie Wilson. "Fatal Couplings of Power and Difference: Notes on Racism and Geography." *Professional Geographer* 54, no. 1 (2002): 15–24. https://doi.org/10.1111/0033-0124.00310.

Gilmore, Ruth Wilson. "In the Shadow of the Shadow State." In *The Revolution Will Not Be Funded: Beyond the Non-profit Industrial Complex.* Edited by INCITE! Duke University Press, 2017.

Goody, Jack. *Cooking, Cuisine, and Class: A Study in Comparative Sociology.* Cambridge University Press, 1982.

Gordon, Lewis. "On Neofascism." DePaul University. Accessed March 2017. https://depaul.hosted.panopto.com/Panopto/Pages/Viewer.aspx?id = 41bd6d41-60fb-4940-b774-4b5998beecc6.

Gottlieb, Robert, and Anupama Joshi. *Food Justice.* MIT Press, 2010.

Graeber, David. *Debt: The First 5,000 Years.* Melville House, 2011.

Greenberg, Jessica R. "When Is Justice Done?" *Fieldsights*, June 9, 2018. https://culanth.org/fieldsights/when-is-justice-done.

Greenhalgh, Susan. "Weighty Subjects: The Biopolitics of the U.S. War on Fat." *American Ethnologist* 39, no. 3 (2012): 471–87.

Gupta, Akhil, and Jessie Stoolman. AAA Presidential Address, 2021. First published September 27, 2022. https://anthrosource.onlinelibrary.wiley.com /doi/abs/10.1111/aman.13775.

Gusterson, Hugh. "Studying Up Revisited." *Polar: Political and Legal Anthropology Review* 20, no. 1 (1997): 114–19.

Guthman, Julie. "Bringing Good Food to Others: Investigating the Subjects of Alternative Food Practice." *Cultural Geographies* 15, no. 4 (2007): 425–41.

Guthman, Julie. "Fast Food/Organic Food: Reflexive Tastes and the Making of 'Yuppie Chow.'" *Journal of Social and Cultural Geography* 4 (2003): 43–56.

Guthman, Julie. Foreword in *Geographies of Race and Food: Fields, Bodies, Markets.* Edited by Rachel Slocum and Arun Saldanha. Ashgate Publishing, 2013.

Guthman, Julie. "How Michael Pollan et al. Made Me Want to Eat Cheetos." *Gastronomica: The Journal of Food and Culture* 7, no. 3 (2007): 75–79.

Guthman, Julie. "'If They Only Knew': Color Blindness and Universalism in California Alternative Food Institutions." *Professional Geographer* 60 (2008): 387–97.

Guthman, Julie. *The Problem with Solutions: Why Silicon Valley Can't Hack the Future of Food*. University of California Press, 2024.

Guthman, Julie, Amy W. Morris, and Patricia Allen. "Squaring Farm Security and Food Security in Two Types of Alternative Food Institutions." *Rural Sociology* 71 (2006): 662–84.

Guyer, Jane I. "Prophecy and the Near Future: Thoughts on Macroeconomic, Evangelical, and Punctuated Time." *American Ethnologist* 34 (2007):409–19.

Halberstam, Jack. "The Wild Beyond: With and for the Undercommons." In *The Undercommons: Fugitive Planning & Black Study*. Edited by Stefano and Fred Moten. Minor Compositions, 2013.

Halvorson, Britt E., and Joshua O. Reno. *Imagining the Heartland: White Supremacy and the American Midwest*. University of California Press, 2022.

Hamilton Kennedy, Scott, dir. *The Garden*. 2008. Black Valley Films.

Hardin, Jessica. "Life before Vegetables: Nutrition, Cash, and Subjunctive Health in Samoa." *Cultural Anthropology* 36, no. 3 (2021): 428–57.

Harney, Stefano, and Fred Moten. *The Undercommons: Fugitive Planning & Black Study*. Minor Compositions, 2013.

Harper, A. Breeze. *Sistah Vegan: Black Female Vegans Speak on Food, Identity, Health, and Society*. Lantern Books, 2009.

Harper, A., A. Shattuck, E. Holt-Gimenez, A. Alkon, and F. Lambrick. *Food Policy Councils: Lessons Learned. Food First: Institute for Food and Development Policy*. Food First Institute for Food and Development Policy, 2009.

Harris, Cheryl. "Reflections on Whiteness as Property." *Harvard Law Review* 134, no. 1 (2020): 8–9.

Harris, Cheryl. "Whiteness as Property." *Harvard Law Review* 106, no. 8 (1993): 1707–91.

Harris, Jessica B. *Beyond Gumbo: Creole Fusion Food from the Atlantic Rim*. Simon and Schuster, 2003.

Harris, Jessica B. *High on the Hog: A Culinary Journey from Africa to America*. Bloomsbury, 2011.

Harrison, Faye V. *Decolonizing Anthropology: Moving Further Toward an Anthropology for Liberation*. First edition. American Anthropological Association, 1991.

Hartigan, John, Jr. "Establishing the Fact of Whiteness." *American Anthropologist* 99, no. 3 (1997): 495–505.

Hartman, Saidiya. *Lose Your Mother: A Journey along the Atlantic Slave Route*. Farrar, Straus, and Giroux, 2007.

Harvey, David. *A Brief History of Neoliberalism*. Oxford University Press, 2005.

Hassberg, Analena Hope. "Nurturing the Revolution: The Black Panther Party and the Early Seeds of the Food Justice Movement." In *Black Food Matters: Racial Justice in the Wake of Food Justice*. Edited by Hanna Garth and Ashanté Reese. University of Minnesota Press, 2020.

Heynen, Nik. "Bending the Bars of Empire from Every Ghetto for Survival: The Black Panther Party's Radical Antihunger Politics of Social Reproduction and Scale." *Annals of the Association of American Geographers* 99, no. 2 (2009): 406–22.

Himmelgreen, David, and Nancy Romero-Daza. "Anthropological Approaches to the Global Food Crisis: Understanding and Addressing the 'Silent Tsunami.'" *Annals of Anthropological Practice* 32, no. 1 (2009): 1–11.

Hinrichs, Claire G. "The Practice and Politics of Food System Localization." *Journal of Rural Studies* 19 (2003): 33–45.

Ho, Karen. *Liquidated: An Ethnography of Wall Street*. Duke University Press, 2009.

Hollan, Doug. "The Relevance of Person-Centered Ethnography to Cross-Cultural Psychiatry." *Transcultural Psychiatry* 34, no. 2 (1997): 219–34. http://doi:10.1177/136346159703400203.

Holt-Giménez, E., and A. Shattuck. "Food Crises, Food Regimes and Food Movements: Rumblings of Reform or Tides of Transformation?" *Journal of Peasant Studies* 38, no. 1 (2011): 109–44.

Hondagneu-Sotelo, Pierrette, and Walter Thompson-Hernandez. "Latino Identity in South Los Angeles—Across the Generations." *PBS SoCal*. July 27, 2016. www.pbssocal.org/shows/departures/latino-identity-in-south-los-angeles-across-the-generations.

Hormann, Matt. "'No Chinese Employed' in Early Pasadena." *Colorado Boulevard*, May 28, 2024. www.coloradoboulevard.net/no-chinese-employed-in-early-pasadena/.

Horne, Gerald. *Fire This Time: The Watts Uprising*. University of Virginia Press, 1995.

Hubler, Shawn. "*Los Angeles Times* Rebuilding the Community: South LA's Poverty Rate Worse Than 65.'" *LA Times*. May 11, 1992. www.latimes.com/archives/la-xpm-1992–05–11-mn-1196-story.html.

Hunt, Darnell. "American Toxicity: Twenty Years after the 1992 Los Angeles 'Riots.'" *Amerasia Journal* 38, no. 1 (2012): ix–xviii.

Hunt, Darnell, and Ana-Christina Ramón. *Black Los Angeles: American Dreams and Racial Realities*. NYU Press, 2010.

Imarisha, Walidah. "Octavia's Brood: Science Fiction Stories from Social Justice Movements." Talk at Lewis & Clark College. April 1, 2016. www.youtube.com/watch?v = vbU6mS9VojM.

INCITE! Women of Color Against Violence, eds. *The Revolution Will Not Be Funded: Beyond the Non-profit Industrial Complex*. South End Press, 2007.

Inclusive Action for the City. Website. 2019. Accessed July 11, 2022. www.inclusiveaction.org/blog/new-name-who-this.

Jackson, John L., Jr. *Racial Paranoia: The Unintended Consequences of Political Correctness*. Basic Civitas, 2008.

Jackson, John L., Jr. *Real Black: Adventures in Racial Sincerity*. University of Chicago Press, 2005.

Jefferson, Anna. "'Not What It Used To Be': Schemas of Class and Contradiction in the Great Recession." *Economic Anthropology* 2 (2015): 310–25.

Joe, Adam, and Mindy Guilford, dirs. *Sprouting Gardens in a Food Desert.* 2012.

Johnson, Cedric G. "The Urban Precariat, Neoliberalization, and the Soft Power of Humanitarian Design." *Journal of Developing Societies* 27, no. 3–4 (2011): 445–75.

Julier, Alice. "The Political Economy of Obesity: The Fat Pay All." In *Food and Culture: A Reader.* Fourth edition. Edited by Carole Counihan, Penny Van Esterik, and Alice Julier. Routledge, 2018.

Jusionyte, Ieva. *Exit Wounds: How America's Guns Fuel Violence across the Border.* University of California Press, 2024.

Kaba, Mariame. *We Do This 'Til We Free Us: Abolitionist Organizing and Transforming Justice.* Haymarket Books, 2021.

KABC. "At Least 6 Injured During Shooting at Grocery Store Shopping Center in South LA, LAFD Says." ABC7. January 1, 2022. https://abc7.com/shopping-center-shooting-south-la-s-avalon-boulevard-superior-grocers-store/11412035/.

Keane, Webb. "Self-Interpretation, Agency, and the Objects of Anthropology: Reflections on a Genealogy." *Comparative Studies in Society and History* 45, no. 2 (2003): 222–48.

Kelley, Robin D. G. "The U.S. v. Trayvon Martin: How the System Worked." *Huffington Post.* July 15, 2013. www.huffingtonpost.com/robin-d-g-kelley/nra-stand-yourground-trayvon-martin_b_3599843.html.

Kelly, Bridget, Victoria M. Flood, and Heather Yeatman. "Measuring Local Food Environments: An Overview of Available Methods and Measures." *Health & Place* 17, no.6 (2011): 1284–93. https://doi.org/10.1016/j.health-place.2011.08.014.

Kendi, Ibram X. *Stamped from the Beginning: The Definitive History of Racist Ideas in America.* Public Affairs, 2016.

Kenner, Robert, dir. *Food, Inc.* Magnolia Home Entertainment, 2009.

Khan, Huma. "Did Michelle Obama Send the Wrong Message with Obesity Comments?" *ABC News.* February 4, 2010. https://abcnews.go.com/Politics/Health/michelle-obama-obesity-comments-bringing-malia-sasha-wrong/story?id=9751138.

Kolb, Kenneth. *Retail Inequality: Reframing the Food Desert Debate.* University of California Press, 2021.

Kumcu, A., and P. Kaufman. "Food Spending Adjustments During Recessionary Times." *Amber Waves.* September 2011. www.ers.usda.gov/amber-waves/2011-september/food-spending.aspx.

Kun, Josh, and Laura Pulido. *Black and Brown in Los Angeles: Beyond Conflict and Coalition.* University of California Press, 2014.

Künzli, Nino, Rob McConnell, David Bates, Tracy Bastain, Andrea Hricko, Fred Lurmann, Ed Avol, Frank Gilliland, and John Peters. "Breathless in Los Angeles: The Exhausting Search for Clean Air." *American Journal of Public Health* 93, no. 9 (2003): 1494–99. https://doi:10.2105/ajph.93.9.1494.

Kwate, Naa Oyo. "Fried Chicken and Fresh Apples: Racial Segregation as a Fundamental Cause of Fast Food Density in Black Neighborhoods." *Health & Place* 14 (2008): 32–44.

Kwate, Naa Oyo A., Ji Meng Loh, Kellee White, and Nelson Saldana. "Retail Redlining in New York City: Racialized Access to Day-to-Day Retail Resources." *Journal Urban Health* 90, no. 4 (2013): 632–52. https://doi:10 .1007/s11524–012–9725–3.

LA Business Journal. "Numero Uno Markets Sold to Private Equity Firms." *LA Business Journal.* May 4, 2009. https://labusinessjournal.com/news/numero -uno-markets-sold-to-private-equity-firms/.

LA Census 2020. "Low Response Area Report." Accessed October 9, 2023. https://census.lacity.org/index.html.

Laclau, Ernesto. *Emancipation(s).* Verso, 2007.

Lang, Tim, and Michael Heasman. *Food Wars: The Global Battle for Minds, Mouths and Markets.* Earthscan, 2004.

Langwick, Stacey A. "A Politics of Habitability: Plants, Healing and Sovereignty in a Toxic World." *Cultural Anthropology* 33, no. 3 (2018): 415–43.

Lappe, Frances Moore, and Anna Lappe. *Hope's Edge: The Next Diet for a Small Planet.* Penguin Putnam, 2002.

Laudan, Rachel. "A Plea for Culinary Modernism: Why We Should Love Fast, New, Processed Food." *Gastronomica: The Journal of Food and Culture* 1, no. 1 (2001): 36–44.

Lazzareschi, Carla, and Stuart Silverstein. "Riot Job-Loss Figure Is Halved." *Los Angeles Times.* May 21, 1992. www.latimes.com/archives/la-xpm -1992–05–21-fi-479-story.html.

Lent, M.R., S.S. Vander Veur, T.A. McCoy, A.C. Wojtanowski, B. Sandoval, S. Sherman, E. Komaroff, and G.D. Foster. "A Randomized Controlled Study of a Healthy Corner Store Initiative on the Purchases of Urban, Low-Income Youth." *Obesity* 22, no. 12 (2014): 2494–500. https://doi.org/10 .1002/oby.20878.

Let's Move! Campaign. "Let's Move! Accomplishments." 2015. Accessed July 18, 2022. https://web.archive.org/web/20151210182547/http://www.letsmove .gov/accomplishments.

Levkoe, Charles Z. "Learning Democracy Through Food Justice Movements." *AgricHum Values* 23 (2006): 89–98. https://doi.org/10.1007/s10460–005 –5871–5.

Lewis, Edna. *The Taste of Country Cooking.* Knopf, 1976.

Lipsitz, George. *The Progressive Investment in Whiteness: How White People Profit from Identity Politics.* Twentieth anniversary edition. Temple University Press, 2018.

Li, Shan. "Five Years in, Fresh & Easy Markets Are a Flop." *Los Angeles Times.* March 21, 2013. www.latimes.com/business/la-fi-fresh-easy-woes-20130321,0,197757.story.

Li, Tania. *The Will To Improve: Governmentality, Development, and the Practice of Politics.* Duke University Press, 2007.

Lloyd, Annie. "A Brief History of LA's Indigenous Tongva People." *LAist.* October 8, 2017. https://laist.com/news/la-history/a-brief-history-of-the-tongva-people.

Logan, Amanda L. *The Scarcity Slot: Excavating Histories of Food Security in Ghana.* University of California Press, 2020.

Los Angeles Food Policy Council (LAFPC) Good Food Economy Working Group. "Recovery Resiliency & Racial Equity," 1–44. In *The Good Food Zone*. www.first5la.org/wp-content/uploads/2021/09/GoodFoodZoneBooklet20 20-2.pdf.

Los Angeles Times. "South L.A." *Mapping L.A.* 2020. Accessed July 1, 2024. http://maps.latimes.com/neighborhoods/region/south-la/#income.

Lui, Earl. "Transforming Food Deserts: A Food Justice Tour of South Los Angeles." California Wellness Foundation, 2020. Accessed July 1, 2024. www.calwellness.org/stories/transforming-food-deserts-a-food-justice-tour -of-south-los-angeles/.

Lusk, Jayson. "The New Food Police Are Out of Touch." *Time Magazine*. May 6, 2013. https://ideas.time.com/2013/05/06/viewpoint-the-new-food-police- are-out-of-touch/.

Mahoney, Adam. "The Environmental Justice Fight To Block the 2028 Olympics in Los Angeles." *Grist*. October 12, 2021. https://grist.org/cities/2028 -olympics-los-angeles-environmental-justice-inglewood/.

Malkki, Liisa H. *The Need To Help: The Domestic Arts of International Humanitarianism*. Duke University Press, 2015.

Marcus, George E. "Ethnography in/of the World System: The Emergence of Multi-Sited Ethnography." *Annual Review of Anthropology* 24 (1995): 95–117. www.jstor.org/stable/2155931.

Masters, Nathan. "How Sepulveda Canyon Became the 405." *PBS SoCal*. June 27, 2017. www.pbssocal.org/shows/lost-la/how-sepulveda-canyon-became -the-405.

Matheson, Victor A., and Robert A. Baade. "Race and Riots: A Note on the Economic Impact of the Rodney King Riots." *Urban Studies* 41, no. 13 (2004): 2691–96. https://doi.org/10.1080/0042098042000294628.

Mamdani, Mahmood. *When Victims Become Killers: Colonialism, Nativism, and the Genocide in Rwanda*. Princeton University Press, 2002.

McChesney, Robert. Introduction to *Profit over People: Neoliberalism and Global Order*. Edited by Noam Chomsky. Seven Stories Press, 2003.

McClintock, Nathan. "Radical, Reformist, and Garden-Variety Neoliberal: Coming to Terms with Urban Agriculture's Contradictions." *Local Environment* 19, no. 2 (2014): 147–71.

McClintock, Nathan, and Micheal Simpson. "Stacking Functions: Identifying Motivational Frames Guiding Urban Agriculture Organizations and Businesses in the United States and Canada." *Agriculture and Human Values* 35 (2018): 19–39.

McGranahan, Carole. "Theorizing Refusal: An Introduction." *Cultural Anthropology* 31, no. 3 (2016): 319–25. https://doi.org/10.14506/ca31.3.01.

McKittrick, Katherine. *Dear Science and Other Stories*. Duke University Press, 2021.

McKittrick, Katherine. "On Plantations, Prisons, and a Black Sense of Place." *Social & Cultural Geography* 12 (2011): 947, 951.

McLaughlin, Sarah. "This Millennial Is Eliminating Food Deserts in South Los Angeles, One Vegan Meal at a Time." *VegNews*, June 11, 2019. https://

vegnews.com/2019/6/this-millennial-is-eliminating-food-deserts-in-south-los-angeles-one-vegan-meal-at-a-time.

McMichael, Philip. "A Food Regime Genealogy." *Journal of Peasant Studies* 36, no. 1 (2009): 139–69.

McNamara, Michael, and Jemaine Love. *Baldwin Hills*. 2007. Black Entertainment Television (BET).

Mejías-Rentas, Antonio. "New Program To Benefit East LA Sidewalk Vendors." *The Eastsider*. Accessed July 13, 2022. www.theeastsiderla.com /neighborhoods/east_los_angeles/new-program-to-benefit-east-la-sidewalk-vendors/article_f13f8cac-02c9-11eb-8a11-efabbb9e7004.html.

Metzl, Jonathan M., and Helena Hansen. "Structural Competency: Theorizing a New Medical Engagement with Stigma and Inequality." *Social Science & Medicine* 103 (2014): 126–33.

Mill, John Stuart. *On Liberty*. John W. Parker and Son, 1859.

Miller, Adrian. *Soul Food: The Surprising Story of an American Cuisine, One Plate at a Time*. University of North Carolina Press, 2013.

Miller, Julius. "City Street Food Merchants Sue L.A. over Rampant 'No Vending Zones.'" *LA Magazine*. December 9, 2022. www.lamag.com/citythink-blog/city-street-food-merchants-sue-l-a-over-rampant-no-vending-zones/.

Mills, Charles W. *The Racial Contract*. Cornell University Press, 1997.

Mills, Charles W. "White Ignorance." In *Race and Epistemologies of Ignorance*. Edited by Shannon Sullivan and Nancy Tuana. SUNY Press, 2007.

Mintz, Sidney. *Sweetness and Power: The Place of Sugar in Modern History*. Penguin Books, 1986.

Miranda, Carolina A. "Of the 63 People Killed During '92 Riots, 23 Deaths Remain Unsolved—Artist Jeff Beall Is Mapping Where They Fell." Los Angeles Times. April 27, 2017. www.latimes.com/entertainment/arts /miranda/la-et-cam-la-riots-jeff-beall-los-angeles-uprising-20170427 -htmlstory.html.

Mitchell, Timothy. *Colonizing Egypt*. University of California, 1988.

Mohanty, Chandra Talpade. "Cartographies of Struggle." In *Third World Women and the Politics of Feminism*. Edited by Chandra Talpade Mohanty, Lourdes Torres, and Ann Russo. Indiana University Press, 1991.

Molina, Natalia. *Fit To Be Citizens: Public Health and Race in Los Angeles 1879–1939*. University of California Press, 2006.

Molina, Natalia. "The Importance of Place and Place-Makers in the Life of a Los Angeles Community: What Gentrification Erases from Echo Park." *Southern California Quarterly* 97, no. 1 (2015): 69–111.

Molina, Natalia. *A Place at the Nayarit: How a Mexican Restaurant Nourished a Community*. University of California Press, 2022.

Morgan, Sandra, and Jeff Maskovsky. "The Anthropology of Welfare 'Reform': New Perspectives on US Urban Poverty in the Post-Welfare Era." *Annual Review of Anthropology* 32 (2003): 315–38.

Moten, Fred. *In the Break: The Aesthetics of the Black Radical Tradition*. University of Minnesota Press, 2003.

Moten, Fred. *Stolen Life*. Duke University Press, 2018.

Mousavi, Amirhosein, Mohammad H. Sowlat, Sina Hasheminassab, Olga Pikelnaya, Andrea Polidori, George Ban-Weiss, and Constantinos Sioutas. "Impact of Particulate Matter (PM) Emissions from Ships, Locomotives, and Freeways in the Communities Near the Ports of Los Angeles (POLA) and Long Beach (POLB) on the Air Quality in the Los Angeles County." *Atmospheric Environment* 195 (2018): 159–69. https://doi.org/10.1016/j.atmosenv.2018.09.044.

Moynihan, Daniel Patrick. *The Negro Family: The Case for National Action*. US Department of Labor, 1965.

Mullings, Leith. *On Our Own Terms: Race, Class and Gender in the Lives of African American Women*. Routledge, 1997.

Narayan, Kirin. "How Native Is a 'Native' Anthropologist?" *American Anthropologist* 95, no. 3 (1993): 671–86.

Nelson, Alondra. *Body and Soul: The Black Panther Party and the Fight against Medical Discrimination*. University of Minnesota Press, 2011.

Nestle, Marion. *Food Politics: How the Food Industry Influences Nutrition and Health*. University of California Press, 2002.

Nettles-Barcelón, Kimberly. "California Soul: Stories of Food and Place from Oakland's Brown Sugar Kitchen." *Boom: A Journal of California* 2, no. 3 (2012): 18–24.

New York Observer. "The Biden Tapes." *The Observer*. January 31, 2007. https://observer.com/2007/01/the-biden-tapes/.

N.W.A. *Straight Outta Compton*. 1998. Ruthless Records, compact disc.

Oh, Angela E. "Rebuilding Los Angeles: 'One Year Later or Why I Did Not Join RLA.'" *Amerasia Journal* 19, no. 2 (1993): 157–60. https://doi:10.17953/amer.19.2.d821721k6u95j12p.

Oldenburg, Ray. *The Great Good Place: Cafés, Coffee Shops, Bookstores, Bars, Hair Salons, and Other Hangouts at the Heart of a Community*. Da Capo Press, 1989.

Oliver, Jamie. *The Naked Chef*. 1999–2001. British Broadcast Company (BBC).

Oliver, Jamie, and Ryan Seacrest. "Chicken Nuggets." Season 1, Episode 1. *Jamie Oliver's Food Revolution*. 2010. ABC studios.

Oluo, Ijeoma. *So You Want To Talk About Race*. Seal Press, 2018.

Omi, Michael, and Howard Winant. *Racial Formation in the United States: From the 1960s to 1990s*. Second edition. Routledge, 1994.

Ong, Paul, and Suzanne Hee. "The Los Angeles Riots/Rebellion and Korean Merchants." In *Losses in the Los Angeles Civil Unrest April 29–May 1, 1992: Lists of the Damaged Properties*. UCLA Center for Pacific Rim Studies, 1993.

Opie, Frederick. *Hog and Hominy: Soul Food from Africa to America*. Columbia University Press, 2008.

Ortega, A.N., S.L. Albert, A.M. Chan-Golston, et al. "Substantial Improvements Not Seen in Health Behaviors Following Corner Store Conversions in Two Latino Food Swamps." *BMC Public Health* 16, no. (2016). https://doi.org/10.1186/s12889-016-3074-1.

Ortner, Sherry B. "Dark Anthropology and Its Others: Theory Since the Eighties." *HAU: Journal of Ethnographic Theory* 6, no. 1 (2016): 47–73.

Oyarzun, Yesmar. "Plantation Politics, Paranoia, and Public Health on the Frontlines of America's COVID-19 Response." *Medical Anthropology Quarterly* 34, no. 4 (2020): 578–90.

Palm, Iman. "The Median Listing Price for Homes in Los Angeles Could Soon Top $1 Million." *KTLA.* Accessed October 9, 2023. https://ktla.com/news /california/the-median-listing-price-for-homes-in-los-angeles-could-soon-top-1-million/amp/.

Park, Kyeyoung. *LA Rising: Korean Relations with Blacks and Latinos after Civil Unrest.* Lexington Books, 2019.

Patel, Raj. "After Words." CSPAN Interview with Evan Kleinman. *CSPAN.* 2008. Accessed July 6, 2022. www.c-span.org/video/?204975-1/after -words-raj-patel#.

Patel, Raj. *Stuffed and Starved: The Hidden Battle for the World Food System.* Melville House, 2008.

Petrini, Carlo. *Slow Food: Slow Food: The Case for Taste.* Columbia University Press, 2001.

Petryna, Adriana. *Horizon Work: At the Edges of Knowledge in an Age of Runaway Climate Change.* Princeton University Press, 2022.

Pierre, Jemima. "The Racial Vernaculars of Development: A View from West Africa." *American Anthropologist* 122, no. 1 (2020): 86–98.

Pollan, Michael. *In Defense of Food: An Eater's Manifesto.* Penguin Press, 2008.

Pollan, Michael. *The Omnivore's Dilemma: A Natural History of Four Meals.* Penguin Press, 2006.

Pollan, Michael. "Out of the Kitchen, onto the Couch. *New York Times Magazine.* 2009. Accessed July 22, 2022. https://michaelpollan.com/articles-archive /out-of-the-kitchen-onto-the-couch/.

Poppendieck, Janet. *Breadlines Knee Deep in Wheat: Food Assistance in the Great Depression.* University of California Press, 2014.

Poppendieck, Janet. *Sweet Charity?: Emergency Food and the End of Entitlement.* Penguin Putnam Books, 1999.

Pottier, J. *Anthropology of Food: The Social Dynamics of Food Security.* Polity Press, 1999.

Povinelli, Elizabeth A. *The Cunning of Recognition: Indigenous Alterities and the Making of Australian Multiculturalism.* Duke University Press, 2002.

Povinelli, Elizabeth A. *Economies of Abandonment: Social Belonging and the Endurance of Late Liberalism.* Duke University Press, 2011.

Povinelli, Elizabeth A. "Radical Worlds: The Anthropology of Incommensurability and Inconceivability." *Annual Review of Anthropology* 30 (2001): 319–34.

Pulido, Laura. *Black, Brown, Yellow, and Left: Radical Activism in Los Angeles.* University of California Press, 2006.

Rae, Issa, Larry Wilmore, Amy Aniobi, Yvonne Orji, Jay Ellis, and Lisa Joyce. *Insecure. The Complete First Season.* 2017. HBO.

Rahoumi, Tamara. "McDonalds Is Changing Its Chicken McNugget Recipe: The Happy Meal Is Getting a Whole Lot Happier." *Delish.* April 28, 2016. www.delish.com/food-news/a47003/the-mcnugget-formula-is-about-to-get -a-major-makeover/.

Ramírez, Margaret. M. "The Elusive Inclusive: Black Food Geographies and Racialized Food Spaces." *Antipode* 47, no. 3 (2015): 748–69.

Ramos, Marco A. "Defining 'Social Justice' at the Academic Medical Center." *Somatosphere*. Accessed January 21, 2018. http://somatosphere.net/?p = 14165.

Rawls, John. *A Theory of Justice*. Harvard University Press, 1971.

Redfin. "South LA Housing Market." 2023. Accessed January 21, 2018. www.redfin.com/neighborhood/92255/CA/Los-Angeles/South-LA/housing-market.

Redmond, Shana, and Damien Sojoyner. "Keywords in Black Protest: A(n Anti-)Vocabulary." *Truth Out*. May 29, 2015. www.truthout.org/opinion/item/31051-keywords-in-black-protest-a-n-antivocabulary.

Reese, Ashanté. *Black Food Geographies: Race, Self-Reliance and Food Access in Washington, DC*. UNC Press, 2019.

Reese, Ashanté. "In the Food Justice World but Not of It: Everyday Black Food Entrepreneurship." In *Black Food Matters: Racial Justice in the Wake of Food Justice*. Edited by Hanna Garth and Ashanté Reese. University of Minnesota Press, 2020.

Reese, Ashanté, and Randolph Carr. "Overthrowing the Food System's Plantation Paradigm." *Civil Eats*. June 19, 2020. https://civileats.com/2020/06/19/op-ed-overthrowing-the-food-systems-plantation-paradigm/.

Reese, Ashanté M. "We Will Not Perish; We're Going To Keep Flourishing: Race, Food Access, and Geographies of Self-Reliance." *Antipode* 50, no. 2 (2018): 407–24.

Reuters. "Los Angeles Council President Steps Down after Audio Leak of Racist Comments." October 11, 2022. www.reuters.com/world/us/los-angeles-council-president-steps-down-after-audio-leak-racist-comments-2022–10–10/.

Reyes-Velarde, Alejandra. "A Community Garden in Watts Provides Solace, Fresh Produce for Immigrants." *LA Times*. January 2, 2023. www.latimes.com/california/story/2023–01–02/watts-community-garden.

Reynolds, Kristin, and Nevin Cohen. *Beyond the Kale: Urban Agriculture and Social Justice Activism in New York City*. University of Georgia Press, 2016.

Riles, Annelise. *The Network Inside Out*. University of Michigan Press, 2000.

Rivera, Carla. "Food Crisis a Measure of Suffering Caused by Riots: Unrest." *LA Times*. June 17, 1992. www.latimes.com/archives/la-xpm-1992–06–17-mn-467-story.html.

Raoul, Peck, dir. *I Am Not Your Negro*. 2016. Magnolia Pictures.

Robbins, Joel. "Beyond the Suffering Subject: Toward an Anthropology of the Good." *Journal of the Royal Anthropological Institute* 19, no. 3 (2013): 447–62.

Robbins, Ocean. "From Food Deserts to Food Oases: Addressing Access to Healthy Food." *Food Revolution Network*. September 11, 2020. https://foodrevolution.org/blog/food-deserts-food-oasis-healthy-food-access/.

Roberts, Dorothy. *Killing the Black Body: Race, Reproduction, and the Meaning of Liberty*. Pantheon Books, 1997.

Roberts, Dorothy. *Shattered Bonds: The Color of Child Welfare*. Basic Books, 2002.

Roberts, Dorothy. *Torn Apart: How the Child Welfare System Destroys Black Families—and How Abolition Can Build a Safer World*. Basic Books, 2022.

Robinson, Cedric. *Black Marxism: The Making of the Black Radical Tradition*. Zed Press, 1983.

Robinson, Paul. "Race, Space, and the Evolution of Black Los Angeles." Chapter 1 in *Black Los Angeles: American Dreams and Racial Realities*. Edited by Darnell Hunt and Ana-Christina Ramón. New York University Press, 2010.

Rodriguez, Cheryl. "Invoking Fannie Lou Hamer: Research, Ethnography and Activism in Low-Income Communities." *Urban Anthropology and Studies of Cultural Systems and World Economic Development* (2003): 231–51.

Roediger, David. *The Wages of Whiteness: Race and the Making of the American Working Class*. Verso, 1991.

Rosa, Jonathan. *Looking Like a Language, Sounding Like a Race: Raciolinguistic Ideologies and the Learning of Latinidad*. Oxford University Press, 2019.

Rosales, Rocio. *Fruteros: Street Vending, Illegality and Ethnic Community in Los Angeles*. University of California Press, 2020.

Rosales, Rocio. "Survival, Economic Mobility and Community among Los Angeles Fruit Vendors." *Journal of Ethnic and Migration Studies* 39, no. 5 (2013): 697–717.

Rosas, Abigail. *South Central Is Home: Race and the Power of Community Investment in Los Angeles*. Stanford University Press, 2019.

Rouse, Carolyn M. "Necropolitics vs. Biopolitics: Spatialization, White Privilege, and Visibility during a Pandemic." *Cultural Anthropology* 36, no. 3 (2021): 360–67.

Rouse, Carolyn M. "Rights, Inequality, and Social Justice." In *A Companion to the Anthropology of Africa*. Edited by Roy Richard Grinker, Stephen C. Lubkemann, Christopher B. Steiner, and Euclides Goncalves. Wiley, 2019.

Satterfield, Stephan. *High on the Hog: How African American Cuisine Transformed America*. 2021–2023. Netflix.

Sbicca, Joshua. "Growing Food Justice by Planting an Anti-Oppression Foundation: Opportunities and Obstacles for a Budding Social movement." *Agriculture and Human Values* 29, no. 4 (2012): 455–66.

Schlosser, Eric. *Fast Food Nation: The Dark Side of the All-American Meal*. Houghton Mifflin, 2001.

Schlosser, Eric, writer. *Fast Food Nation*. 2006. Searchlight Pictures, Inc.

Schlosser, Eric. "Still a Fast Food Nation: Eric Schlosser Reflects on 10 Years Later." *Daily Beast*. 2017. Accessed July 26, 2022. www.thedailybeast.com /still-a-fast-food-nation-eric-schlosser-reflects-on-10-years-later.

SCOPE. "Climate Equity from the Grassroots." 2017. Accessed July 28, 2022. https://scopela.org/climate-equity-from-the-grassroots/.

SCOPE. "A New Economy for South Los Angeles—SCOPE." 2020. Accessed July 2, 2024. http://scopela.org/our-work/campaigns/.

Scully, Matthew. *Dominion: The Power of Man, the Suffering of Animals, and the Call to Mercy*. St. Martin's Press, 2003.

Sen, Amartya. "Food and Freedom." Sir John Crawford Memorial Lecture, Washington, DC. 1987. Accessed July 2, 2024. http://wphna.org/wp-content /uploads/2015/02/1985-Sen-Food-and-freedom.pdf.

Shah, Nayan. *Contagious Divides: Epidemics and Race in San Francisco's Chinatown*. University of California Press, 2001.

Shah, Sonia. *The Body Hunters: Testing New Drugs on the World's Poorest Patients*. New Press, 2012.

Shange, Savannah. *Progressive Dystopia: Abolition, Antiblackness, and Schooling in San Francisco*. Duke University Press, 2019.

Shange, Savannah, and Roseann Liu. "Solidarity-as-Debt: Fugitive Publics and the Ethics of Multiracial Coalition." *Fieldsights*. July 31, 2019. https:// culanth.org/fieldsights/solidarity-as-debt-fugitive-publics-and-the-ethics-of-multiracial-coalit.

Sharp, Steven. "Renderings Revealed for the First Apartments at Inglewood's Hollywood Park Development: The Wesley and The Crosby Will Feature 314 Units." *Urbanize LA*. November 17, 2022. https://la.urbanize.city /post/renderings-revealed-first-apartments-inglewoods-hollywood-park -development.

Sharpe, Christina. *In the Wake: On Blackness and Being*. Duke University Press, 2016.

Shelby Report. "Big Deal in SoCal: Superior Grocers Acquires Numero Uno." *Shelby Report*. July 13, 2022. https://theshelbyreport.com/2022/07/13/big-deal-in-socal-superior-grocers-acquires-numero-uno/.

Shelby Report. "CEO Song Honored As Superior Grocers Celebrates 40th Anniversary." *Shelby Report*. January 1, 2021. www.theshelbyreport.com/2021 /01/21/ceo-song-honored-as-superior-grocers-celebrates-40th-anniversary/.

Shelby Report. "Superior's CEO Immigrated from South Korea with Early Designs on a Different Path." *Shelby Report*. January 21, 2021. www.theshelbyreport .com/2021/01/21/mimi-song-fashions-successful-grocery-career/.

Sides, Josh. *LA City Limits: African American Los Angeles from the Great Depression to the Present*. University of California Press, 2003.

Silverstein, Stuart, and Nancy Brooks. "Shoppers in Need of Stores (Lack of Retail Industries and Other Businesses in South Los Angeles, California)." *Los Angeles Times*. November 24, 1991.

Shiva, Vandana. *Soil Not Oil: Environmental Justice in a Time of Climate Crisis*. South End Press, 2008.

Shiva, Vandana, ed. *Manifestos on the Future of Food and Seed*. South End Press, 2007.

Short, Anne, Julie Guthman, and Samuel Raskin, "Food Deserts, Oases or Mirages?" *Journal of Planning Education and Research* 26, no. 3 (2007): 352–64.

Simpson, Audra. *Mohawk Interruptus: Political Life across the Borders of Settler States*. Duke University Press, 2014.

Simpson, Audra. "On Ethnographic Refusal: Indigeneity, 'Voice' and Colonial Citizenship." *Junctures: The Journal for Thematic Dialogue* 9 (2007): 67–80.

Singleton, John, dir. *Boyz n the Hood*. 1991. Sony Pictures.

Slocum, Rachel. "Anti-racist Practice and the Work of Community Food Organizations." *Antipode* 38 (2006): 327–49.

Slocum, Rachel. "Thinking Race Through Corporeal Feminist Theory: Divisions and Intimacies at the Minneapolis Farmers' Market." *Social & Cultural Geography* 9, no. 8 (2008): 849–69.

Slocum, Rachel. "Whiteness, Space, and Alternative Food Practice." *Geoforum* 38 (2007): 520–33.

Slocum, Rachel, and Arun Saldanha, eds. *Geographies of Race and Food: Fields, Bodies, Markets.* Ashgate Publishing, 2013.

Slocum, Rachel, Jerry Shannon, Kirsten Valentine Cadieux, and Matthew Beckman. "Properly, with Love, from Scratch: Jamie Oliver's Food Revolution." *Radical History Review Issue* 110 (2011): 178–91.

Smart-Grosvenor, Vertamae. *Thursdays and Every Other Sunday Off: A Domestic Rap by Verta Mae.* Doubleday, 1972.

Smart-Grosvenor, Vertamae. *Vibration Cooking: Or, The Travel Notes of a Geechee Girl.* University of Georgia Press, 1970.

Smedley, Audrey. *Race in North America: The Origins and Evolution of a Worldview.* Westview, 1993.

Smith, Linda Tuhiwai. *Decolonizing Methodologies: Researching and Indigenous Peoples.* Zed Books Ltd., 1999.

Smoler, Ryan. "A Visit to South LA's Village Market Place Food Hub." *Long Beach Fresh.* 2018. Accessed July 11, 2022. http://lbfresh.org/news/a-visit-to-south-las-village-market-place-food-hub/.

Social Enterprise Alliance. "About." Accessed March 12, 2023. https://socialenterprise.us/about.

Social Justice Learning Institute (SJLI). Website. Accessed July 11, 2022. https://sjli.org/.

Sojoyner, Damien M. "Another Life Is Possible: Black Fugitivity and Enclosed Places." *Cultural Anthropology* 32, no. 4 (2017): 514–36.

Sojoyner, Damien M. *First Strike: Educational Enclosures in Black Los Angeles.* University of Minnesota Press, 2016.

Sojoyner, Damien M. *Joy and Pain: A Story of Black Life and Liberation in Five Albums.* University of California Press, 2022.

Sojoyner, Damien M. "You Are Going To Get Us Killed: Fugitive Archival Practice and the Carceral State." *American Anthropologist* 123, no. 3 (2021): 658–70.

Soon-Shiong, Patrick. "The *Times*' Reckoning on Race and Our Commitment To Meaningful Change." *Los Angeles Times.* September 17, 2020. www.latimes.com/opinion/story/2020–09–27/los-angeles-times-reckoning-on-race.

South Central Farm. Website. Accessed July 14, 2022. www.southcentralfarm.org/farm-his-herstory.

Spurlock, Morgan, dir. *Super Size Me.* 2004. The Con Productions.

Stallworth, Leo, and Grace Manthey. "Homicides in Los Angeles Reach Highest Level in 15 Years During 1st Half of 2022: Report." *ABC News.* July 13, 2022. Accessed November 11, 2022. https://abc7.com/los-angeles-homicides-crime-report/12046605/.

STAND LA. "Urban Oil Sites." *Stand-LA*. Accessed July 28, 2022. www.stand
.la/drill-sites-in-la.html.

Stark, Michael L., and Wendy Kennedy. *Vons Grocery Company: Images of
America*. Arcadia Publishing, 2014.

Stephens, Pamela, and Manuel Pastor. "What's Going On?: Black Experiences
of Latinization and Loss in South Los Angeles." *Du Bois Review: Social Science Research on Race* 17, no. 1 (2020): 1–32. https://vdOI:10.1017
/s1742058x20000053.

Stovall, Tyler. *White Freedom: The Racial History of an Idea*. Princeton University Press, 2021.

Strathern, Marilyn, ed. *Audit Cultures: Anthropological Studies in Accountability, Ethics and the Academy*. Routledge, 2000.

Strings, Sabrina. *Fearing the Black Body: The Racial Origins of Fat Phobia*.
New York University Press, 2019.

Sturm, Roland, and Aiko Hattori. "Diet and Obesity in Los Angeles County
2007–2012: Is There a Measurable Effect of the 2008 'Fast-Food Ban'?"
Social Science and Medicine 133 (2015): 205–11.

Susaneck, Adam Paul. "Los Angeles Metro 2020–2060: The Future and Growth
of Los Angeles Rail Transit." April 6, 2020. Accessed October 26, 2023.
https://medium.com/@adamasusaneck/los-angeles-metro-2020–2060
-f44ado4ffofa4.

Sze, Julie, and Jonathan K. London. "Environmental Justice at the Crossroads."
Sociology Compass 2, no. 4 (2008): 1331–54.

Tate, Allison, and Signe Okkels Larsen, dirs. *Urban Harvest*. 2015.

Taylor, Keeanga-Yamahtta. *From #BlackLivesMatter to Black Liberation*.
Haymarket Books, 2017.

Taylor, Keeanga-Yamahtta. *How We Get Free: Black Feminism and the Combahee River Collective*. Haymarket Books, 2017.

Taylor, Keeanga-Yamahtta. *Race for Profit: How Banks and the Real Estate
Industry Undermined Black Homeownership*. University of North Carolina
Press, 2021.

Terry, Bryant. *Afro-Vegan: Farm-fresh African, Caribbean & Southern Flavors
Remixed*. Ten Speed Press, 2014.

Terry, Bryant. *Vegan Soul Kitchen: Fresh, Healthy, and Creative African-
American Cuisine*. Da Capo Lifelong Books, 2009.

Thomas, Deborah. *Political Life in the Wake of the Plantation: Sovereignty,
Witnessing, Repair*. Duke University Press, 2019.

Tipton-Martin, Toni. *The Jemima Code: Two Centuries of African American
Cookbooks*. University of Texas Press, 2015.

Torres-Rouff, David. *Before L.A.: Race, Space, and Municipal Power in Los
Angeles, 1781–1894*. Yale University Press, 2013.

Trapp, Micah M. "Performing Vegetable Nutrition: Rethinking School Food
and Health." *Culture, Agriculture, Food and Environment* 44, no. 2 (2022):
120–31.

TRD Staff. "Archeon Group To Join 180 Apartments and Grocery Store in
South LA: Koreatown-Based Developer Seeks To Buy 2.8 Acres from City

for Approved Project." *Urbanize LA*. January 11, 2023. https://therealdeal
.com/la/2023/01/11/archeon-group-to-join-180-apartments-and-grocery
-store-in-south-la/.

Trechter, Sara, and Mary Bucholtz. "White Noise: Bringing Language into Whiteness Studies." *Journal of Linguistic Anthropology* 11, no. 1 (2001): 3–21.

Trouillot, Michel-Rolph. "Anthropology and the Savage Slot: The Poetics and
Politics of Otherness." In *Recapturing Anthropology: Working in the
Present*. Edited by Richard G. Fox. School for Advances Research Press,
1991.

Trouillot, Michel-Rolph. "The Anthropology of the State in the Age of Globalization: Close Encounters of the Deceptive Kind." *Current Anthropology* 42,
no. 1 (2001): 125–38.

Tsing, Anna Lowenhaupt. *The Mushroom at the End of the World: On the Possibility of Life in Capitalist Ruins*. Princeton University Press, 2015.

Tuck, Eve, and K. Wayne Yang. "Decolonization Is Not a Metaphor." *Decolonization: Indigeneity, Education & Society* 1, no. 1 (2012): 1–40

Tuttle, Brad. "Tale of Two Supermarkets: Why Fresh & Easy Flopped and
Fairway Flies High." April 18, 2013. http://business.time.com/2013/04/18
/tale-of-two-supermarkets-why-fresh-easy-flopped-and-fairway-flies-high/.

Twitty, Michael W. *The Cooking Gene: A Journey Through African American
Culinary History in the Old South*. Amistad/Harper Collins, 2017.

UN Food and Agriculture Organization (FAO). *The State of Food Insecurity in
the World*. Rome, 2009.

US Census Bureau. "American Community Survey 1-year Estimates." *Census
Reporter*. 2021. Accessed November 1, 2022. http://censusreporter.org
/profiles/79500US0603751-los-angeles-county-south-central-la-city-south
-centralwatts-puma-ca/.

US Census Bureau. "Census Urban Land Area List." Accessed October 9, 2020.
https://www2.census.gov/geo/docs/reference/ua/ua_list_all.txt.

US Environmental Protection Agency. "Annual Air Quality Los Angeles County
Air Quality Days by Year, 1980–2021." *Los Angeles Almanac*. 2021.
Accessed July 15, 2022. www.laalmanac.com/environment/evo1b.php.

Valdez, Natali. *Weighing the Future: Race, Science, and Pregnancy Trials in the
Postgenomic Era*. University of California Press, 2022.

Vallianatos, Mark. "Food Justice and Food Retail in Los Angeles." *Ecology
Law Currents* 36 (2009): 186–94.

Vargas, João Costa. *Catching Hell in the City of Angels: Life and Meanings of
Blackness in South Central Los Angeles*. First edition. University of Minnesota Press, 2006.

Vargas, João Costa. "The *Los Angeles Times*' Coverage of the 1992 Rebellion:
Still Burning Matters of Race and Justice." *Ethnicities* 4, no. 2 (2004):
209–36.

Vargas, João Costa, and Joy A. James. "Refusing Blackness-as-Victimization:
Trayvon Martin and the Black Cyborgs." In *Pursuing Trayvon Martin: His-
torical Contexts and Contemporary Manifestations of Racial Dynamics*.
Edited by George Yancy and Janine Jones. Lexington Books, 2012.

Vick, Karl. "L.A. Official Wants a Change of Menu." *Washington Post*. July 12, 2008. www.washingtonpost.com/wp-dyn/content/article/2008/07/12 /AR2008071201557_2.html.

Wallach, Jennifer Jensen. *Dethroning the Deceitful Pork Chop: Rethinking African American Foodways from Slavery to Obama*. University of Arkansas Press, 2015.

Wallach, Jennifer Jensen. *Getting What We Need Ourselves: How Food Has Shaped African American Life*. Rowman & Littlefield, 2019.

Washington, Karen, and Leah Penniman. "You Belong to the Land: A Conversation with Karen Washington and Lean Penniman." *Resilience*. September 10, 2019. www.resilience.org/stories/2019–09–10/you-belong-to-the-land-a-conversation-with-karen-washington-and-leah-penniman/.

Wells, Jernard, series host. *New Soul Kitchen*. 2019.

West, Paige. *Dispossession and the Environment: Rhetoric and Inequality in Papua New Guinea*. Columbia University Press, 2016.

Weston, Phoebe. "'This Is No Damn Hobby': The 'Gangsta Gardener' Transforming Los Angeles." *The Guardian*. April 28, 2020. www.theguardian .com/environment/2020/apr/28/ron-finley-gangsta-gardener-transforming -los-angeles.

White House Archive. "FACT SHEET: Obama Administration Announces More Than $4 Billion in Private Sector Commitments and Executive Actions To Scale Up Investment in Clean Energy Innovation." Obama White House Archives. June 16, 2015. https://obamawhitehouse.archives.gov/the-press -office/2015/06/16/fact-sheet-obama-administration-announces-more-4 -billion-private-sector.

White House Archive. "Obama Administration Details Healthy Food Financing Initiative." February 19, 2010. https://home.treasury.gov/news/press-releases/tg555.

White House Archive. "Taking on 'Food Deserts'." Obama White House Archives. February 24, 2010. https://obamawhitehouse.archives.gov /blog/2010/02/24/taking-food-deserts.

White, George. "Riot Impact Worse Than Predicted." *Los Angeles Times*. September 11, 1992.

White, Monica M. "D-Town Farm: African American Resistance to Food Insecurity and the Transformation of Detroit." *Environmental Practice* 13, no. 4 (2011): 406–17.

Whitehead, Tony L. "In Search of Soul Food and Meaning: Culture, Food, and Health." In *African Americans in the South: Issues of Race, Class, and Gender*. Edited by Hans A. Baer and Yvonne Jones. University of Georgia Press, 1992.

Wikipedia. "Crime in Los Angeles." Accessed November 11, 2022. https:// en.wikipedia.org/wiki/Crime_in_Los_Angeles.

Wilkerson, Isabel. *The Warmth of Other Suns: The Epic Story of America's Great Migration*. Random House, 2010.

Wilkins, Emma L., Michelle A. Morris, Duncan Radley, and Claire Griffiths. "Using Geographic Information Systems To Measure Retail Food Environments: Discussion of Methodological Considerations and a Proposed

Reporting Checklist (Geo-FERN)." *Health & Place* 44 (2017): 110–17. https://doi.org/10.1016/j.healthplace.2017.01.008.

Williams-Forson, Psyche. *Building Houses out of Chicken Legs*. University of North Carolina Press, 2006.

Williams-Forson, Psyche. *Eating While Black: Food Shaming and Race in America*. University of North Carolina Press, 2022.

Williams-Forson, Psyche. "Other Women Cooked for My Husband: Negotiating Gender, Food and Identities in an African American/Ghanaian Household." In *Taking Food Public: Redefining Foodways in a Changing World*. Edited by Psyche Williams-Forson and Carole Counihan. Routledge, 2012.

Winant, Howard. *The New Politics of Race: Globalism, Difference, and Justice*. University of Minnesota Press, 2004.

Winant, Howard. "White Racial Projects." In *The Making and Unmaking of Whiteness*. Edited by Birgit Brander Rasmussen, Eric Klinenberg, Irene J. Nexica, and Matt Wray. Duke University Press, 2001.

Wright Ann. "Interactive Web Tool Maps Food Deserts, Provides Key Data." *USDA Blog*. May 3, 2011. www.usda.gov/media/blog/2011/05/03/interactive-web-tool-maps-food-deserts-provides-key-data#:~:text = In%20the%20Food%20Desert%20Locator,supermarket%20or%20large%20grocery%20store.

Yu, E. Y., ed. *Black-Korean Encounter: Toward Understanding and Alliance*. Los Angeles: Institute for Asian American and Pacific Asian Studies, 1994.

Zafar, Rafia. *Recipes for Respect: African American Meals and Meaning*. Southern Foodways Alliance Studies in Culture, People, and Place. University of Georgia Press, 2019.

Zamora, Sylvia. *Racial Baggage: Mexican Immigrants and Race Across the Border*. Stanford University Press, 2022.

Zilberg, Elana. "A Troubled Corner: The Ruined and Rebuilt Environment of a Central American Barrio in Post-Rodney-King-Riot Los Angeles." *City and Society* 14, no. 2 (2002): 31–55.

Zumper. 2022. Rental listing. www.zumper.com/apartments-for-rent/los-angeles-ca/south-central-la/2-beds.

Index

academic language: moralized and slippery signifiers, 110; structural framing in food justice, xiv–xv

access to healthy food: grocery store expansion, 194–96; increasing efforts, 2; problems with upscale retail models, 198; racialized inequality in access, 194, 205, 217n11; volunteer labor and CSA models, xiv. *See also* food deserts and food swamps

activism: food justice activist contradictions, xiii–xvii, 4–6, 197–209; grassroots vs. outsider-led organizing, xiv–xviii; misunderstandings of South Central, 6–7; radical vs. liberal models, 4–5, 205–6; shifting priorities, 209

Adams, Lindsay (Food for All), 69–71, 73, 92, 165

African American Hebrew Israelites of Jerusalem, 6

Afro-Vegan (Terry), 7

Alejandra (food justice activist), 136–37

allyship in food justice: performative allyship, xiv–xv, 203; possibilities of multiracial coalitions, 206, 209

ancestral and community knowledge: African diasporic food traditions, 207–8; Black and Brown community foodways, 203–4; rejection of deficit models, 208; resistance rooted in historical traditions, 206–9

Anderson, Josh, 8, 111–16, 119, 125, 233nn38–39

Andrés (South Central resident), 8–10, 109

Barrio Bite (nonprofit organization), 87, 140–41. *See also* Jimenez, Federico (Barrio Bite)

Beliso-De Jesús, Aisha M., 109, 234n48, 236n21

Benjamin, Ruha, 109, 221n64

Benjamin, Walter, 106

Bettering Life (organization), 87, 104–5, 131, 144–49. *See also* David (Bettering Life); Smith, Matt (Bettering Life)

Black communities: cultural foodways, 203, 207–8; depictions as deficient, 202; displacement and gentrification, 196–98; exclusion from food systems, 197–98; food sovereignty organizing, 206–7; Great Migration and, 37–38; historic nourishment practices, xvi; misrepresentation by outsiders, xvi–xvii; stereotyping and saviorism, xvii; targeting by food justice projects, 198

Black cultural and political movements: African Hebrew Israelites of Jerusalem, 7; Black Panther Party (BPP), 6, 21, 81, 202, 207; BUGS (Black Urban Growers & Farmers), 9, 206–7

Black Lives Matter uprisings, 189–90

Black Panther Party (BPP), 6, 21, 81, 202, 207
Black Urban Growers (BUGS), 9, 206–7
Black veganism and plant-based diets: cultural and political dimensions, 7, 121, 167, 189; healthy eating and, 6–7, 56, 65, 156
Bledsoe, Chase (Produce Power), 8, 80–81, 83, 111, 119–21, 126, 179, 191–92
Borneman, John, 72
Bourdieu, Pierre, 232n22
Brodkin, Karen, 140, 230nn9,10
brown, adrienne maree, 163, 165, 171–72, 173, 175–76, 180, 190, 192
Brown, Autumn, 171
Brown communities. *See* Latinx/Brown communities
Build It Better (organization), 90–94, 135. *See also* Johnson, Randy (Build It Better)
Butler, Octavia, 165, 172–73, 236n3, 237n22

Candace (Produce Power), 127, 128
capitalism and food justice: charity vs. justice frameworks, 5; critiques of nonprofit industrial complex, 205; racial capitalism and food inequality, 205
Catching Hell in the City of Angels (Vargas), 45–46
Chadburn, Melissa, 50
Chandrasekaran, Priya, 172
the Chef, 75–76, 95
Coates, Ta-Nehisi, 107
Combahee River Collective, 107
commensality and cultural food practices: Black and Brown traditions, xvi, 105; community gatherings and nourishment, 6–7; forms of, 24; shared eating as political, cultural act, 203
community and grassroots organizing: centering impacted communities, 206–9; community engagement and extractive models, 6–7; comparison with outsider-led projects, xvi–xvii; mutual aid vs. charity, xvii. *See also* grassroots vs. outsider approaches; mutual aid vs. charity
Community Based Participatory Action Research (CBPR), 149–50
community gardens and urban agriculture: access and cost-efficiency, 198–99; gentrification concerns, 195–98; historical use of, 4; plans for, 2–3; racial dynamics and white-led models, 198

community supported agriculture (CSA) programs, xiv, 59, 128, 181, 198–99
Compton, 15, 17, 218n15, 219n27
Cooper, Brittney, 107
Costa Vargas, João H., 41, 45, 223–24n48
Coulombe, Joe, 42
COVID-19 pandemic lockdowns, 143, 153, 189–91, 200
Crenshaw District (Los Angeles), 6, 14*map*, 65, 84, 129
crisisification, 202, 221n59
Cristianos (investigator), 145
cultural appropriation and disconnect: ethnic food marginalization, 201; between food justice programming and residents, 203–4; white racial project dynamics in cooking workshops, 203
Cunningham, Sarah (Produce Power), 8–9, 23, 80–89, 94–95, 119, 122, 137–38, 188–89

dark anthropology, xiv
David (Bettering Life), 131–33, 144–49, 157–58
Davies, Carole Boyce, 27
Davis, Angela, 81, 82, 107
Davis, Mike, 35–37
deficit models, 202, 208
Desmond, Matthew, 232n22
De Souza, Rebecca, 86
development and gentrification: antigentrification, 178; displacement through food projects, 194–98; causes of, 75, 142, 197; green gentrification, 196–97; media portrayals and, 46; rent increases and mixed-use development, 194–95; SoFi Stadium and Olympics 2028 impacts, 194–97; violence and, 46–47
DiAngelo, Robin, 107
diet and health narratives: behavioral models and their limit, 201–3; critiques of American diet, 19; healthy food and racialized concept, 6–7, 88, 104, 201–3; moralization and depoliticization of health, 56–57, 205–6. *See also* access to healthy food; Black veganism and plant-based diets
DuBois, W.E.B., 107, 110

El Super, 44, 45*fig.*, 51, 52*map*, 53, 55
Emergent Strategy (brown), 163, 165, 171, 175
Emirbayer, Mustafa, 232n22

empowerment and justice language: co-optation and vagueness of, 205–6; education and, 149–153; placemaking and, 133–35, 146, 157–58; strategic use in nonprofit discourse, 5, 94, 131; youth and, 148

environmental and food justice: contrasting lineages of environmental justice and Black food justice, 207; eco-central and entrepreneurial motivational frames, 5; effects on, 238n6

Fall Fest, 127–28

Fanon, Franz, 81, 82

Ferguson, James, 12, 62

Finley, Ron, 61–62

Floyd, George, 107, 190, 231n20

food access. *See* access to healthy food

food apartheid: community interpretations and misuses, 194–98, 201; critiques of term and structural framing, 24, 45, 149, 202; food justice and, 25, 157, 209; misunderstood by activists, xv, 7–13, 92, 157, 201, 203; racial capitalism and, 163; responses to, 18, 113, 163. *See also* food deserts and food swamps

Food Day, 66–68, 69, 70, 71, 73

food deserts and food swamps: definitions of, 9; identification of, 60, 226n90; oversimplification of systemic issues, 51–56, 87–88, 113, 146, 202–3, 220n49; symbolic narratives of lack, 2, 7–8, 62–63, 221n50, 230n6

Food for All (organization), xi–xii, 3, 69, 73, 94, 181, 184, 186–88, 199. *See also* Adams, Lindsay (Food for All); Miguel (Food for All); Sunny (Food for All)

food justice: definitions and origins, 3–6; liberal vs. radical approaches, 4–5, 197–98; rise of in LA, 18–23; seen as service work, 5–6; tensions and ideological contradictions, 4–5, 197–98; use of "justice" as branding, 5; vacant lot metaphor in, 1–2, 6–7, 61–62

food justice movement: lack of cohesion and unity, 200–205; multiracial coalitions potential, 4; outsider-led vs. community-led tensions, xiii–xviii; power struggles and value gaps, 205–6; structural violence reproduction, xvii

food justice organizations: fragmented motivations, xiii–xv; grassroots models, xvi–xvii; Rooting Change and CSA program example, 198–99

food sovereignty, 20, 168, 206–7, 217n5, 237n31

food systems: equitable food systems, 199–200, 206, 228n9; liberation of, 170–173; outsider approach problems of, 118; placemaking and, 133; political nature of, 143–44; reimagination through placemaking and praxis, 209; structural inequalities in access, labor, and land use, 4, 18, 227n4; unsustainable solutions, 200–205

Foucault, Michel, 107

Frankenberg, Ruth, 230n10, 231n18

Freire, Paolo, 81, 133, 185

Frey, Lawrence R., 229n18

Garcetti, Eric, 67, 68, 69, 71, 72, 87, 94, 227nn1,2

gentrification. *See* development and gentrification

Gilmore, Ruthie Wilson, 217n10

Gold, Jonathan, 75

Gordon, Lewis, 109

Gottlieb, Robert, 21–22

Graeber, David, 239n10

grassroots vs. outsider approaches: co-optation of grassroots movement language, 5, 206; depoliticizing of problems and, 119; diverse food justice projects and, 59, 60–63, 91, 108, 178; grass-roots organizing, 68–69, 131, 134, 155, 185; local knowledge devaluation, xvi, 25, 89, 91, 118, 126; outsiders, xviii, 5, 13, 63, 86, 89, 91, 108, 197–98; placemaking and, 134–35, 138–39; radical approach, 26, 29, 178, 206, 209; social justice and, 82; tensions and harm from non-resident interventions, xiv–xviii, 25–28, 86, 170, 197–98; South Central Farm and, 58–59

Great Society programs, 41, 168

Green, Jamarcus (Rooting Change), 23–24, 123, 149–53, 157–58, 198–99, 207–9

Growing Health (organization), 87. *See also* Julian (food justice activist)

Gupta, Akhil, 12, 237n37

Gusterson, Hugh, 215n2

Guthman, Julie, 22, 23, 27, 215n1, 232n21

Harlins, Latasha, 34–35, 43, 61, 63, 174

Harper, A. Breeze, 6–7

Harris, Cheryl, 110, 170

Harvey, David, 83

Hazel (food justice activist), 10, 26

health and nutritionism: cultural knowledge of, 6–7; definitions and vagueness, 105, 201, 206; food justice movement and, 9, 28, 66, 76–77, 80, 84, 95, 105; moral ideologies about, 23, 35, 37, 126, 205, 222n16,17; obesity, 20–21, 59–60, 102, 113, 117, 145–46, 209, 220nn46,47, 221n59; public health and, xv, 17, 21, 35, 37, 88, 146, 227n1; racial notions of, 37, 105, 106, 175, 225n82; socioeconomic and racial disparities in, 7, 39, 88, 152, 157, 234n41; structural racism obscured by individualism, 130, 201–3, 205. *See also* access to healthy food

Ho, Karen, 215n2

Horne, Gerald, 47

How to Survive the End of the World (podcast), 171

Hunt, Darnell, 48, 218nn18,20, 218n, 219–20n35

Hussle, Nipsey, 3, 13, 15, 129

Imarisha, Walidah, 165, 171, 236n19

INCITE! Women of Color Against Violence collective, 184

Indigenous food practices, 4, 24, 105, 170

In the Liberated Future (booklet), 163–64

Jackson, John, 231n13

Javier (Barrio Bite), 87, 88, 140–41

Jimenez, Federico (Barrio Bite), 87, 88, 140, 141–43, 144, 157–58, 188–91, 199

Johnson, Randy (Build It Better), 82, 90–94, 124–25, 135–37

Johnson administration, 41, 168

Jordan Downs Housing Complex, 194

Jorge (research assistant), 53–55, 138

Joshi, Anupama, 21–22

Journee (South Central resident), 30–32, 209

Julian (food justice activist), 1–5, 7–8, 10–11, 13

Kaba, Mariame, 47–48

Kendi, Ibram X., 107

Kim, Hyejin (Produce Power), 173–80, 188, 191, 192, 193, 197, 199, 204

King, Rodney, 34, 48, 57, 172

Korean community: 1992 LA uprising, 44, 48–49; Black-Korean relations in food justice, 43–44, 197; radical food futures and, 179–80; transformative relationship building and, 173–79. *See also* Kim, Hyejin (Produce Power)

Kween (South Central resident), 127–28

LANCER (Los Angeles City Energy Recovery Project), 57–58

land and placemaking: land access and justice, 4, 170, 178–79, 206; placemaking as politicized, co-opted concept, 129–37, 204–5; redlining and historical injustices, 18, 38, 43, 46, 76, 79, 142, 146, 204, 219n35

Latinx/Brown communities: cultural foodways and resistance, xvi, 53–57, 203; food justice work and, xiii, 60, 104, 106, 169, 176, 179; grocery stores and, 42–44, 54–56; impacts of food shaming and crisisification, 202; migrant demographics, 39; misrepresentation in programming, xvi–xvii, 104, 106, 108, 203; in South Central/South LA, 15, 39, 174–175, 176, 219n22; youth in, 74

Lipsitz, George, 15, 61, 106

Locke, John, 108, 228n10

Los Angeles Food Policy Council (LAFPC), 66, 219n27, 226–27n1

Mackey, John, 42

Magdely (Barrio Bite), 140–41

Marx, Karl, 82, 167

Mary Louise (bus participant), 74

McDonald's, 19, 130, 220n38, 226n87

McKittrick, Katherine, 26–27, 219n34

media and popular narratives: *The Garden* (2008 film), 57; lack of structural analysis in mainstream media, 200; mainstream books on US food system, 18–20; outsider understanding shaped by TV/news, 6; *The Parable Series* (Butler), 172; portrayals of South LA in rap music and movies, 15, 45–46, 57

Melissa (nonprofit employee), 101–4, 125

methodology and positionality: ethnographic practices, xv–xvi, 6–7; polymorphous engagement, 215n2; positionality and whiteness, xv–xvi; pseudonym use, ix, 216n1; reflectivity and researcher embeddedness, xiii–xvii

Miguel (Food for All), xi, xii, 69

Mission Marathon, 129–31, 141, 157

Molina, Natalia, 37, 134, 137, 222n17, 225n83

Ms. Bernetta (South Central resident), 159–60

Ms. Corrinne (South Central resident), 56, 160

Ms. Judy (South Central resident), 56, 160
Ms. Mary (Mission Marathon), 129–31, 133, 134, 141, 157–58
Ms. Veronica (South Central resident), 97–100, 114, 117, 234n39
mutual aid vs. charity: commensality and, 24; food insecurity and, 20–21, 154–55; historic and current examples in South Central, xvii, 6–7; justice framework and, 5, 72–73, 166, 229n18; placemaking framework and, 133; population focus for, 43, 176; stigmatizing charity, 89; stakeholders and, 85

narratives and symbolism: food deserts and food swamps, 2, 7–9, 21, 51, 60, 87–88, 146, 202–3, 220n49, 221n50, 230n6; framing of community need, 6–7; vacant lots and, 1–2, 6–7, 61–62, 195; Whole Foods and, 194, 198, 209
Nation of Islam, 6, 81
Newton, Huey P., 6
NGO (nongovernmental organization) work, 112, 115, 234n39
nutrition education (K-12): cooking demonstrations, 11; educational interventions, xiii, 2, 26, 60, 97; disconnect from cultural relevance, 203; gardening labor and, 3; school programs influenced by BPP, 6; social justice interventions, 153–57
Nzinga (food justice activist), 166–70, 192

Obama, Barack, 228n8
Obama, Michelle, 21, 60
Obama administration, 21, 60, 106–7, 226n90
obesity, 20–21, 59–60, 102, 113, 117, 145–46, 209, 220nn46,47, 221n59
Octavia's Brood (brown and Imarisha, eds.), 171, 236n19
Oliver, Jamie, 59
Oluo, Ijeoma, 107
Olympics (Los Angeles): 1932, 39; 1984, 39, 50; 2028, 194, 238nn1,2
organic food, 8, 9, 109–10, 232n21
Ortner, Sherry, xiv

The Parable Series (Butler), 172
Patel, Raj, 19
Penniman, Leah, 9, 206
Pierre, Jemima, 109, 234n48
placemaking. *See* land and placemaking

plant-based diets. *See* Black veganism and plant-based diets
Pollan, Michael, 19, 220n38
Poppendieck, Janet, 20
Povinelli, Elizabeth, 27, 180, 221n59, 232–33n23
Power Politics (Brodkin), 140
Produce Power (organization), 8, 30–31, 87, 94, 119, 120, 127–28. *See also* Bledsoe, Chase (Produce Power); Cunningham, Sarah (Produce Power); Kim, Hyejin (Produce Power)

Queen Afua, 6

race issues. *See* white supremacy in food systems
racial capitalism and inequity: liberation from, 163, 166, 180; as root of food system injustice, 24, 181, 205; social justice projects and, 108, 193; structural causes vs. surface symptoms, 4; as support of privilege and power, 36, 205
Raimi (food justice activist), 10–11, 26
Ramón, Ana-Christina, 218n20
Rana, Junaid, 109
Rawls, John, 80–81, 228n10, 229nn11,12
Rebuild LA (RLA), 50, 120, 225nn77,78
reclamation and resistance: community-based resistance to displacement, 56, 206–9, 217n5; organizations supporting, 24; spiritual health and, 6–7
Reese, Ashanté, 18
residents of South Central: demographics of, 15–16; lack of inclusion in project design, xviii; seen as deficient or in need of saving, xvi–xvii; slotted into stereotypes by activists, xvii. See also *specific residents*
retail and grocery development: corner stores and redevelopment, 137–39; food retail in South LA, 51–56; racialized retail environments, 40–44; racial tensions and, 43–49; rebuilding efforts, 50–51
The Revolution Will Not Be Funded (INCITE! Women of Color Against Violence, eds.), 184
Ronica (food justice organizer), 153–57, 189
Rooting Change (organization), 23–24, 123, 149–50, 151, 152–53, 157, 198, 208. *See also* Green, Jamarcus (Rooting Change)

saviorism and white virtue: narratives of
benevolence and "helping," 89, 112–13,
116, 202; in staffing and leadership,
204; white food justice activists and,
xiv–xv, 231n20
Schlosser, Eric, 19
Seale, Bobby, 6
segregation, 38, 217n11, 231n13
Shakur, Tupac, 63
Shange, Savannah, 81, 166, 216n2, 233n23
Shiva, Vandana, 19
Sistah Vegan (Harper), 6–7
slippery signifiers, 110, 205–6
Slocum, Rachel, 22, 23, 232n21
slotting, xvii
Smith, Barbara, 107
Smith, Matt (Bettering Life), 8, 87, 88–90,
111, 116–19, 125, 125–26
SoFi Stadium, 194–97
Sojoyner, Damien, 216n2, 237n35
South Central Farm, 57–59
South Central Los Angeles: brief history of,
35–39; bus tour of, 73–75; demograph-
ics of, 37–39; distinct cultural and
political history, 6–7; divergent
understandings of, 13–16; naming
politics and resident perspectives,
xvii–xviii, 237n38
South LA (imaginary): food access in,
16–18; naming politics and resident
perspectives, xvii–xviii, 237n38;
racialization of space and, 15
Spurlock, Morgan, 19
street food, 135–37, 235n8
Sunny (Food for All), 181–87, 188, 191–92,
199, 237n38
Supplemental Nutritional Assistance
Program (SNAP), 20, 52–53, 220n42
sustainability: elite discourse around, 76,
78, 79, 83; lack of long-term, 139, 140,
202, 204
systemic inequity, 36, 88, 150, 233

Tacos for Teachers campaign, 135–37
Taylor, Keeanga-Yamahtta, 47
Terry, Bryant, 7

The Theory of Justice (Rawls), 81, 228n10
third spaces, 130–31
Thomas, Deborah A., xvi
Trader Joe's, 18, 42, 46–47, 51, 199
Trouillot, Michel-Rolph, 27

Ueberroth, Peter, 50
urban agriculture. *See* community gardens
and urban agriculture
USDA Food Desert Locator, 60, 226n90

vacant lots: placemaking and, 151, 195,
224n71; used symbolically by activists,
1–2, 6–7, 61–62
Vargas, João H. Costa, 41, 45, 223–24n48
veganism. *See* Black veganism and
plant-based diets
Vegan Soul Food (Terry), 7
violence: media portrayals of, 15, 46; 1992
uprising, 48–50; racial healing from,
174, 179; structural and systemic, xvii,
36, 44, 63, 109, 223n48; violence of
displacement and food injustice, xvii,
35, 44, 45–47, 227n4; Watts Rebellion,
47–48; of whiteness, 107, 109

Wacquant, Loic, 232n22
Walmart, 41, 51, 65, 84–85, 129, 131
War on Poverty, 41, 168
Washington, Karen, 9
Watts District, 14*map*, 35, 37, 195, 218n15
Watts Rebellion, 47–48
Wells, Ida B., 71, 81, 83, 207, 227n4
Wendy (South Central resident), 64–65
West LA, 9, 17–18, 56, 92, 105, 106
white supremacy in food systems:
entanglement in, 24, 71, 169, 179,
192–93; invisibility of whiteness, 22,
107, 109–10, 120–124, 231n20,
232n21; liberal white racial projects, 24,
126, 202–6; nonprofit and philanthropic
influence, 205; whiteness in leadership
and vision, xv–xvi, 232n21. *See also*
saviorism and white virtue
Whole Foods Market, 18, 42, 51, 194, 198,
199, 209

CALIFORNIA STUDIES IN FOOD AND CULTURE

Darra Goldstein, Editor

1. *Dangerous Tastes: The Story of Spices*, by Andrew Dalby

2. *Eating Right in the Renaissance*, by Ken Albala

3. *Food Politics: How the Food Industry Influences Nutrition and Health*, by Marion Nestle

4. *Camembert: A National Myth*, by Pierre Boisard

5. *Safe Food: The Politics of Food Safety*, by Marion Nestle

6. *Eating Apes*, by Dale Peterson

7. *Revolution at the Table: The Transformation of the American Diet*, by Harvey Levenstein

8. *Paradox of Plenty: A Social History of Eating in Modern America*, by Harvey Levenstein

9. *Encarnación's Kitchen: Mexican Recipes from Nineteenth-Century California: Selections from Encarnación Pinedo's* El cocinero español, by Encarnación Pinedo, edited and translated by Dan Strehl, with an essay by Victor Valle

10. *Zinfandel: A History of a Grape and Its Wine*, by Charles L. Sullivan, with a foreword by Paul Draper

11. *Tsukiji: The Fish Market at the Center of the World*, by Theodore C. Bestor

12. *Born Again Bodies: Flesh and Spirit in American Christianity*, by R. Marie Griffith

13. *Our Overweight Children: What Parents, Schools, and Communities Can Do To Control the Fatness Epidemic*, by Sharron Dalton

14. *The Art of Cooking: The First Modern Cookery Book*, by the Eminent Maestro Martino of Como, edited and with an introduction by Luigi Ballerini, translated and annotated by Jeremy Parzen, and with fifty modernized recipes by Stefania Barzini

15. *The Queen of Fats: Why Omega-3s Were Removed from the Western Diet and What We Can Do To Replace Them*, by Susan Allport

16. *Meals to Come: A History of the Future of Food*, by Warren Belasco

17. *The Spice Route: A History*, by John Keay

18. *Medieval Cuisine of the Islamic World: A Concise History with 174 Recipes*, by Lilia Zaouali, translated by M. B. DeBevoise, with a foreword by Charles Perry

19. *Arranging the Meal: A History of Table Service in France*, by Jean-Louis Flandrin, translated by Julie E. Johnson, with Sylvie and Antonio Roder; with a foreword to the English-language edition by Beatrice Fink

20. *The Taste of Place: A Cultural Journey into Terroir*, by Amy B. Trubek

21. *Food: The History of Taste*, edited by Paul Freedman

22. *M. F. K. Fisher among the Pots and Pans: Celebrating Her Kitchens*, by Joan Reardon, with a foreword by Amanda Hesser

23. *Cooking: The Quintessential Art*, by Hervé This and Pierre Gagnaire, translated by M. B. DeBevoise

24. *Perfection Salad: Women and Cooking at the Turn of the Century*, by Laura Shapiro

25. *Of Sugar and Snow: A History of Ice Cream Making*, by Jeri Quinzio

26. *Encyclopedia of Pasta*, by Oretta Zanini De Vita, translated by Maureen B. Fant, with a foreword by Carol Field

27. *Tastes and Temptations: Food and Art in Renaissance Italy*, by John Varriano

28. *Free for All: Fixing School Food in America*, by Janet Poppendieck

29. *Breaking Bread: Recipes and Stories from Immigrant Kitchens*, by Lynne Christy Anderson, with a foreword by Corby Kummer

30. *Culinary Ephemera: An Illustrated History*, by William Woys Weaver

31. *Eating Mud Crabs in Kandahar: Stories of Food during Wartime by the World's Leading Correspondents*, edited by Matt McAllester

32. *Weighing In: Obesity, Food Justice, and the Limits of Capitalism*, by Julie Guthman

33. *Why Calories Count: From Science to Politics*, by Marion Nestle and Malden Nesheim

34. *Curried Cultures: Globalization, Food, and South Asia*, edited by Krishnendu Ray and Tulasi Srinivas

35. *The Cookbook Library: Four Centuries of the Cooks, Writers, and Recipes That Made the Modern Cookbook*, by Anne Willan, with Mark Cherniavsky and Kyri Claflin

36. *Coffee Life in Japan*, by Merry White

37. *American Tuna: The Rise and Fall of an Improbable Food*, by Andrew F. Smith

38. *A Feast of Weeds: A Literary Guide to Foraging and Cooking Wild Edible Plants*, by Luigi Ballerini, translated by Gianpiero W. Doebler, with recipes by Ada De Santis and illustrations by Giuliano Della Casa

39. *The Philosophy of Food*, by David M. Kaplan

40. *Beyond Hummus and Falafel: Social and Political Aspects of Palestinian Food in Israel*, by Liora Gvion, translated by David Wesley and Elana Wesley

41. *The Life of Cheese: Crafting Food and Value in America*, by Heather Paxson

42. *Popes, Peasants, and Shepherds: Recipes and Lore from Rome and Lazio*, by Oretta Zanini De Vita, translated by Maureen B. Fant, foreword by Ernesto Di Renzo

43. *Cuisine and Empire: Cooking in World History*, by Rachel Laudan

44. *Inside the California Food Revolution: Thirty Years That Changed Our Culinary Consciousness*, by Joyce Goldstein, with Dore Brown

45. *Cumin, Camels, and Caravans: A Spice Odyssey*, by Gary Paul Nabhan

46. *Balancing on a Planet: The Future of Food and Agriculture*, by David A. Cleveland

47. *The Darjeeling Distinction: Labor and Justice on Fair-Trade Tea Plantations in India*, by Sarah Besky

48. *How the Other Half Ate: A History of Working-Class Meals at the Turn of the Century*, by Katherine Leonard Turner

49. *The Untold History of Ramen: How Political Crisis in Japan Spawned a Global Food Craze*, by George Solt

50. *Word of Mouth: What We Talk About When We Talk About Food*, by Priscilla Parkhurst Ferguson

51. *Inventing Baby Food: Taste, Health, and the Industrialization of the American Diet*, by Amy Bentley

52. *Secrets from the Greek Kitchen: Cooking, Skill, and Everyday Life on an Aegean Island*, by David E. Sutton

53. *Breadlines Knee-Deep in Wheat: Food Assistance in the Great Depression*, by Janet Poppendieck

54. *Tasting French Terroir: The History of an Idea*, by Thomas Parker

55. *Becoming Salmon: Aquaculture and the Domestication of a Fish*, by Marianne Elisabeth Lien

56. *Divided Spirits: Tequila, Mezcal, and the Politics of Production*, by Sarah Bowen

57. *The Weight of Obesity: Hunger and Global Health in Postwar Guatemala*, by Emily Yates-Doerr

58. *Dangerous Digestion: The Politics of American Dietary Advice*, by E. Melanie DuPuis

59. *A Taste of Power: Food and American Identities*, by Katharina Vester

60. *More Than Just Food: Food Justice and Community Change*, by Garrett M. Broad

61. *Hoptopia: A World of Agriculture and Beer in Oregon's Willamette Valley*, by Peter A. Kopp

62. *A Geography of Digestion: Biotechnology and the Kellogg Cereal Enterprise*, by Nicholas Bauch

63. *Bitter and Sweet: Food, Meaning, and Modernity in Rural China*, by Ellen Oxfeld

64. *A History of Cookbooks: From Kitchen to Page over Seven Centuries*, by Henry Notaker

65. *Reinventing the Wheel: Milk, Microbes, and the Fight for Real Cheese*, by Bronwen Percival and Francis Percival

66. *Making Modern Meals: How Americans Cook Today*, by Amy B. Trubek

67. *Food and Power: A Culinary Ethnography of Israel*, by Nir Avieli

68. *Canned: The Rise and Fall of Consumer Confidence in the American Food Industry*, by Anna Zeide

69. *Meat Planet: Artificial Flesh and the Future of Food*, by Benjamin Aldes Wurgaft

70. *The Labor of Lunch: Why We Need Real Food and Real Jobs in American Public Schools*, by Jennifer E. Gaddis

71. *Feeding the Crisis: Care and Abandonment in America's Food Safety Net*, by Maggie Dickinson

72. *Sameness in Diversity: Food and Globalization in Modern America*, by Laresh Jayasanker

73. *The Fruits of Empire: Art, Food, and the Politics of Race in the Age of American Expansion*, by Shana Klein

74. *Let's Ask Marion: What You Need to Know about the Politics of Food, Nutrition, and Health*, by Marion Nestle, in conversation with Kerry Trueman

75. *The Scarcity Slot: Excavating Histories of Food Security in Ghana*, by Amanda L. Logan

76. *Gastropolitics and the Specter of Race: Stories of Capital, Culture, and Coloniality in Peru*, by María Elena García

77. *The Kingdom of Rye: A Brief History of Russian Food*, by Darra Goldstein

78. *Slow Cooked: An Unexpected Life in Food Politics*, by Marion Nestle

79. *Yerba Mate: The Drink That Shaped a Nation*, by Julia J. S. Sarreal

80. *Wonder Foods: The Science and Commerce of Nutrition*, by Lisa Haushofer

81. *Ways of Eating: Exploring Food through History and Culture*, by Benjamin A. Wurgaft and Merry I. White

82. *From Label to Table: Regulating Food in America in the Information Age*, by Xaq Frohlich

83. *Intoxicating Pleasures: The Reinvention of Wine, Beer, and Whiskey after Prohibition*, by Lisa Jacobson

84. *The Quinoa Bust: The Making and Unmaking of an Andean Miracle Crop*, by Emma McDonell

85. *On Hunger: Violence and Craving in America, from Starvation to Ozempic*, by Dana Simmons

86. *The Pierogi Problem: Cosmopolitan Appetites and the Reinvention of Polish Food*, by Fabio Parasecoli, Agata Bachórz, and Mateusz Halawa

87. *Nile Nightshade: Tomato, A Kitchen History of Modern Egypt*, by Anny Gaul

88. *Food Justice Undone: Lessons for Building a Better Movement*, by Hanna Garth

Founded in 1893,
UNIVERSITY OF CALIFORNIA PRESS
publishes bold, progressive books and journals
on topics in the arts, humanities, social sciences,
and natural sciences—with a focus on social
justice issues—that inspire thought and action
among readers worldwide.

The UC PRESS FOUNDATION
raises funds to uphold the press's vital role
as an independent, nonprofit publisher, and
receives philanthropic support from a wide
range of individuals and institutions—and from
committed readers like you. To learn more, visit
ucpress.edu/supportus.